New Longman Shakespeare

Romeo and Juliet

William Shakespeare

edited by John O'Connor

LONGMAN

Pearson Education Limited
Edinburgh Gate
Harlow
Essex
CM20 2JE
England and Associated Companies throughout the World

ISBN 0582 36579 1

First published 1999
Printed in Singapore

The Publisher's policy is to use paper manufactured from sustainable forests.

Acknowledgements

We are grateful to the following for permission to reproduce photographs:

Catherine Ashmore page 76 below; Capital Pictures page 8; Mary Evans Picture Library/Ultrecht University Library page 240; Ronald Grant Archive pages 76 above, 112, 146, 188, 189, 208, 221; Robbie Jack page 103; 20th Century Fox (Courtesy Kobal) pages 182, 202; Paul Mulcahy page 224; The Shakespeare Centre Library, Stratford-Upon-Avon pages 74, 84, 98, 122; John Tramper page 241.

Cover Aquarius

Contents

Introduction

To the student

Shakespeare wrote *Romeo and Juliet* so that it could be performed by actors and enjoyed by audiences. To help you get the most out of the play, this edition includes:
- a complete **script**;
- **notes** printed next to the script which explain difficulties and point out important features;
- **activities** on the same page which will help you to focus on the scene you are reading;
- page-by-page **summaries** of the plot;
- **exam questions** after each Act, which will give you practice at the right level;
- **background information** about *Romeo and Juliet*, Shakespeare's theatre and the verse he uses; and
- **advice** on how to set out titles and quotations in your essays.

To the teacher

New Longman Shakespeare has been designed to meet the varied and complex needs of students working throughout the 11–16 age-range.

The textual notes

These have been newly written to provide understandable explanations which are easily located on the page:
- notes are placed next to the text with clear line references
- explanations of more complex words are given in context and help is provided with key imagery and historical references.

The activities

1 **Activities accompanying the text**

There are based on the premise that the text is best enjoyed and understood as a script for performance:

- In addition to a wide variety of reading, writing, listening and speaking activities, students are encouraged to: improvise, learn the script for performance, freeze-frame, rehearse, hot-seat, devise graphs and charts and create various forms of artwork, including storyboards, collages and cartoons.
- To provide a clear structure, activities are placed opposite the section of text to which they refer and come under five headings:
  - **i Character reviews** help students to think about the many different aspects of a given character which are presented in the course of the play. There might be as many as twenty of these activities on a single major character.
  - **ii Actors' interpretations** draw upon actual performances and ask students to consider comments from actors and directors in film and stage productions.
  - **iii Shakespeare's language** activities, focusing on everything from imagery to word-play, enable students to understand how the dramatist's language works to convey the central ideas of the play.
  - **iv Plot reviews** help students to keep in mind the essential details of what is happening in the story as well as asking them to consider how the plot is structured.
  - **v Themes** are explored according to their predominance in each play.
- 'Serial activities' (Macbeth 1, ... 2, ... 3, for example) enable students to focus in detail on a single key feature.

In addition, students who find extended tasks on Shakespeare a daunting prospect can combine several of these more focused activities – each in itself free-standing – to form the basis of a fuller piece of work.

2 Exam-style activities

At the end of each Act – and also at the end of the book – there are activities which require SATs and GCSE style responses and offer opportunities for assessment.

3 Summative activities

Thinking about the play as a whole ... is a section which offers a wide range of summative activities suitable for all levels.

Differentiation
Many students using this edition will be approaching Shakespeare for the first time; some might be studying the play for their Key Stage 3 SATs exam; others will be working towards GCSE.

Introduction

To answer their very different needs and interests, many of the activities have been differentiated to match the National Curriculum Level Descriptions and GCSE criteria. Activities of this kind are presented in three levels:

A Foundation level activities, which support an initial reading of the play and help students to build a solid basic knowledge and understanding.
B Activities geared towards the needs of Year 9 Key Stage 3 students preparing for SATs.
C More advanced activities in line with GCSE requirements.

Plot summaries

As students work through the play, their understanding of the play's plot is supported by:
• a brief headline summary at the top of each spread
• regular Plot Review activities
• a final detailed summary, scene by scene.

Background

Details are provided on:
• Shakespeare's England
• Plays and playhouses
• The Globe theatre
• The social and historical background (to each particular play)
• Shakespeare's life and his times

Studying and writing about the play

To help students who are studying the play for examinations, there are sections on:
• Shakespeare's verse (with examples from the particular play)
• Study skills: titles and quotations

ROMEO AND JULIET
CHARACTERS IN THE PLAY

The CHORUS

The house of Capulet
LORD CAPULET
LADY CAPULET
JULIET, their daughter
TYBALT, Juliet's cousin
Juliet's NURSE
Capulet's SERVANT
PETER, the Nurse's servant
an old COUSIN
SAMPSON, a servant
GREGORY, a servant
other servants and followers

The house of Montague
LORD MONTAGUE
LADY MONTAGUE
ROMEO, their son
BENVOLIO, Romeo's friend
BALTHASAR, Romeo's servant
ABRAHAM, a servant
other servants

The Prince's household
ESCALUS, PRINCE of Verona
MERCUTIO, a relative of the Prince
PARIS, another relative
Paris's PAGE
Mercutio's page
attendants

also from Verona
FRIAR LAWRENCE, a Franciscan friar
FRIAR JOHN, his friend
an OFFICER
a CAPTAIN of the watch
members of the watch
musicians
guests at the Capulet feast
citizens

in Mantua
an APOTHECARY

The story is set in Verona, except for 5.1, which takes place in Mantua.

1.1 Prologue

The Chorus introduces the story, set in Verona: a long-standing feud between the Montagues and Capulets will be ended only by the deaths of two ill-fated lovers, Romeo and Juliet.

Activities

Shakespeare's language: the sonnet

The Prologue is written in the form of a sonnet (which you can learn more about on page 48 and page 56), a fourteen-line poem often divided, as this one is, into three sections, the third of which ends in a 'rhyming couplet'.

1. In groups of four, create freeze-frames to show the main events of the story as they are highlighted in the Prologue. Then read out the Prologue as each group shows its tableau.

2. Note down what information is provided in each of the three sections by completing the statements:
   - Section 1 (1–4):
     This is a story about two families . . .
   - Section 2 (5–8):
     A boy from one family and a girl from the other fall in love . . .
   - Section 3 (9–12):
     In our two-hour play you will see . . .
   - Rhyming couplet (13–14):
     If our actors don't give a very good performance . . .

Learn the Prologue by heart and produce a performance of it in groups, perhaps with different people performing different sections.

1 **households** families

1 **alike in dignity** as noble as each other

3 **ancient grudge** long-term hatred

3 **mutiny** outburst of violence

4 **civil** to do with citizens

5 **From forth . . . foes** born from these two enemies, who are lethal to one another

6 **star-crossed** ill-fated; doomed by the influence of the stars

7 **misadventured . . . overthrows** unfortunate tragic accidents

9 **passage** course

9 **death-marked** doomed to death

11 **but . . . end** except for the deaths of their children

12 **traffic** business *('two hours' is perhaps not to be taken literally, but simply suggests that the play will not be long enough to bore the audience)*

14 **What . . . mend** the actors' hard work will try to make up for any deficiencies in the play

Prologue

Enter CHORUS.

CHORUS   Two households, both alike in dignity,
  In fair Verona where we lay our scene,
From ancient grudge break to new mutiny,
  Where civil blood makes civil hands unclean,
From forth the fatal loins of these two foes 5
  A pair of star-crossed lovers take their life;
Whose misadventured piteous overthrows
  Doth with their death bury their parent's strife.
The fearful passage of their death-marked love,
  And the continuance of their parents' rage, 10
Which, but their children's end, nought could remove,
  Is now the two hours' traffic of our stage;
The which, if you with patient ears attend,
  What here shall miss, our toil shall strive to mend.

Exit.

1.1 A street in Verona

Two Capulet servants, Sampson and Gregory, brag about their part in the feud with the Montagues.

Activities

Actors' interpretations (1): the boastful servants

The play starts with two servants from the house of Capulet. First of all, decide what it is they are boasting about (lines 1–30). Then improvise a modern conversation, deciding first where it is going to take place, based upon Shakespeare's dialogue. Sampson's lines might start off like this;
you will need to expand upon them and add Gregory's replies:

• 1–6: Nobody insults me and gets away with it . . .
• 7–15: I hate the Montagues . . .
• 16–26: Of course, the Montagues' women are a different matter . . .
• 27–30: It's well known I'm a great lover . . .

bucklers small shields

1–4 **coals . . .** *Wordplay based on*: (1) **carry coals** = be humiliated; (2) **colliers** = coal-miners (considered dirty and dishonest); (3) **choler** (pronounced collar) = anger; (4) **collar** = hangman's noose.

3 **and** if

3 **draw** draw our swords

5–10 **moved . . .** *More wordplay*: (1) angry; (2) moved to run away (behave like a coward).

5 **I strike . . .** When I am angry (**moved**), I am quick to fight.

8 **stand** stand and fight *(But **stir** (have sex) and **stand** (have an erection: see line 27) also introduce the sexual language.)*

11 **take the wall . . .** keep to the clean side of the pavement, nearest the wall, forcing the Montagues into the road

12–13 **goes to the wall** is defeated by the strong

14–15 **weaker vessels** 'the weaker sex' *(from the Bible)*

16–17 **thrust . . .** *another sexual meaning*

20 **'T is all one** It makes no difference.

24 **maidenheads** virginity

25–26 **sense** (1) meaning; (2) feeling

Act 1

Scene 1

A street in Verona.

Enter SAMPSON and GREGORY, servants of the Capulet household, armed with swords and bucklers.

SAMPSON   Gregory, on my word, we'll not carry coals.

GREGORY   No, for then we should be colliers.

SAMPSON   I mean, and we be in choler, we'll draw.

GREGORY   Ay, while you live, draw your neck out of collar.

SAMPSON   I strike quickly, being moved.   5

GREGORY   But thou art not quickly moved to strike.

SAMPSON   A dog of the house of Montague moves me.

GREGORY   To move is to stir, and to be valiant is to stand: therefore, if thou art moved thou runn'st away.

SAMPSON   A dog of that house shall move me to stand: I will   10 take the wall of any man or maid of Montague's.

GREGORY   That shows thee a weak slave, for the weakest goes to the wall.

SAMPSON   'Tis true, and therefore women, being the weaker vessels, are ever thrust to the wall: therefore I will   15 push Montague's men from the wall, and thrust his maids to the wall.

GREGORY   The quarrel is between our masters, and us their men.

SAMPSON   'T is all one. I will show myself a tyrant: when I   20 have fought with the men, I will be civil with the maids; I will cut off their heads.

GREGORY   The heads of the maids?

SAMPSON   Ay, the heads of the maids, or their maidenheads; take it in what sense thou wilt.   25

1.1 A street in Verona

Two Montague servants approach, and the Capulets try to provoke a fight while keeping the law on their side.

Activities

Shakespeare's language: bawdy wordplay

Use the following explanations to help you to understand the wordplay in the exchanges between Sampson and Gregory:

- 'carry coals' (1) can mean 'do menial jobs' or 'be humiliated'
- 'choler' (3) (anger) is pronounced the same as 'collar' which could mean a hangman's noose
- 'moved' (5) could mean aroused sexually, or encouraged to run away
- 'stir' (8) can mean to have sex, and 'stand' (8, 27) can mean to have an erection
- 'the weakest goes to the wall' (12–13) is a proverb meaning that weak people are thrown aside by strong ones; Sampson boasts that he will 'thrust' Montague's maids to the wall (16–17)
- 'maidenheads' (24) means the maids' virginities
- 'sense' (25, 26) means 'feeling' as well as 'meaning'
- 'a pretty piece of flesh' (28) is Sampson's boast about his sexual prowess
- 'poor John' (30) is dried salted hake – in other words, shrivelled up
- 'tool' (30) and 'weapon' (32) are common slang terms for the penis.

28 **pretty piece of flesh** (1) attractive man; (2) well endowed

30 **poor John** a dried fish *(an insult to Sampson's virility as it would be too floppy to stand up)*

30 **tool** weapon *(and another sexual term)*

36 **marry** *a mild oath*: 'By the virgin Mary'

36 **I fear thee!** I'm afraid that's exactly what you will do (run away)!

37 **take the law ...** keep on the right side of the law

38–39 **take ... list** interpret it as they wish

40 **bite my thumb** *an insulting gesture, made by putting the thumb behind the top teeth and jerking it outwards, clicking the teeth*

41 **bear it** put up with it

GREGORY	They must take it in sense that feel it.	
SAMPSON	Me they shall feel while I am able to stand; and 't is known I am a pretty piece of flesh.	
GREGORY	'T is well thou art not fish; if thou hadst, thou hadst been poor John. Draw thy tool: here comes two of the house of Montagues.	30

Enter ABRAHAM and another servant, both of the Montague household.

SAMPSON	My naked weapon is out. Quarrel; I will back thee.	
GREGORY	How? Turn thy back and run?	
SAMPSON	Fear me not.	35
GREGORY	No, marry; I fear thee!	
SAMPSON	Let us take the law of our sides; let them begin.	
GREGORY	I will frown as I pass by, and let them take it as they list.	
SAMPSON	Nay, as they dare. I will bite my thumb at them, which is disgrace to them if they bear it.	40
ABRAHAM	Do you bite your thumb at us, sir?	
SAMPSON	I do bite my thumb, sir.	
ABRAHAM	Do you bite your thumb at us, sir?	
SAMPSON	(*Aside to* GREGORY) Is the law of our side if I say "Ay"?	45
GREGORY	(*Aside to* SAMPSON) No.	
SAMPSON	(*Replying to* ABRAHAM) No, sir, I do not bite my thumb at you, sir, but I bite my thumb, sir.	
GREGORY	Do you quarrel, sir?	50
ABRAHAM	Quarrel sir? No, sir.	

 1.1 A street in Verona

Sampson and Gregory become bolder when they see Tybalt (a Capulet) approaching and the brawl begins. Benvolio, a Montague, tries to prevent the violence, but Tybalt is eager for a fight and the ensuing riot is stopped only by the arrival of the Prince's officers.

Activities

Character review: Tybalt (1)

The actor playing Tybalt can establish his character in a number of ways: through his language, through his appearance and in the way he moves.

1. In pairs, one person takes the part of Benvolio, the other Tybalt. Pick just one word from each of the seven lines of their exchange (64–70) and improvise a scene, using the seven words to convey the difference between the two characters.

2. What can you tell about the character of Tybalt (centre) from this photograph?

3. How might the Montague servants react when they see Tybalt approaching? If you get a chance, look at the way they behave in the 1997 film, directed by Baz Luhrmann.

4. What kind of role do you think he might play in the story outlined by the Prologue?

52 **I am for you** I'm your man! (I accept your challenge)

61 **swashing** slashing

63 **Put up** sheathe (put your swords away)

64 **heartless hinds** (1) servants (hinds) lacking courage; (2) female deer without males (hartless)

66 **I do but keep** I am only keeping

67 **manage it** use it

66 **part** separate

71 **bills and partisans** axes and spears

73 **long sword** heavy, old-fashioned weapon

SAMPSON   But if you do, sir, I am for you. I serve as good a
man as you.

ABRAHAM   No better?

SAMPSON   Well, sir –   55

Enter BENVOLIO.

GREGORY   (*Interrupting* SAMPSON *as he sees* TYBALT *approaching*)
Say "Better"; here comes one of my master's
kinsmen.

SAMPSON   (*To* ABRAHAM) Yes, better, sir.

ABRAHAM   You lie.

SAMPSON   Draw, if you be men. Gregory, remember thy   60
swashing blow.

They fight. BENVOLIO draws his sword and tries to separate them.

BENVOLIO   Part, fools!
Put up your swords; you know not what you do.

Enter TYBALT.

TYBALT   What, art thou drawn among these heartless hinds?
Turn thee, Benvolio; look upon thy death.   65

BENVOLIO   I do but keep the peace. Put up thy sword
Or manage it to part these men with me.

TYBALT   What, drawn, and talk of peace? I hate the word
As I hate hell, all Montagues, and thee.
Have at thee, coward!   70

They fight. Enter an OFFICER with three or four armed citizens.

OFFICER   Clubs, bills and partisans, strike! Beat them down!
Down with the Capulets! Down with the
Montagues!

Enter CAPULET in his nightgown, with LADY CAPULET, his wife.

CAPULET   What noise is this? Give me my long sword, ho!

1.1 A street in Verona

Escalus, the Prince of Verona, angrily rebukes Montague and Capulet: this is the third riot to have taken place and the Prince threatens the death penalty for anyone caught fighting in the streets again.

Activities

Actors' interpretations (2): the riot

In groups of seven or eight, freeze-frame the moment when Tybalt draws his sword against Benvolio (70). Each person then explains what his or her character is thinking or feeling at that moment. Then do the same with the moment when the Prince enters (79).

Plot review (1)

A The Prince makes it very clear why he is so angry and why strict measures have to be taken.

1. Work in pairs to express the main points of his pronouncement in your own words, using the following as a structure:
   - 79–82: This is what I think of you . . .
   - 84–86: This is what you must do . . .
   - 87–93: This is what you have done . . .
   - 94–101: If it happens again . . .

2. Perform the speech in groups of four, with one person responsible for each section, thinking carefully about the changes in tone from one part of the speech to the next.

B Write tomorrow's front-page news report for the *Verona Independent*

Continued on page 12

76 **in spite of me** to mock me, in defiance of me

80 **Profaners ...** The Montagues and Capulets have misused (profaned) their swords (**steel**) by staining them with their neighbours' blood.

82 **quench ... rage** who put out the fire of your destructive anger

84–85 **On pain ...** You will be tortured if you do not throw down your weapons.

85 **mistempered** (1) in a bad temper; (2) badly made (poorly tempered steel)

86 **movèd** angry

87 **civil brawls** public riots

87 **bred of ...** caused by some trivial comment

91 **Cast by ...** reject their appropriately sober (**grave beseeming**) behaviour

93 **Cankered with ...** *their weapons have become rusty with lack of use in peacetime*

93 **cankered hate** cancerous hatred

95 **... pay the forfeit ...** you will be executed, for having broken the peace

99 **our farther pleasure** what else I decide to do

102 **Who set ...** Who set off this old quarrel again?

Act 1 Scene 1

LADY CAPULET	A crutch, a crutch! Why call you for a sword?
CAPULET	My sword I say! Old Montague is come, 75 And flourishes his blade in spite of me.

Enter MONTAGUE and LADY MONTAGUE, his wife.

MONTAGUE	Thou villain, Capulet. (*To his wife*) Hold me not; let me go.
LADY MONTAGUE	Thou shalt not stir one foot to seek a foe.

Enter PRINCE ESCALUS with his train.

PRINCE   Rebellious subjects, enemies to peace,
Profaners of this neighbour-stainèd steel –   80
Will they not hear? What ho! you men, you beasts,
That quench the fire of your pernicious rage
With purple fountains issuing from your veins,
On pain of torture, from those bloody hands
Throw your mistempered weapons to the ground,   85
And hear the sentence of your movèd Prince.
Three civil brawls bred of an airy word
By thee, old Capulet, and Montague,
Have thrice disturbed the quiet of our streets,
And made Verona's ancient citizens   90
Cast by their grave beseeming ornaments
To wield old partisans in hands as old,
Cankered with peace, to part your cankered hate.
If ever you disturb our streets again,
Your lives shall pay the forfeit of the peace.   95
For this time, all the rest depart away.
You, Capulet, shall go along with me,
And Montague, come you this afternoon,
To know our farther pleasure in this case,
To old Freetown, our common judgement-place.   100
Once more, on pain of death, all men depart.

Exeunt all except MONTAGUE, LADY MONTAGUE and BENVOLIO.

MONTAGUE Who set this ancient quarrel new abroach?
Speak, nephew. Were you by when it began?

1.1 A street in Verona

Benvolio tells Romeo's mother and father how the riot started. Then they discuss Romeo's recent behaviour: he has been keeping to himself and seems depressed.

Activities

newspaper. Decide first whether it is a serious broadsheet, like the *Guardian* or *The Times*, or a popular tabloid, such as the *Sun* or *Daily Mirror*. Include:

- an account of the riot
- quotes from men on the two sides
- quotes from passers-by
- a summary of the Prince's declarations.

C Write the 'leader' editorial (the article in which the newspaper expresses its own opinions) for the *Verona Independent*. Include:

- an account of the origin of the feud (which you will have to invent) and the three recent uprisings
- the newspaper's opinions on the Prince's actions so far in trying to curb the conflict
- opinions on the chances of success for his latest measures (lines 94–96)
- suggestions for further measures to secure peace.

Character review: Romeo (1)

Benvolio and Romeo's father have both noticed Romeo's recent strange behaviour.

Imagine you were making a film of *Romeo and Juliet*. Draw three frames of a storyboard, based on lines 116–123, 129–131 and 132–138.

107 **prepared** already drawn

110 **... nothing hurt withal** The winds were not hurt by Tybalt's strokes.

112 **on part and part** some on one side, some on the other

116–117 **an hour before ... east** an hour-before dawn

118 **walk abroad** go for a walk

120 **westward rooteth ...** grows to the west from this side of the city

123 **stole ... covert** crept into the shadows

124–128 **measuring ... from me** Judging his feelings by the way I felt myself – wanting most of all to be alone – and feeling that even my own company was too much for me, I did what I wanted (**Pursued my humour**) which was what he wanted too, and happily kept away from someone who was trying to escape from me.

130 **augmenting** adding to

132–134 **But all ... bed** 'But as soon as it was dawn'. (*Aurora was the goddess of the dawn.*)

139 **portentous** ill-omened

139 **humour** mood

140 **Unless ...** Unless we can help him get over it by offering some good advice.

1.1

BENVOLIO	Here were the servants of your adversary
	And yours, close fighting ere I did approach. 105
	I drew to part them; in the instant came
	The fiery Tybalt, with his sword prepared,
	Which, as he breathed defiance to my ears,
	He swung about his head and cut the winds,
	Who, nothing hurt withal, hissed him in scorn. 110
	While we were interchanging thrusts and blows,
	Came more and more, and fought on part and part,
	Till the Prince came, who parted either part.
LADY MONTAGUE	O where is Romeo? Saw you him to-day?
	Right glad I am he was not at this fray. 115
BENVOLIO	Madam, an hour before the worshipped sun
	Peered forth the golden window of the east,
	A troubled mind drive me to walk abroad,
	Where, underneath the grove of sycamore
	That westward rooteth from this city side, 120
	So early walking did I see your son.
	Towards him I made, but he was ware of me,
	And stole into the cover of the wood.
	I, measuring his affections by my own,
	Which then most sought where most might not be found, 125
	Being one too many by my weary self,
	Pursued my humour not pursuing his,
	And gladly shunned who gladly fled from me.
MONTAGUE	Many a morning hath he there been seen,
	With tears augmenting the fresh morning's dew, 130
	Adding to clouds more clouds with his deep sighs;
	But all so soon as the all-cheering sun
	Should in the farthest east begin to draw
	The shady curtains from Aurora's bed,
	Away from light steals home my heavy son, 135
	And private in his chamber pens himself,
	Shuts up his windows, locks fair daylight out,
	And makes himself an artificial night.
	Black and portentous must this humour prove,
	Unless good counsel may the cause remove. 140
BENVOLIO	My noble uncle, do you know the cause?

1.1 A street in Verona

Benvolio promises to try to discover the cause of Romeo's unhappiness and the Capulets leave, seeing their son approach. Romeo explains his depression: his love for a girl (later called Rosaline) is not being returned.

Activities

Shakespeare's language: imagery

In many of his plays Shakespeare uses images from the world of nature. Draw a picture, or create one from magazine cuttings, to illustrate Montague's image in lines 149–151. Make sure that you get across the idea that there is something harmful and unnatural in Romeo's behaviour, as his father sees it.

Character review: Romeo (2)

In pairs, act out the first exchange between Benvolio and Romeo (158–166). Decide first whether Benvolio is sitting or standing, and how he reacts when Romeo enters. Then discuss: (a) what mood Romeo seems to be in; (b) what you can tell from the fact that he plays with words when describing his situation.

142 **of** from

143 **importuned** asked

145 **his own affections' counsellor** discussing his feelings about love only with himself

147–148 **so secret ...** he is so secretive and mysterious, so hard to 'sound out' and get the truth out of

149 **envious** harmful

152–153 **Could we ... as know** If we could only find the cause of his unhappiness, we would be as happy to help him get over it as to know what it is.

155 **I'll know ...** I'll find out what's the matter with him, unless he keeps on refusing to tell me.

156–157 **I would ... shrift** I only hope that, by staying here, you will hear a true confession.

158 **... so young?** *Romeo has been up a long time and is surprised that it is still morning (**morrow**).*

159 **But new-struck nine** It has only just gone nine o'clock.

166 **Out of her favour ...** I love her, but she doesn't love me.

1.1

MONTAGUE	I neither know it, nor can learn of him.
BENVOLIO	Have you importuned him by any means?

MONTAGUE   Both by myself and many other friends:
But he, his own affections' counsellor,   145
Is to himself – I will not say how true –
But to himself so secret and so close,
So far from sounding and discovery
As is the bud bit with an envious worm
Ere he can spread his sweet leaves to the air,   150
Or dedicate his beauty to the sun.
Could we but learn from whence his sorrows grow,
We would as willingly give cure as know.

Enter ROMEO.

BENVOLIO   See where he comes. So please you, step aside;
I'll know his grievance or be much denied.   155

MONTAGUE   I would thou wert so happy by thy stay
To hear true shrift. Come, madam, let's away.

Exeunt MONTAGUE and LADY MONTAGUE.

BENVOLIO   Good morrow, cousin.

ROMEO   Is the day so young?

BENVOLIO   But new-struck nine.

ROMEO   Ay me, sad hours seem long.
Was that my father that went hence so fast?   160

BENVOLIO   It was. What sadness lengthens Romeo's hours?

ROMEO   Not having that which, having, makes them short.

BENVOLIO   In love?

ROMEO   Out –

BENVOLIO   Of love?   165

ROMEO   Out of her favour where I am in love.

1.1 A street in Verona

When Romeo notices the aftermath of the riot, he is as depressed about the violence as he is by love. Love seems to him to be a contradictory and confusing emotion. Benvolio asks who the girl is.

167–168 **Alas that Love ... proof** It's a shame that love, which looks so pleasant, should prove to be so difficult when we experience it.

169–170 **... whose view is muffled ...** *A reference to Cupid, son of the love goddess Venus, who, though blindfolded, can still find a way to fulfil his desires.*

173 **Here's much to do ...** *Hate causes the turmoil in the streets, but love causes the turmoil inside Romeo.*

175 **O anything ...** anything created out of nothing in the first place

176 **serious vanity** weighty emptiness

177 **well-seeming forms** shapes which appear attractive

179 **Still-waking** always awake

180 **This love feel I ...** I am in love, but am not loved in return.

182 **oppression** unhappiness

183 **such is love's transgression** This is the kind of sin that love makes you commit.

184–186 **Griefs of ... thine** My own griefs are weighing me down, but you will increase them by adding some of your own.

188 **fume** vapour

189 **purged** cleared, cleansed

192 **gall** bitter-tasting poison

193 **Soft** Wait a moment

BENVOLIO	Alas, that Love, so gentle in his view,
	Should be so tyrannous and rough in proof.

ROMEO	Alas, that Love, whose view is muffled still,	
	Should without eyes see pathways to his will.	170
	Where shall we dine? O me! What fray was here?	
	Yet tell me not, for I have heard it all.	
	Here's much to do with hate, but more with love.	
	Why then, O brawling love, O loving hate,	
	O anything of nothing first create,	175
	O heavy lightness, serious vanity,	
	Misshapen chaos of well-seeming forms,	
	Feather of lead, bright smoke, cold fire, sick health,	
	Still-waking sleep that is not what it is,	
	This love feel I, that feel no love in this.	180
	Dost thou not laugh?	

BENVOLIO	No, coz, I rather weep.

ROMEO	Good heart, at what?

BENVOLIO	At thy good heart's oppression.

ROMEO	Why, such is love's transgression.	
	Griefs of mine own lie heavy in my breast,	
	Which thou wilt propagate to have it pressed	185
	With more of thine. This love that thou hast shown	
	Doth add more grief to too much of mine own.	
	Love is a smoke made with the fume of sighs:	
	Being purged, a fire sparkling in lovers' eyes;	
	Being vexed, a sea nourished with loving tears.	190
	What is it else? A madness most discreet,	
	A choking gall, and a preserving sweet.	
	Farewell, my coz.	

BENVOLIO	Soft, I will go along;
	And if you leave me so, you do me wrong.

ROMEO	Tut, I have lost myself; I am not here.	195
	This is not Romeo; he's some other where.	

BENVOLIO	Tell me in sadness, who is that you love?

ROMEO	What, shall I groan and tell thee?

1.1 A street in Verona

Romeo explains that Rosaline is not interested in love and cannot be won over: her beauty will die with her. He rejects Benvolio's suggested cure: that he should forget Rosaline and take an interest in other girls.

Activities

Character review: Romeo (3)

The actor Ray Fearon, who played Romeo with the Royal Shakespeare Company in 1998, said: 'I like Romeo's wit. He's fast and furious. He's got a way with words. He's passionate and he goes for what he believes in, where some people might stop and think.'

Look back at the witty exchange between Romeo and Benvolio which is based on the idea of shooting arrows (203–209).

1. How does the wordplay build up? The following structure will help you to follow it:
   - 203: My aim was quite good . . .
   - 204: You're a good shot . . .
   - 205: It's easy to hit a clear target . . .
   - 206: You've missed this time . . .
2. How does the reference to Cupid fit the wordplay? Think about the way Cupid made people fall in love.
3. Why is it appropriate that Diana was the Roman goddess of hunting, as well as of chastity?

199 **sadly** seriously

203 **I aimed so near** I guessed as much

205 **right fair mark . . .** a good target is easiest to hit

207 **Dian's wit** *Diana was the Roman archer goddess, who had enough 'wit' (good sense) to remained unaffected by love.*

208–212 **And in strong proof . . .** Her sexual purity is strong armour against Cupid's arrows. She refuses to listen to love-talk, or put up with loving glances, or accept bribes (gold that might win over a saint).

214 **when she dies . . .** her ability to hand on her beauty to a child will die with her

216–218 **in that sparing . . . posterity** By 'saving herself', she is guilty of waste – by not handing on her beauty to children (**posterity**).

220 **To merit bliss . . .** She will go to heaven for her sexual purity, but I will go to hell, guilty of the sin of despair.

221 **forsworn to** sworn that she will not

228–229 **These happy masks . . .** The black masks that ladies wear at dances – fortunate (**happy**) because they can touch their faces – remind us how beautiful they really are.

BENVOLIO	Groan? Why no.
	But sadly tell me who.
ROMEO	A sick man in sadness makes his will 200
	A word ill urged to one that is so ill.
	In sadness, cousin, I do love a woman.
BENVOLIO	I aimed so near when I supposed you loved.
ROMEO	A right good mark-man! And she's fair I love.
BENVOLIO	A right fair mark, fair coz, is soonest hit. 205
ROMEO	Well, in that hit you miss. She'll not be hit
	With Cupid's arrow; she hath Dian's wit,
	And in strong proof of chastity well-armed,
	From Love's weak childish bow she lives uncharmed.
	She will not stay the siege of loving terms, 210
	Nor bide th' encounter of assailing eyes,
	Nor ope her lap to saint-seducing gold.
	O, she is rich in beauty; only poor
	That when she dies, with beauty dies her store.
BENVOLIO	Then she hath sworn that she will still live chaste? 215
ROMEO	She hath, and in that sparing makes huge waste,
	For beauty, starved with her severity,
	Cuts beauty off from all posterity.
	She is too fair, too wise, wisely too fair,
	To merit bliss by making me despair. 220
	She hath forsworn to love, and in that vow
	Do I live dead, that live to tell it now.
BENVOLIO	Be ruled by me; forget to think of her.
ROMEO	O, teach me how I should forget to think!
BENVOLIO	By giving liberty unto thine eyes: 225
	Examine other beauties.
ROMEO	'T is the way
	To call hers – exquisite – in question more.
	These happy masks that kiss fair ladies' brows,
	Being black, puts us in mind they hide the fair.
	He that is strucken blind cannot forget 230

1.1 A street in Verona

Benvolio remains determined to help Romeo forget Rosaline. Meanwhile Count Paris is seeking Capulet's approval to marry Juliet. Capulet tells him that he considers his thirteen-year-old daughter to be too young for marriage, but will follow Juliet's wishes.

Activities

Character review: Romeo (4)

1 (a) How accurately do you think each of the following words describes Romeo in this scene? bored; confused; obsessed; dazed; unhappy; bitter; blinkered; obstinate. Find references to support your views. Are there other adjectives that you would add to this list?

(b) Look back at lines 206–222 and discuss why the girl is refusing to accept Romeo's love (in his opinion).

2 Discuss the difference between love and infatuation. From what Romeo says, and from the way he has behaved, would you say that he was genuinely in love, or just infatuated? Write the letter that Romeo might send to an 'agony aunt' (or 'uncle') of a teenage magazine, In which he explained his problem and asked for advice.

232–234 **Show me ...** Show me any exceedingly attractive woman and her exceeding beauty will simply remind me that the girl I love exceeds her in beauty!

236 **I'll pay that doctrine ...** I'll teach you to forget her or die in the attempt.

Clown He is usually the same servant as Peter, who appears with the Nurse in 2.4.

1–2 **bound** ordered to keep the peace

4 **reckoning** reputation

5 **at odds** as enemies

6 **suit** request

8 **... a stranger in the world** Juliet has led a sheltered life.

9 **She hath not seen ...** she is not yet fourteen

12 **Younger ...** Girls younger than Juliet have become happy mothers.

13 **marred** spoiled *(perhaps by giving birth to children)*

14–15 **Earth hath swallowèd ...** *Juliet is the sole Capulet heir.*

17–19 **My will ... voice** You must get her agreement to marry; it is not just a question of what I want. Once she has agreed, I will approve of whatever choice she has made.

22 **store** number

The precious treasure of his eyesight lost.
Show me a mistress that is passing fair:
What doth her beauty serve, but as a note
Where I may read who passed that passing fair?
Farewell; thou canst not teach me to forget.   235

BENVOLIO   I'll pay that doctrine, or else die in debt.

Exeunt.

Scene 2

The same.

Enter CAPULET, PARIS and, Capulet's SERVANT.

CAPULET   But Montague is bound as well as I,
In penalty alike, and 't is not hard, I think,
For men so old as we to keep the peace.

PARIS   Of honourable reckoning are you both,
And pity 't is you lived at odds so long.   5
But now, my lord, what say you to my suit?

CAPULET   But saying o'er what I have said before:
My child is yet a stranger in the world;
She hath not seen the change of fourteen years;
Let two more summers wither in their pride   10
Ere we may think her ripe to be a bride.

PARIS   Younger than she are happy mothers made.

CAPULET   And too soon marred are those so early made.
Earth hath swallowèd all my hopes but she;
She's the hopeful lady of my earth.   15
But woo her, gentle Paris, get her heart;
My will to her consent is but a part.
And she agreed, within her scope of choice
Lies my consent and fair according voice.
This night I hold an old accustomed feast,   20
Whereto I have invited many a guest,
Such as I love; and you among the store,
One more most welcome, makes my number more.
At my poor house look to behold this night

21

1.2 A street in Verona

Capulet invites Paris to a family feast to be held that night and gives his servant a list of people to be invited. Unfortunately the servant cannot read.

Activities

Character review: Capulet (1)

What impression have you have formed of Capulet from his first appearance? In pairs, discuss how far you would agree with each of the following statements, grading them from 1 (seriously disagree) to 5 (totally agree). Then compare your gradings with another pair, justifying your decisions. Capulet seems to be:

(a) prepared to accept peace between his family and the Montagues;

(b) a protective father;

(c) a doting father;

(d) a father who is willing to take his daughter's wishes into account;

(e) somebody who likes to show off his wealth and social status;

(f) somebody who had a lot of girl-friends when he was a young man.

Finally, how old is Capulet, as far as you can tell?

---

25 **Earth-treading stars** stars (beautiful women) who walk on Earth

26 **comfort** happiness

27–28 **well apparelled ... limping ...** April is 'well dressed' in the new spring leaves; winter 'limps away' slowly to give way to spring.

29 **female buds** young girls

30 **Inherit** possess, enjoy

31 **like her most ...** admire the one whom you think is best

32–33 **Which one ... number** When you have viewed all these girls, of whom my daughter will be one, you might place her first.

33 **though in reckoning none** *(possibly:)* though you might not judge her so highly

38–41 **It is written ...** It is said that people should stick to what they do best.

45 **learned** somebody educated (who can read)

47 **Tut** an expression used when someone is disagreeing

47–52 **one fire ...** *A new love will help Romeo to forget the torment of the old one.*

48 **another's anguish** the suffering of a second pain

49 **holp** helped

53 **plantain leaf** leaf used to help cuts heal

	Earth-treading stars that make dark heaven	
	light.	25
	Such comfort as do lusty young men feel	
	When well-apparelled April on the heel	
	Of limping winter treads, even such delight	
	Among fresh female buds shall you this night	
	Inherit at my house; hear all, all see,	30

Earth-treading stars that make dark heaven
   light.   25
Such comfort as do lusty young men feel
When well-apparelled April on the heel
Of limping winter treads, even such delight
Among fresh female buds shall you this night
Inherit at my house; hear all, all see,   30
And like her most whose merit most shall be:
Which one more view of many, mine being one,
May stand in number, though in reckoning none.
Come, go with me. (*To the* CLOWN, *giving him a paper*)
   Go, sirrah, trudge about
Through fair Verona; find those persons out   35
Whose names are written there, and to them say
My house and welcome on their pleasure stay.

                      Exeunt CAPULET and PARIS.

SERVANT   Find them out whose names are written here? It is
written that the shoemaker should meddle with
his yard and the tailor with his last, the fisher   40
with his pencil and the painter with his nets. But I
am sent to find those persons whose names are
here writ, and cap never find what names the
writing person hath here writ. I must to the
learned. (*He sees* BENVOLIO *and* ROMEO *approaching*)   45
In good time!

   Enter BENVOLIO and ROMEO.

BENVOLIO   Tut, man, one fire burns out another's burning,
One pain is lessened by another's anguish;
Turn giddy, and be holp by backward turning.
One desperate grief cures with another's languish: 50
Take thou some new infection to thy eye,
And the rank poison of the old will die.

ROMEO   Your plantain leaf is excellent for that.

BENVOLIO   For what, I pray thee?

ROMEO   For your broken shin.

BENVOLIO   Why, Romeo, art thou mad?   55

1.2 **A street in Verona**

The servant asks Romeo for help in reading the guest-list for the feast and invites him to attend. Romeo reads the name of Rosaline among those invited.

56–58 **bound ... tormented** tied up ... (*This describes the ways in which the insane were dealt with in Shakespeare's time – see the treatment of Malvolio in* Twelfth Night.)

58 **Good e'en** Good afternoon. ('*evening' being any time after midday*)

59 **God gi' good e'en** God give you good evening.

59–60 **read** *Romeo replies that he can 'read' (foretell) his fortune by looking at his misery.*

61 **without book** (1) by heart; (2) from experience

64 **rest you merry** 'Goodbye and good luck.'

67 **County** Count

84 **crush** drink down

24

ROMEO	Not mad, but bound more than a madman is; Shut up in prison, kept without my food, Whipped and tormented, and – Good e'en, good fellow.
SERVANT	God gi' good e'en. I pray, sir, can you read?
ROMEO	Ay, mine own fortune in my misery. 60
SERVANT	Perhaps you have learned it without book. But I pray, can you read anything you see?
ROMEO	Ay, if I know the letters and the language.
SERVANT	Ye say honestly; rest you merry. (*He moves off*)
ROMEO	Stay, fellow; I can read. (*He reads the list*) 65 "Signor Martino and his wife and daughters; County Anselme and his beauteous sisters; The lady widow of Vitruvio; Signor Placentio and his lovely nieces; Mercutio and his brother Valentine; 70 Mine uncle Capulet, his wife and daughters, My fair niece Rosaline and Livia; Signor Valentio and his cousin Tybalt; Lucio and the lively Helena." A fair assembly, Whither should they come? 75
SERVANT	Up –
ROMEO	Whither? To supper?
SERVANT	To our house.
ROMEO	Whose house?
SERVANT	My master's. 80
ROMEO	Indeed, I should have asked thee that before.
SERVANT	Now I'll tell you without asking. My master is the great rich Capulet; and if you be not of the house of Montagues, I pray come and crush a cup of wine. Rest you merry. 85

Exit SERVANT.

1.3 A room in Capulet's house

Romeo accepts Benvolio's suggestion that they should attend the Capulet feast, but refuses to believe that he will find anyone there more beautiful than Rosaline. In the Capulet household, Juliet is being called for.

Activities

Themes: love

Several times in this scene Benvolio offers Romeo advice on how he might deal with his 'unrequited' (not returned) love for Rosaline (47–52, 86–91 and 98–103).

1. Do you think he gives wise advice? Would you follow Benvolio's advice, if you were in Romeo's position?
2. Imagine that Romeo has written to a magazine about his problem (see the activity on page 18). Using Benvolio's advice as a basis, write the reply that an 'agony aunt' (or 'uncle') might offer.

89   **unattainted** unbiased, unprejudiced

92–95   **When the devout ... liars** When my religion (of looking at Rosaline), lies in that way, then may tears turn to fire and my eyes – often drowned but never dead – be burned as obvious heretics (people who turn away from the true religion).

97   **match** equal

98   **none else ...** when there were no other beauties present

99–103   **Herself poised ... best** Her image was in both your eyes (like the pans of a set of scales) and you had no one to compare her with. Take one eye off her to look at another girl and the new one's beauty would outweigh Rosaline's.

103   **scant** scarcely, hardly

2   **by my maidenhead ...** *The Nurse swears by the fact that she was still a virgin when she was twelve years old.*

4   **God forbid!** *The Nurse suddenly remembers that 'lady-bird' can mean prostitute.*

BENVOLIO	At this same ancient feast of Capulet's
	Sups the fair Rosaline whom thou so loves,
	With all the admiréd beauties of Verona.
	Go thither, and with unattainted eye,
	Compare her face with some that I shall show, 90
	And I will make thee think thy swan a crow.
ROMEO	When the devout religion of mine eye
	Maintains such falsehood, then turn tears to fire;
	And these, who, often drowned, could never die,
	Transparent heretics, be burnt for liars. 95
	One fairer than my love? The all-seeing sun
	Ne'er saw her match since first the world begun.
BENVOLIO	Tut, you saw her fair, none else being by,
	Herself poised with herself in either eye;
	But in that crystal scales let there be weighed 100
	Your lady's love against some other maid
	That I will show you shining at this feast,
	And she shall scant show well that now seems best.
ROMEO	I'll go along, no such sight to be shown,
	But to rejoice in splendour of mine own. 105

Exeunt.

Scene 3

A room in Capulet's house.

Enter LADY CAPULET and NURSE.

LADY CAPULET	Nurse, where's my daughter? Call her forth to me.
NURSE	Now, by my maidenhead at twelve year old, I bade
	her come. What, lamb! What, lady-bird! God
	forbid! Where's this girl? What, Juliet!

Enter JULIET.

JULIET	How now? Who calls?	5
NURSE	Your mother.	
JULIET	Madam, I am here. What is your will?	

1.3 A room in Capulet's house

Lady Capulet and the Nurse discuss Juliet's age. The Nurse reminisces about an incident from Juliet's childhood.

Activities

Actors' interpretations (4): calling back the Nurse

In some productions of the play, the Nurse is called back because she lets Lady Capulet see how upset she is at being excluded from the conversation.

1. In threes, act out lines 1–17, with the Nurse (a) showing how upset she is; (b) leaving obediently and quietly.
2. How differently does Lady Capulet have to behave in the two versions?
3. Finally compare your performances with other groups'. Which interpretation do you prefer as the audience's introduction to the Nurse? Why?
4. What does this sequence reveal about the relationship between Lady Capulet and the Nurse? Think particularly about their different positions in the household.

8 **... the matter** This is what I want to talk about.

10 **thou's** you must

11 **pretty** suitable

14 **teen** grief

16 **Lammas-tide** *The 1st of August; a feast to celebrate the harvest*

19 **Susan** the Nurse's own daughter

22 **Lammas-Eve** *Juliet's birthday is therefore the 31st of July.*

27 **laid wormwood ...** *Mothers would put a bitter-tasting substance on the nipple (dug) to put the child off sucking.*

33 **"Shake" ...** The dove-house shakes in the earthquake.

34 **'Twas no need ...** Believe me (**I trow**), there was no need to tell me to get out of the way!

36 **stand high-lone** stand up by herself

36 **by the rood** *an oath*: 'By the holy cross'

39 **'a** he

40 **took up** picked up

41–42 **when thou hast ...** when you know a bit more!

42–43 **by my holidame** *an oath*: 'By my holiness' (or possibly: holy mother – the Virgin Mary)

43 **left** stopped

LADY CAPULET	This is the matter. Nurse, give leave a while;
	We must talk in secret. (*NURSE begins to leave*)
	Nurse, come back again;
	I have remembered me, thou's hear our counsel. 10
	Thou know'st my daughter's of a pretty age.
NURSE	Faith, I can tell her age unto an hour.
LADY CAPULET	She's not fourteen.
NURSE	I'll lay fourteen of my teeth – and yet, to my teen
	be it spoken, I have but four – she's not fourteen. 15
	How long is it now to Lammas-tide?
LADY CAPULET	A fortnight and odd days.
NURSE	Even or odd, of all days in the year come
	Lammas-Eve at night shall she be fourteen. Susan
	and she – God rest all Christian souls – were of 20
	an age. Well, Susan is with God; she was too good
	for me. But, as I said, on Lammas-Eve at night
	shall she be fourteen; that shall she, marry; I
	remember it well. 'T is since the earthquake now
	eleven years, and she was weaned – I never shall 25
	forget it – of all the days of the year, upon that
	day; for I had then laid wormwood to my dug,
	sitting in the sun under the dove-house wall. My
	lord and you were then at Mantua – nay, I do bear
	a brain! But, as I said, when it did taste the 30
	wormwood on the nipple of my dug and felt it
	bitter, pretty fool, to see it tetchy, and fall out
	with the dug! "Shake", quoth the dove-house.
	'Twas no need, I trow, to bid me trudge. And since
	that time it is eleven years for then she could 35
	stand high-lone; nay, by the rood, she could have
	run and waddled all about, for even the day
	before, she broke her brow, and then my husband
	– God be with his soul, 'a was a merry man –
	took up the child. "Yea," quoth he, "dost thou fall 40
	upon thy face? Thou wilt fall backward when
	thou hast more wit, wilt thou not, Jule?" And, by
	my holidame, the pretty wretch left crying, and

1.3 A room in Capulet's house

Having persuaded the Nurse to cease her reminiscing, Lady Capulet introduces the subject of marriage and informs Juliet that Paris wants to marry her.

Activities

Character review: the Nurse (1)

Quite apart from giving an audience information about the Nurse, the speech paints a wonderful picture of the domestic life of the Capulets.'

A Look carefully at the Nurse's speech and note down what information it provides about life in the Capulet household.

B In threes, learn what amuses the Nurse so much by performing the incident that she describes: one person reads the speech (from 37: 'even the day before . . .'), while others play the parts of the Nurse's husband and the baby Juliet. Alternatively you could storyboard it as a flashback in a film version.

C Write directors' notes to assist an actress playing the Nurse with this lengthy speech and the continued exchanges with Lady Capulet and Juliet (through to 61), giving advice on how she should bring out:
- the Nurse's love for Juliet
- her extrovert, bawdy, down-to-earth character
- the contrast between the Nurse and Lady Capulet.

44–45 **come about** come true eventually *(as Juliet is now ready for marriage and sex)*

45 **I warrant, and I should** I promise you, even if I were to live

52 **it** its

53 **stone** testicle

53 **perilous knock** dangerous bump

55–56 **when thou comest to age** when you're old enough

59 **God mark thee to his grace** May God make you one of the chosen souls!

60–61 **And I might** If only I could

61 **once** one day

62 **theme** subject

64 **How stands . . .?** How would you respond to the idea of getting married?

66–67 **. . . thine only nurse . . .** If I were not the only woman who had breastfed you, I'd say you had sucked in wisdom with your milk!

69 **ladies of esteem** society women

70 **count** calculation

71 **much upon these years** at roughly the same age

75 **a man of wax** the very model of manhood; the ideal man

said "Ay". To see now how a jest shall come
about! I warrant, and I should live a thousand   45
years, I never should forget it. "Wilt thou not,
Jule?" quoth he; and, pretty fool, it stinted, and
said "Ay".

| LADY CAPULET | Enough of this. I pray thee hold thy peace. |

| NURSE | Yes, madam; yet I cannot choose but laugh, to   50 |

think it should leave crying, and say "Ay"; and yet
I warrant it had upon it brow a bump as big as a
young cockerel's stone – a perilous knock – and it
cried bitterly. "Yea," quoth my husband, "fall'st
upon thy face? Thou wilt fall backward when   55
thou comest to age, wilt thou not, Jule? It stinted,
and said "Ay".

| JULIET | And stint thou too, I pray thee, Nurse, say I. |

| NURSE | Peace, I have done. God mark thee to his grace, |

thou wast the prettiest babe that e'er I nursed. And I   60
might live to see thee married once, I have my wish.

| LADY CAPULET | Marry, that "marry" is the very theme |

I came to talk of. Tell me, daughter Juliet,
How stands your dispositions to be married?

| JULIET | It is an honour that I dream not of.   65 |

| NURSE | An honour! Were not I thine only nurse, I would |

say thou hadst sucked wisdom from thy teat.

| LADY CAPULET | Well, think of marriage now. Younger than you, |

Here in Verona, ladies of esteem,
Are made already mothers. By my count,   70
I was your mother much upon these years
That you are now a maid. Thus then in brief,
The valiant Paris seeks you for his love.

| NURSE | A man, young lady! Lady, such a man as all the |

world . . . why, he's a man of wax!   75

| LADY CAPULET | Verona's summer hath not such a flower. |

1.3 A room in Capulet's house

Lady Capulet praises Paris and gives Juliet persuasive reasons for marrying him. Juliet agrees to consider Paris as a potential husband and promises to obey her mother's wishes.

Activities

Character review: Lady Capulet (1)

How do you think Lady Capulet should react while the Nurse is telling her story and repeating it?

1. Make brief notes on what she might be feeling and thinking at certain moments (e.g. at lines 12, 18, 21, 38, 48, 57 and 61).
2. What does the scene reveal about the relationship between Juliet and her mother?
3. If you get the chance, look at the way in which Lady Capulet behaves in the Zeffirelli film.
4. What does Lady Capulet's speech (78–93) reveal about her view of love? In order to gain a deeper understanding of the picture that she is painting, work in pairs to express its main points in your own words, using the following as a structure:
   * 80–87: Imagine that Paris's face were a book – with lines (82), a margin (85), but no cover (87)
   * 88–89: Fish, which are beautiful, need to live in the sea, also beautiful
   * 90–93: Books look better with gold clasps.

80 **Read o'er the volume ...** *(See the activity on this page.)*

82–83 **every married lineament ... content** all his features, joined in harmony with one another, each one complementing the other

84 **what obscured** whatever you cannot see clearly

86 **unbound** (1) without a cover; (2) unmarried

88–89 **... 't is much pride ... hide** Just as the fish lives in the sea, the contents of a book live within the covers.

90–93 **That book ... less** Just as a book is admired for its contents and its gold clasps, so you will share in Paris's glory when you are married to him.

94 **Women grow ...** Women get pregnant by men.

96 **I'll look to like ... move** I expect I shall like him if I am attracted by looking at him.

97–98 **But no more deep ... fly** But I will not fall in love except with your permission.

101 **in extremity** in a mess, needing urgent attention

102 **I must hence to wait** I have to go off and serve at table.

103 **straight** immediately

104 **the County stays** The Count (Paris) is waiting.

105 **to** to add to

1.3

NURSE	Nay, he's a flower; in faith, a very flower.
LADY CAPULET	What say you? Can you love the gentleman?
	This night you shall behold him at our feast.
	Read o'er the volume of young Paris' face, 80
	And find delight writ there with beauty's pen;
	Examine every married lineament,
	And see how one another lends content;
	And what obscured in this fair volume lies,
	Find written in the margent of his eyes. 85
	This precious book of love, this unbound lover,
	To beautify him, only lacks a cover.
	The fish lives in the sea; and 't is much pride
	For fair without, the fair within to hide.
	That book in many's eyes doth share the glory 90
	That in gold clasps locks in the golden story:
	So shall you share all that he doth possess
	By having him, making yourself no less.
NURSE	No less? Nay, bigger! Women grow by men.
LADY CAPULET	Speak briefly: can you like of Paris' love? 95
JULIET	I'll look to like, if looking liking move;
	But no more deep will I endart mine eye
	Than your consent gives strength to make it fly.

Enter CLOWN.

CLOWN	Madam, the guests are come, supper served up,
	you called, my young lady asked for, the Nurse 100
	cursed in the pantry, and everything in extremity.
	I must hence to wait. I beseech you, follow
	straight.
LADY CAPULET	We follow thee. Juliet, the County stays.
NURSE	Go, girl; seek happy nights to happy days. 105

Exeunt.

1.4 Outside Capulet's house

Romeo, Benvolio and their friend Mercutio pause outside Capulet's house to plan how to make their entrance to the feast. Romeo is still love-sick and Mercutio tries to cheer him up.

Activities

Actors' interpretations (5): props and costumes

Romeo and his friends are planning to gate-crash the Capulets' party. In those days, groups of young men invited to banquets and balls were expected to perform some kind of brief entertainment or 'masque', and although Benvolio argues that such things are now out of date (3), he and the others give us a good idea of what such performances might have been like. Look through lines 1–30 and discuss in pairs what you have learned about:

- the appearance of Cupid, who might introduce the masque (4–6)
- the speaking of a prologue (7–8)
- dancing in masques (9–10)
- lighting (11–12)
- the wearing of masks (30).

1 **for our excuse** *to introduce themselves and apologise for gate-crashing*

3 **The date ...** These days, such long-winded speeches are unfashionable.

5 **Tartar's ... bow ...** *typical Cupid's bow, made of wood* (**lath**)

6 **crow-keeper** someone acting as a scarecrow

7 **without-book** learnt by heart

7–8 **faintly spoke ...** spoken without much spirit, and with the help of the prompter *(who helps the actors when they forget their lines)*

10 **measure them a measure** give them a dance

11 **ambling** dancing

19 **too sore empiercèd ...** too seriously wounded by Cupid's arrow

21 **bound a pitch** jump to the height that a falcon can soar

23–24 **to sink in it ... love** *Sexual wordplay.* To enjoy lovemaking, you would have to be a heavy weight on (**burden**) the woman you love.

26 **rude** rough, violent

28 **Prick love ...** If love is hurting you: (1) hurt it back; (2) have sex.

29 **... a case ...** Give me a mask to put my face in.

Scene 4

Outside Capulet's house.

Enter torchbearers, followed by ROMEO, MERCUTIO, BENVOLIO and five or six other masked men.

ROMEO	What, shall this speech be spoke for our excuse,
	Or shall we on without apology?
BENVOLIO	The date is out of such prolixity:
	We'll have no Cupid hoodwinked with a scarf,
	Bearing a Tartar's painted bow of lath,
	Scaring the ladies like a crow-keeper;
	Nor no without-book prologue, faintly spoke
	After the prompter, for our entrance.
	But let them measure us by what they will,
	We'll measure them a measure and be gone.
ROMEO	Give me a torch: I am not for this ambling;
	Being but heavy, I will bear the light.
MERCUTIO	Nay, gentle Romeo, we must have you dance.
ROMEO	Not I, believe me. You have dancing shoes
	With nimble soles: I have a soul of lead
	So stakes me to the ground I cannot move.
MERCUTIO	You are a lover: borrow Cupid's wings,
	And soar with them above a common bound.
ROMEO	I am too sore empiercèd with his shaft
	To soar with his light feathers; and so bound,
	I cannot bound a pitch above dull woe.
	Under love's heavy burden do I sink.
MERCUTIO	And to sink in it should you burden love –
	Too great oppression for a tender thing.
ROMEO	Is love a tender thing? It is too rough,
	Too rude, too boisterous, and it pricks like thorn.
MERCUTIO	If love be rough with you, be rough with love:
	Prick love for pricking, and you beat love down.
	Give me a case to put my visage in:
	A visor for a visor! What care I

Line numbers: 5, 10, 15, 20, 25, 30

1.4 Outside Capulet's house

Romeo is anxious about attending the feast: he has had a disturbing dream and Mercutio tells him that he must have been visited by Queen Mab, the fairies' midwife.

Activities

Shakespeare's language: wordplay

Mercutio is another of the characters who loves playing with words.

1. Discuss the meaning of the wordplay In lines 9–10 ('measure'); 12 (an oxymoron: see page 14); 15 ('soles/soul'); 18–19 ('soar/sore'); 20–21 ('bound'); 26–28 (a bawdy innuendo); 30 ('visor'); 39–41 ('done/dun/Dun'); 51 ('lie').

2. What do you think the effect of all this wordplay might be at this stage of the play? Discuss each of the following possibilities and compare your responses with other people's. The repeated wordplay suggests that:
   • the young men are light-hearted
   • they are extremely intelligent and witty
   • they are confused about whether to gate-crash the Capulets' party or not
   • they have the ability to see the connections between different parts of their experience.

3. Very often these days people groan at puns, and yet it seems clear that Shakespeare and his audience must have liked them. How do you react to the wordplay yourself?

32 **the beetle brows ...** a mask with overhanging eyebrows

34 **betake him to his legs** start dancing straightaway

36 **senseless rushes** the rushes strewn on the floor, trodden down by 'senseless' people

37–38 **proverbed with ... on** the old proverb applies to me: 'the onlooker gets the best view'

39 **The game was ...** I have had the best of the game; let's quit while we are ahead.

40 **dun's the mouse ...** *A proverb meaning: 'Keep quiet; keep your head down!'* '**Dun**' = grey; *therefore: inconspicuous, as a constable should be.*

41 **draw thee from ...** Pull you out of the mud. **Dun** was also a common name for a horse.

42 **save your reverence** *a common expression used in apologies*

43 **burn daylight** waste time

46–47 **Take our ... wits** Understand the words in the meaning that I intended.

48–49 **And we mean well ... go** We may have good intentions in going to the Capulets' feast. but I do not think it is a sensible thing to do.

55 **midwife** nurse who assists at the birth of a baby – *Queen Mab acts as midwife to help sleepers 'give birth' to their dreams*

What curious eye doth quote deformities?
Here are the beetle brows shall blush for me.

He puts on a mask.

BENVOLIO Come, knock and enter; and no sooner in,
But every man betake him to his legs.

ROMEO A torch for me: let wantons light of heart   35
Tickle the senseless rushes with their heels,
For I am proverbed with a grandsire phrase:
I'll be a candle-holder and look on.
The game was ne'er so fair, and I am done.

MERCUTIO Tut, dun's the mouse, the constable's own word;   40
If thou art Dun, we'll draw thee from the mire,
Or, save your reverence, love, wherein thou stickest
Up to the ears. Come, we burn daylight, ho.

ROMEO Nay, that's not so.

MERCUTIO   I mean, sir, in delay
We waste our lights in vain, like lights by day.   45
Take our good meaning, for our judgement sits
Five times in that, ere once in our five wits.

ROMEO And we mean well in going to this masque,
But 't is no wit to go.

MERCUTIO   Why, may one ask?

ROMEO I dreamt a dream tonight.

MERCUTIO   And so did I.   50

ROMEO Well, what was yours?

MERCUTIO   That dreamers often lie.

ROMEO In bed asleep while they do dream things true.

MERCUTIO O then I see Queen Mab hath been with you.

BENVOLIO Queen Mab? What's she?

MERCUTIO She is the fairies' midwife, and she comes   55

1.4 Outside Capulet's house

Mercutio explains who Queen Mab is and what she does while people are asleep.

Shakespeare's language: the Queen Mab speech

1. As a group, draw an illustration of Queen Mab, as Mercutio describes her, labelling each detail with quotations from the script.
2. Also as a group, work on a modern version of the description of Queen Mab. Think what her coach might be made up of these days, rather than objects from the natural world.
3. After this point (72) the description becomes more satirical (mocking people through humour). Draw a cartoon of your favourite description of what Queen Mab does to people (73–89), using thought-bubbles to represent their dreams, as Mercutio describes them.
4. Suggest some modern versions of the dreamers described by Mercutio (what would a teacher dream of, for example?) and compose some lines in the style of the Queen Mab speech.

58 **atomies** tiny creatures

60 **spinners'** spiders'

62 **traces** harness

64 **film** gossamer

69 **joiner-squirrel** *The squirrel hollows out nuts like a carpenter.*

70 **Time out o' mind** for as long as people can remember

71 **state** splendour

73 **straight** immediately

79 **smelling out a suit** being paid to argue someone's case at court

80–81 **tithe-pig ...** *pigs were sometimes given as the tenth of a person's income which had to go to the parson*

82 **benefice** appointment in church *(to bring him more income)*

85 **breaches, ambuscadoes ...** attacks through holes made in castle walls, ambushes, high-quality swords made in Spain

86 **healths ...** drinking heavily, toasting people's health

91–92 **bakes the elf-locks ... bodes** makes untidy people's hair matted, which is very unlucky

94 **to bear** (1) to bear the weight of a man: (2) to bear children

95 **of good carriage** Women (1) carry themselves gracefully; (2) carry children; (3) bear the weight of their lover.

In shape no bigger than an agate stone
On the forefinger of an alderman,
Drawn with a team of little atomies
Athwart men's noses as they lie asleep.
Her waggon spokes made of long spinners' legs,   60
The cover of the wings of grasshoppers,
Her traces of the smallest spider-web,
Her collars of the moonshine's watery beams,
Her whip of cricket's bone, the lash of film,
Her waggoner a small grey-coated gnat,   65
Not half so big as a round little worm
Pricked from the lazy finger of a maid.
Her chariot is an empty hazel-nut,
Made by the joiner-squirrel or old grub,
Time out o' mind the fairies' coachmakers.   70
And in this state she gallops night by night
Through lovers' brains, and then they dream of love;
O'er courtiers' knees, that dream on curtsies straight;
O'er lawyers' fingers, who straight dream on fees;
O'er ladies' lips, who straight on kisses dream,   75
Which oft the angry Mab with blisters plagues,
Because their breaths with sweetmeats tainted are.
Sometime she gallops o'er a courtier's nose
And then dreams he of smelling out a suit;
And sometime comes she with a tithe-pig's tail,   80
Tickling a parson's nose as 'a lies asleep,
And then dreams he of another benefice;
Sometime she driveth o'er a soldier's neck,
And then dreams he of cutting foreign throats,
Of breaches, ambuscadoes, Spanish blades,   85
Of healths five fathom deep, and then anon
Drums in his ear, at which he starts and wakes,
And being thus frighted, swears a prayer or two,
And sleeps again. This is that very Mab
That plaits the manes of horses in the night,   90
And bakes the elf-locks in foul sluttish hairs,
Which once untangled, much misfortune bodes;
This is the hag, when maids lie on their backs,
That presses them and learns them first to bear,
Making them women of good carriage;   95
This is she –

1.5 The hall in Capulet's house

Romeo interrupts Mercutio's description of Queen Mab. Mercutio dismisses dreams as meaningless fantasies, and despite Romeo's profound misgivings, they enter the Capulets' house. Inside the servants are rushing around in disorder.

Activities

Character review: Romeo (5)

At the end of the scene Romeo talks about a premonition that he will die as a result of events that will take place that night. Earlier (50), he was about to describe a troubling dream, which perhaps gave rise to this premonition. Based upon the words that he uses here (107–112), discuss what you think Romeo's dream might have been about and either write it up as though recounted by Romeo (perhaps in the form of a poem), or create a picture which represents it (using your own drawing skills, or creating a collage from images cut from magazines).

Plot review (2)

1. Who are Benvolio and Mercutio? List the most important things that we know about each one.
2. Which one of them actually has an invitation to the party? Why should he have an invitation, but not the others? It will help to check the list of characters on page 1.
3. What plan have they formed, to do with the Capulet party?
4. What seems to be troubling Romeo as they approach the party? What are his worries concerning 'fate' or 'the stars'?

99 **Begot of ...** born of nothing more than idle dreaming

101–104 **more inconstant ... south** *The changeable wind is imagined as a fickle lover who woos the north, but, finding it cold and unresponsive, turns to the warm south.*

105 **blows us from ourselves** distracts us from our intentions (to go to the party)

107–110 **misgives Some consequence ... revels** I have an uneasy feeling that this party will give rise to something bad, fated to happen, but not yet revealed.

110–112 **and expire ... death** and put an end to a hated existence, by making me pay the awful penalty of an early death

113 **steerage of my course** He who has control over the direction in which I sail *(God)*

1 **take away** remove the dirty dishes

2 **He shift a trencher?** Do you expect him to move a plate?

3–5 **one or two ...** *They feel that they have not got enough helpers.*

6 **joint-stools** stools made by joiners (carpenters)

6–7 **court-cupboard** sideboard

7 **look to the plate** deal with the sliverware

7 **Good thou** Be a good man and ...

ROMEO	Peace, peace, Mercutio, peace! Thou talk'st of nothing.	
MERCUTIO	True, I talk of dreams, Which are the children of an idle brain, Begot of nothing but vain fantasy, Which is as thin of substance as the air, And more inconstant than the wind, who woos Even now the frozen bosom of the north, And being angered, puffs away from thence, Turning his face to the dew-dropping south.	100
BENVOLIO	This wind you talk of blows us from ourselves: Supper is done, and we shall come too late.	105
ROMEO	I fear, too early, for my mind misgives Some consequence, yet hanging in the stars, Shall bitterly begin his fearful date With this night's revels, and expire the term Of a despisèd life closed in my breast, By some vile forfeit of untimely death: But He that hath the steerage of my course Direct my sail. On, lusty gentlemen.	110
BENVOLIO	Strike, drum.	115

Exeunt.

Scene 5

The hall in Capulet's house.

Enter ROMEO and the other maskers and stand at one side of the stage.
Enter two SERVANTS.

FIRST SERVANT	Where's Potpan, that he helps not to take away? He shift a trencher? He scrape a trencher?	
SECOND SERVANT	When good manners shall lie all in one or two men's hands, and they unwashed too, 'tis a foul thing.	5
FIRST SERVANT	Away with the joint-stools, remove the court-cupboard, look to the plate. Good thou, save me a	

1.5 The hall in Capulet's house

Capulet welcomes his guests noisily and then sits down to reminisce with an old cousin about their youth.

8   **march-pane** marzipan

14–15   **Cheerly . . . all** Cheer up and let him who lives longest take the lot.

     maskers masked dancers

17   **walk a bout** have a dance

19   **deny** refuse

19   **makes dainty** seems reluctant; makes a fuss

20   **Am I come near . . .** Have I hit the nail on the head? Have I guessed the truth?

26   **A hall, a hall!** Make some space!

26   **foot it** dance away

27   **turn the tables up** pack away the trestle tables

29   **this unlooked-for sport . . .** this unexpected entertainment *(the maskers)* is welcome

33   **By'r lady** By our Lady *(the Virgin Mary)*

piece of march-pane, and, as thou loves me, let the
porter let in Susan Grindstone and Nell. (*He calls*)
Antony and Potpan!   10

Enter the servants, ANTONY and POTPAN.

ANTONY   Ay, boy, ready.

FIRST   You are looked for and called for, asked for and
  SERVANT   sought for, in the great chamber.

POTPAN   We cannot be here, and there too. Cheerly, boys;
                be brisk a while, and the longer liver take all.   15

Exeunt SERVANTS.

*Enter LORD and LADY CAPULET, JULIET, TYBALT, NURSE, the guests and
musicians at one side of the stage, meeting the maskers who are at the other side.*

CAPULET   Welcome, gentlemen. Ladies that have their toes
                Unplagued with corns will walk a bout with you.
                Ah ha, my mistresses! which of you all
                Will now deny to dance? She that makes dainty,
                She, I'll swear, hath corns. Am I come near ye now? 20
                Welcome, gentlemen. I have seen the day
                That I have worn a visor, and could tell
                A whispering tale in a fair lady's ear
                Such as would please; 't is gone, 't is gone, 't is gone.
                You are welcome, gentlemen. Come, musicians,
                    play!   25

Music plays and they dance.

                A hall, a hall! Give room, and foot it, girls
                (*To the servants*) More light you knaves, and turn the
                    tables up,
                And quench the fire, the room is grown too hot.
                (*To himself*) Ah, sirrah, this unlooked-for sport
                    comes well.
                (*To his COUSIN*) Nay sit, nay sit, good cousin Capulet 30
                For you and I are past our dancing days.
                How long is 't now since last yourself and I
                Were in a mask?

COUSIN   By 'r lady, thirty years.

1.5 The hall in Capulet's house

Romeo notices Juliet and is stunned by her beauty. Tybalt identifies him in the crowd and angrily reports his discovery of the gate-crasher to Capulet.

Activities

Actors' interpretations (7): blocking the scene

At some point during rehearsals, actors will agree on their positions and moves on stage; this is known as 'blocking a scene'. Sketch a copy of the stage plan on page 239 and mark on it the positions of all the main characters at line 42 ('What lady's that ...'). Then draw arrows on the plan to show what moves the characters make through to line 61, when Capulet addresses Tybalt.

Compare your decisions with someone else and discuss the differences.

What was the best way of letting the audience see the exchange between Capulet and Tybalt while other things were going on?

Character review: Romeo (6)

Re-read Romeo's words on first seeing Juliet (45–54) and note (a) all the words and phrases which show that Romeo is thinking of her beauty in terms of brightness, in contrast to the surrounding dark; (b) the line which suggests that there is something holy about her.

What does this language tell you about the nature of Romeo's feelings?

35 **nuptial** wedding

36 **Come Pentecost** when Whitsun comes round

39 **Will you tell me that?** Really?

40 **but** only

40 **a ward** a minor *(under twenty-one)* with a guardian

42–43 **enrich the hand** she makes the hand 'richer' by holding it

47 **Ethiop** Ethiopian *(but a term in those days for any black African)*

48 **too rich ...** too fine for everyday use and too precious for this Earth

49–50 **So shows ... shows** In a crowd of other ladies, she looks like a snow-white dove in the company of crows.

51–52 **The measure done ...** Once this dance is over, I'll watch where she stands and bless my coarse hand by touching hers.

53 **Forswear it** Swear that it was not so

56 **rapier** light sword for fencing

57 **antic face** comic, grotesque mask

58 **fleer ...** mock our celebrations **(solemnity)**

59 **by the stack ...** by the honour of my ancestry and family name

60 **hold** consider

61 **Wherefore storm ...?** Why are you behaving so angrily?

63 **in spite** in contempt

CAPULET	What, man? 'T is not so much, 't is not so much:
	'T is since the nuptial of Lucentio – 35
	Come Pentecost as quickly as it will –
	Some five and twenty years, and then we masked.
COUSIN	'T is more, 't is more; his son is elder, sir:
	His son is thirty.
CAPULET	Will you tell me that?
	His son was but a ward two years ago. 40
	(*Observing the dancers*) Good youth i' faith. O
	youth's a jolly thing.
ROMEO	(*To a* SERVANT) What lady's that which doth enrich
	the hand of yonder knight?
SERVANT	I know not, sir.
ROMEO	(*To himself*) O she doth teach the torches to burn
	bright! 45
	It seems she hangs upon the cheek of night
	As a rich jewel in an Ethiop's ear;
	Beauty too rich for use, for earth too dear.
	So shows a snowy dove trooping with crows,
	As yonder lady o'er her fellows shows. 50
	The measure done, I'll watch her place of stand,
	And, touching hers, make blessèd my rude hand.
	Did my heart love till now? Forswear it, sight,
	For I ne'er saw true beauty till this night.
TYBALT	This, by his voice, should be a Montague. 55
	Fetch me my rapier, boy. (*Exit page*) What dares the
	slave
	Come hither, covered with an antic face,
	To fleer and scorn at our solemnity?
	Now, by the stock and honour of my kin,
	To strike him dead, I hold it not a sin. 60
CAPULET	Why, how now, kinsman! Wherefore storm you so?
TYBALT	Uncle, this is a Montague, our foe;
	A villain that is hither come in spite,
	To scorn at our solemnity this night.
CAPULET	Young Romeo is it?

1.5 The hall in Capulet's house

Capulet has heard good reports of Romeo and angrily rebukes Tybalt for threatening to cause a disturbance in his house. Tybalt withdraws but privately threatens revenge on Romeo.

Activities

Actors' interpretations (8): the argument

Capulet and Tybalt have a spirited argument about Romeo's presence at the party. Write directors' notes to help the actors, giving advice on:
- how the characters are feeling, and why
- how they should say particular lines, and why
- where to pause
- movements and actions they could make at certain points, and why
- facial expressions
- reactions you want the audience to have, and why.

Character review: Tybalt (2)

In this, his second appearance, Tybalt once again shows himself to be short-tempered and violent. In groups of three improvise a scene in which, having stormed out of the party, he tells his followers what has happened and what he now plans to do to get his revenge on Romeo.

67 **'A bears him . . .** he behaves like a dignified gentleman

69 **well-governed** good-mannered

70–71 **I would not . . . disparagement** I would not want to treat him badly in my house, for all the wealth in Verona.

73–75 **It is my will . . . feast** If you respect my wishes, you will behave pleasantly and stop frowning.

78 **goodman boy** *a double insult*: **goodman** = not a gentleman; **boy** = immature

78 **Go to!** *An impatient and angry expression*: 'Stop!'

80 **God shall mend** 'God save us!'

81 **mutiny** disturbance

82 **set cock-a-hoop** cause a fuss

82 **be the man** You have to play the macho man!

84 **saucy** insolent *(a much stronger meaning than nowadays)*

85 **scathe you** do you harm

85 **I know what** unless I'm greatly mistaken

86 **contrary** oppose

87 **Well said** Well done

88 **princox** young upstart

90–91 **Patience . . . greeting** I am shaking because my natural feelings of anger **(wilful choler)** are in conflict with the need to restrain myself.

93 **gall** poison

TYBALT	'T is he, that villain, Romeo.	65

CAPULET	Content thee, gentle coz, let him alone;
	'A bears him like a portly gentleman:
	And to say truth, Verona brags of him
	To be a virtuous and well-governed youth.

I would not, for the wealth of all this town, 　70
Here in my house do him disparagement;
Therefore be patient, take no note of him.
It is my will, the which if thou respect,
Show a fair presence and put off these frowns,
An ill-beseeming semblance for a feast. 　75

TYBALT　　It fits when such a villain is a guest.
I'll not endure him.

CAPULET　　　　　　　He shall be endured.
What, goodman boy? I say he shall. Go to!
Am I the master here, or you? Go to!
You'll not endure him! God shall mend my soul, 　80
You'll make a mutiny among my guests!
You will set cock-a-hoop! You'll be the man!

TYBALT　　Why, uncle, 't is a shame.

CAPULET　　　　　　　Go to, go to!
You are a saucy boy. Is 't to indeed?
This trick may chance to scathe you, I know what. 　85
You must contrary me! Marry, 't is time –
(*To the dancers*) Well said, my hearts! (*To* TYBALT)
　You are a princox; go
Be quiet, or – (*To the servants*) More light, more
　light, for shame! –
(*To* TYBALT) I'll make you quiet. – (*To the dancers*)
　What, cheerly, my hearts!

He leaves TYBALT and moves among the guests.

TYBALT　　(*To himself*) Patience perforce with wilful choler
　meeting, 　90
Makes my flesh tremble in their different greeting.
I will withdraw, but this intrusion shall,
Now seeming sweet, convert to bitterest gall.

　　　　　　　　　　　　　　　　　　　Exit.

1.5 The hall in Capulet's house

Romeo and Juliet meet, exchange loving words and then kiss. The Nurse interrupts, summoning Juliet to her mother. When she has left, Romeo finds out from the Nurse who Juliet is.

94 **profane** desecrate, make dirty

95 **holy shrine** sacred place of worship *(Juliet's hand)*

98 **you do wrong your hand . . .** Your hand is not as rough as you say it is (and therefore you do not need to smooth my hand by kissing it).

99 **mannerly** good-mannered and fitting; proper

101 **palm to palm . . .** *Palmers (pilgrims who had returned from Jerusalem, with a palm leaf as a token) would touch a holy statue's hand, not kiss it.*

105 **They pray . . .** Let our lips ask for our prayers (for a kiss) to be answered, so that we will not fall into the sin of despair.

106 **Saints do not move . . .** Even though saints answer prayers. their statues do not move.

107 **Then move not . . .** So keep still, while I receive the answer to my prayer (a kiss).

108 **purged** cleansed, purified

109 **O trespass . . .** You encouraged (**urged**) this sin (**trespass**) very sweetly.

111 **Give . . . again** Give me my sin back.

111 **by the book** like an expert *(who has learned the art of kissing from books)*

113 **Marry, bachelor** Goodness, young man!

ROMEO	(*Taking* JULIET's *hand*) If I profane with my unworthiest hand	
	This holy shrine, the gentle sin is this:	95
	My lips, two blushing pilgrims, ready stand	
	To smooth that rough touch with a tender kiss.	

JULIET   Good pilgrim, you do wrong your hand too much,
Which mannerly devotion shows in this;
For saints have hands that pilgrims' hands do
     touch,   100
And palm to palm is holy palmers' kiss.

ROMEO   Have not saints lips, and holy palmers too?

JULIET   Ay, pilgrim, lips that they must use in prayer.

ROMEO   O then, dear saint, let lips do what hands do:
They pray, "Grant thou, lest faith turn to despair."   105

JULIET   Saints do not move, though grant for prayers' sake.

ROMEO   Then move not, while my prayer's effect I take.
Thus from my lips, by thine, my sin is purged.

He kisses her.

JULIET   Then have my lips the sin that they have took.

ROMEO   Sin from my lips? O trespass sweetly urged!   110
Give me my sin again.

He kisses her again.

JULIET   You kiss by the book.

NURSE comes to JULIET from the side of the stage.

NURSE   Madam, your mother craves a word with you.

JULIET joins her mother at the side of the stage.

ROMEO   What is her mother?

NURSE   Marry, bachelor,
Her mother is the lady of the house,
And a good lady, and a wise and virtuous.   115

1.5 The hall in Capulet's house

Romeo leaves the feast with the knowledge that he loves a Capulet. Juliet herself then discovers that she has fallen in love with her supposed enemy, a Montague.

Activities

Actors' interpretations (9): the maskers whisper

Actors performing this scene usually decide what it is that they whisper in Capulet's ear. It seems to be an excuse for having to leave, but it is strange that they do not speak it openly. Discuss what they might be saying, remembering that it has to be something that Capulet will understand and accept, but apparently not something that they want others to hear.

Character review: Romeo (7)

How seriously should we take Romeo's change of heart? Discuss whether there is anything in his language here which might encourage us to believe that he is now genuinely in love. Does the religious imagery help to give this impression, or do his involved arguments make him seem too clever and hypocritical, in your opinion? If you have seen an actor performing this scene (Leonard Whiting or Leonardo DiCaprio, for example), try to recall whether or not they seemed sincere, and how they conveyed that impression.

116 **withal** with

118 **the chinks** plenty of money *(because Juliet is Capulet's only heir)*

119 **O dear account ...** What a terrible price to have to pay! My life is now owed to my family's enemy.

120 **The sport ...** Let's quit while we are ahead. *(See 1.4.39.)*

121 **Ay, so I fear ...** Yes. I fear that whatever else happens will be disturbing for me.

123 **... trifling foolish banquet towards** There are light refreshments about to be served.

124 **Is it e'en so?** Oh, I see.

125 **honest** honourable

127 **by my fay, it waxes ...** by my faith, it's getting late

129 **yond gentleman** that gentleman over there

133 **would not** did not want to

136 **My grave ... bed** I will die unmarried.

136 **like** likely

139 **My only love ...** The only man I love is the offspring of the one thing I hate: the Montagues.

I nursed her daughter that you talked withal.
I tell you, he that can lay hold of her
Shall have the chinks.

ROMEO   Is she a Capulet?
O dear account! My life is my foe's debt.

BENVOLIO   Away, be gone! The sport is at the best.   120

ROMEO   Ay, so I fear; the more is my unrest.

CAPULET   Nay, gentleman, prepare not to be gone:
We have a trifling foolish banquet towards.

The maskers whisper their excuses to him.

Is it e'en so? Why, then I thank you all.
I thank you, honest gentlemen; good night.   125
(*To the servants*) More torches here! Come on, then
  let's to bed.

Torchbearers show the maskers out

(*To himself*) Ah, sirrah, by my fay, it waxes late.
I'll to my rest.

Exeunt all except JULIET and NURSE

JULIET   Come hither, Nurse. What is yond gentleman?

NURSE   The son and heir of old Tiberio.   130

JULIET   What's he that now is going out of door?

NURSE   Marry, that I think be young Petruchio.

JULIET   What's he that follows there, that would not dance?

NURSE   I know not.

JULIET   Go ask his name. (*Exit NURSE*) If he be marrièd,   135
My grave is like to be my wedding bed.

NURSE   (*Returning*) His name is Romeo, and a Montague,
The only son of your great enemy.

JULIET   (*To herself*) My only love sprung from my only hate!

1.5 The hall in Capulet's house

As the feast ends, Juliet is called to her room, hiding her thoughts and feelings from the Nurse.

Activities

Character review: Juliet (1)

What have you learned about Juliet from this scene? In pairs, discuss each of the following statements about Juliet, deciding how far you agree with them. Juliet:

- falls in love as easily as Romeo
- really wanted Romeo to kiss her, but had to pretend to be unwilling
- is as clever with words as Romeo
- always tells the Nurse her innermost secrets
- feels that she can never love a Montague.

140 **Too early . . .** I saw him before I knew who he was; now that I know, it's too late: I am already in love with him!

141–142 **Prodigious birth . . . enemy** The fact that I have to fall in love with a hated enemy is a very ill-omened (**prodigious**) start to our love.

144 **Anon, anon!** Coming!

Too early seen unknown, and known too late!   140
Prodigious birth of love it is to me,
That I must love a loathèd enemy.

NURSE   What's this, what's this?

JULIET   A rhyme I learnt even now
Of one I danced withal.

JULIET's mother calls her from another room.

NURSE   Anon, anon!
Come let's away; the strangers all are gone.   145

Exeunt.

Exam practice

Plot review (3)

Most of Shakespeare's plays do not begin with a Prologue (a kind of introduction). Here the dramatist has chosen to give us an idea of what to expect of his story.

1. What does he tell us will happen in this play? What kind of story will it be? Although the Prologue gives us some information, he still leaves a number of questions unanswered. For example:
2. What do you think might have first sparked off the 'ancient grudge' between the two families? (You have a wide choice here: it might help to think about other long-standing hostilities that you know about from different parts of the world.)
3. What do you think 'star-crossed' might mean? Can you give examples of other people (from history, literature or films) whom you would think of as 'star-crossed'?
4. Are there any other questions that you would like the Prologue to have answered?
5. Do you think the Prologue has given too much away?
6. Do you think it is a good idea to start the play off like this?

Plot review (4): characters

A The history of the characters in this story is important, as it affects the way they think and behave in the present day. To check that you know all the important facts established so far, answer the following questions in pairs:

1. In which city is this story set?
2. What are the names of the two feuding families?
3. Which of Romeo's friends tries to be a peacemaker?
4. How many recent 'civil brawls' have there been?
5. What threat does the Prince utter after the latest riot?
6. Who is Romeo in love with when the play starts?
7. Who is having discussions with Juliet's father about marriage? What is his rank?
8. How old is Juliet?
9. When will her birthday be?
10. Who was Susan?
11. How old was Juliet's mother when she got married, and how old is she now?
12. How old, roughly, is Juliet's father? (See 1.5.31–39.)

B Write an article for Verona's version of a magazine such as *Hello!*, reporting on the well-known society figures at the Capulet party and some of the things they were seen doing. Base your report on:

- the list of people invited (1.2.66–74) and others who you know were present

- the maskers' entertainment
- incidents such as the argument between Capulet and Tybalt (would the reporter know what it was about?) and Juliet's meeting with a young man.

Characters such as the Nurse might provide some interesting gossip.

C Write a few lines from the diaries of Capulet, the Nurse and Benvolio, and a brief note scribbled by Tybalt to one of his followers, each of which contains something about the main incidents that affected them at the party and gives a different perspective from the others. Rosaline was at the party too: what would she write in her diary? Draft all the entries in appropriate handwriting on interesting-looking paper and put them together to create a collage, entitled 'After the Capulet party . . .'.

Plot review (5): time line

It becomes clear from a conversation between Capulet and Paris later in the play (3.4.18–19) that the party at which the lovers meet takes place on a Sunday. Draw up the beginning of a time line, marking on it the main events of Act 1. from early Sunday morning (the riot happens before nine – see 1.1.159) through to late evening when Romeo leaves the Capulet house.

Character review: Mercutio (1)

When John McEnery played Mercutio in the 1968 film, he gave the impression that the character had become carried away with his imaginings and had to be stopped by Romeo; a similar interpretation was seen in Harold Perrineau's performance in the 1997 film, where the Queen Mab speech seems to be a drug-induced fantasy. Roger Allam played it quite differently and felt that Romeo and Mercutio were having an argument about feeling versus intellect: 'Mercutio is disgusted . . . that Romeo is putting his faith in love and dreams: "dreamers often lie". This argument between them continues right to the end of the scene.'

1. Discuss which of these three interpretations you find most interesting: that Mercutio is:
   (a) a highly emotional young man who finds himself getting completely out of control and carried away by his imaginings (McEnery);
   (b) somebody in the grip of drugs, hallucinating (Perrineau);
   (c) a thinker and intellectual who wants to convince Romeo that it is foolish to believe dreams and follow your feelings all the time (Allam).
2. What do lines 93–95 add to your picture of Mercutio?

② Prologue

The Chorus describes the switch in Romeo's affections, from Rosaline to Juliet, and comments on the obstacles in the way of Romeo and Juliet's love. Outside the Capulets' walled garden, Benvolio and Mercutio are looking for Romeo.

Activities

Shakespeare's language: the sonnet

Look back at the earlier activities on the sonnet (pages 2 and 48) and remind yourself about its usual structure. The sonnet which opens Act 2 reports the main points of the story so far. Work in pairs to express it in your own words, using the following as a guide:

- Section 1 (1–4):
  Off with the old love, on with the new
  . . .
  Romeo and Rosaline . . .

- Section 2 (5–8):
  Romeo and Juliet . . .
  But . . .

- Section 3 (9–12):
  Meeting . . .

- Rhyming couplet (13–14):
  But their love gives them strength . . .

---

1 **old Desire** *Romeo's old love for Rosaline*

2 **young Affection . . .** his new love longs, open-mouthed (**gapes**) to take its place (**be his heir**)

3 **fair** Rosaline's beauty

4 **with tender . . .** seems less beautiful, now that it is compared with sweet Juliet

5 **loves again** loves in return

6 **Alike** *Both Juliet and Romeo are equally enchanted by love.*

7 **foe-supposed** the one supposed to be his enemy

7 **complain** express his feelings; plead for love

8 **fearful** frightening

9 **held** considered, seen as

10 **use to swear** usually swear

11 **means** opportunities

14 **Tempering . . .** softening the extreme difficulty with the great sweetness of their meetings

2 **dull earth** his physical body (lacking a soul without Juliet)

2 **centre** core (or heart, now in Juliet's possession)

4 **stolen him** crept off secretly

6 **conjure** call him up, like a spirit

7 **humours** odd moods

7 **liver** *thought to be the origin of passion*

8 **in the likeness of** looking like *(spirits had to take on a physical shape when they appeared)*

Act 2

Prologue

Enter CHORUS.

CHORUS   Now old Desire doth in his death-bed lie,
     And young Affection gapes to be his heir;
That fair for which love groaned for and would die,
     With tender Juliet matched, is now not fair.
Now Romeo is beloved and loves again,   5
     Alike bewitchèd by the charm of looks,
But to his foe-supposed he must complain,
     And she steal love's sweet bait from fearful hooks:
Being held a foe, he may not have access
     To breathe such vows as lovers use to swear;   10
And she as much in love, her means much less
     To meet her new-belovèd anywhere;
But passion lends them power, time means, to meet,
     Tempering extremities with extreme sweet.

Scene 1

A street beside the wall of Capulet's garden.

Enter ROMEO walking away from Capulet's house.

ROMEO   Can I go forward when my heart is here?
Turn back, dull earth, and find thy centre out.

He climbs over the wall into the garden.

Enter MERCUTIO and BENVOLIO in the street. ROMEO listens from inside the garden.

BENVOLIO   Romeo! my cousin Romeo! Romeo!

MERCUTIO   He is wise,
And on my life hath stolen him to bed.

BENVOLIO   He ran this way and leapt this orchard wall.   5
Call, good Mercutio.

MERCUTIO   Nay, I'll conjure too.
Romeo! humours! madman! passion! liver!
Appear thou in the likeness of a sigh;
Speak but one rhyme and I am satisfied;

2.1 A street beside the wall of Capulet's garden

Mercutio pretends to conjure Romeo magically and teases him about his failed love for Rosaline.

10 **Cry but "Ay me"** only utter the sound of a lover's sigh

10 **"love" and "dove"** *rhyming words typical of love poetry*

12 **purblind son and heir** Cupid, the blindfolded son of Venus, goddess of love

13 **Young Abraham** *No one really knows what this means. Possibly: Cupid is both young (he is a child) and also old (as he has been around for a very long time) like Abraham in the Bible.*

13 **trim** suitably

14 **King Cophetua** *a king in an old ballad who fell in love with a beggar maid*

16 **ape** *Romeo is 'playing dead' like a performing ape.*

20 **demesnes ... adjacent** *literally:* nearby estates, lands

21 **in thy likeness** looking like yourself *(see line 8)*

27 **That were some spite** that would make him angry

27 **invocation** conjuring spell

31 **To be consorted with** to spend time with; associate with

31 **humorous** (1) damp and humid; (2) putting people into moods

32 **befits** suits

37 **that she were** if only she were

39 **truckle-bed** child's bed on wheels

40 **field-bed** *wordplay:* (1) camp bed; (2) sleeping out in the open

Cry but "Ay me", pronounce but "love" and "dove"   10
Speak to my gossip Venus one fair word,
One nickname for her purblind son and heir,
Young Abraham Cupid, he that shot so trim
When King Cophetua loved the beggar maid.
He heareth not, he stirreth not, he moveth not;   15
The ape is dead, and I must conjure him.
(*Addressing* ROMEO) I conjure thee by Rosaline's bright
   eyes,
By her high forehead and her scarlet lip,
By her fine foot, straight leg and quivering thigh,
And the demesnes that there adjacent lie,   20
That in thy likeness thou appear to us.

BENVOLIO   And if he hear thee, thou wilt anger him.

MERCUTIO   This cannot anger him. 'T would anger him
To raise a spirit in his mistress' circle,
Of some strange nature, letting it there stand   25
Till she had laid it, and conjured it down;
That were some spite. My invocation
Is fair and honest: in his mistress' name
I conjure only but to raise up him.

BENVOLIO   Come; he hath hid himself among these trees   30
To be consorted with the humorous night;
Blind is his love, and best befits the dark.

MERCUTIO   If love be blind, love cannot hit the mark.
Now will he sit under a medlar tree,
And wish his mistress were that kind of fruit   35
As maids call medlars when they laugh alone.
O Romeo, that she were! O that she were
An open-arse and thou a Poperin pear!
Romeo, good night. I'll to my truckle-bed:
This field-bed is too cold for me to sleep.   40
Come, shall we go?

BENVOLIO   Go then, for 't is in vain.
To seek him here that means not to be found.

Exeunt MERCUTIO and BENVOLIO.

2.2 Inside Capulet's garden

Inside the Capulets' garden, Romeo spies Juliet through her bedroom window and talks about her beauty. Then suddenly she utters his name.

Activities

Character review: Romeo (8)

A Romeo's descriptions of Juliet are very powerful and dramatic. Pick one of the following and draw a picture to illustrate what he is saying:

- 4–9: Arise, fair sun . . .
- 15–22: Two of the fairest . . .
- 26–32: O speak again, bright angel . . .

B Romeo's descriptions of Juliet in this scene focus very heavily on images of light and brightness. Find these references and discuss what they seem to suggest about the nature of Romeo's feelings at this point. Look back at lines 2–6, 15–17, 19–22, 26.

C How would you answer someone who suggested that Romeo's language (all the references to brightness, the dramatic images . . .) is totally overdone, as (a) Juliet is neither a saint nor a goddess; and (b) he has only just met her.

Themes: love

There is an enormous contrast between Romeo's language to Juliet in 1.5 and 2.2, and Mercutio's language in 2.1. Look back at what the two characters say. What does their language reveal about their very different attitudes to love?

1 **He . . .** *people like Mercutio, who have not experienced love . . .*

2 **soft** wait

2 **yonder window** that window over there

4 **envious** *(that Juliet is more beautiful)*

6 **her maid** *as a virgin, Juliet is a 'handmaid' of Diana, goddess of both the moon and chastity*

8 **vestal livery** *the pale green clothes she wears as a virgin serving at Diana's temple*

9 **fools** *professional fools also often wore green (and yellow)*

11 **O that . . .** I wish she knew that she were my love!

12 **What of that?** It doesn't matter.

13 **discourses** speaks clearly

15–17 **. . . Having some business . . .** Two stars are absent on business and they beg (**entreat**) Juliet's eyes to shine in their places in heaven (**spheres**) until they return.

18 **What if . . .** What if her eyes were in heaven and the stars in her head?

21 **airy region** sky, heavens

28 **wingèd messenger** angel

29 **white-upturnèd . . . eyes** eyes looking up, so that the whites show

31 **lazy-pacing** slow-moving

33 **Wherefore** Why

34 **refuse** give up

Scene 2

Inside Capulet's garden.

ROMEO He jests at scars that never felt a wound.
(*He sees* JULIET) But soft! What light through yonder
    window breaks?
It is the east, and Juliet is the sun.
Arise, fair sun, and kill the envious moon,
Who is already sick and pale with grief   5
That thou her maid art far more fair than she.
Be not her maid, since she is envious;
Her vestal livery is but sick and green,
And none but fools do wear it; cast it off.
It is my lady, O it is my love!   10
O that she knew she were!
She speaks, yet she says nothing, What of that?
Her eye discourses: I will answer it.
I am too bold; 't is not to me she speaks.
Two of the fairest stars in all the heaven,   15
Having some business, do entreat her eyes
To twinkle in their spheres till they return.
What if her eyes were there, they in her head?
The brightness of her cheek would shame those stars
As daylight doth a lamp; her eyes in heaven   20
Would through the airy region stream so bright
That birds would sing and think it were not night.
See how she leans her cheek upon her hand.
O that I were a glove upon that hand,
That I might touch that cheek!

JULIET   Ay me!

ROMEO   She speaks.   25
O speak again, bright angel, for thou art
As glorious to this night, being o'er my head,
As is a wingèd messenger of heaven
Unto the white-upturnèd wondering eyes
Of mortals that fall back to gaze on him   30
When he bestrides the lazy-pacing clouds,
And sails upon the bosom of the air.

JULIET O Romeo, Romeo! Wherefore art thou Romeo?
Deny thy father and refuse thy name:

2.2 Inside Capulet's garden

Not realising she is being overheard, Juliet declares that she loves Romeo despite the fact that he is a Montague. He calls out to her and she recognises his voice, fearing for his safety if he is caught.

35 **be but** only be; just be

39 **though not** even if you were not a Montague; whatever you call yourself

46 **owes** owns, possesses

47 **doff** remove *(like a hat)*; cast off

48 **for that name** in exchange for your name

50 **new baptized** renamed in a second baptism

51 **Henceforth** from this time on

52 **bescreened in** covered by the screen of

53 **counsel** secret and private thoughts

61 **thee dislike** if you don't like either of them

66 **o'erperch** fly over

67 **limits** walls

| | Or if thou wilt not, be but sworn my love | 35 |
| | And I'll no longer be a Capulet. | |

ROMEO (*Aside*) Shall I hear more, or shall I speak at this?

JULIET 'T is but thy name that is my enemy.
Thou art thyself, though not a Montague.
What's "Montague"? It is nor hand, nor foot, 40
Nor arm, nor face, nor any other part
Belonging to a man. O be some other name!
What's in a name? That which we call a rose
By any other word would smell as sweet.
So Romeo would, were he not Romeo called, 45
Retain that dear perfection which he owes
Without that title. Romeo, doff thy name,
And for that name, which is no part of thee,
Take all myself.

ROMEO (*To JULIET*)   I take thee at thy word.
Call me but "Love", and I'll be new baptized; 50
Henceforth I never will be Romeo.

JULIET What man art thou, that thus bescreened in night,
So stumblest on my counsel?

ROMEO   By a name
I know not how to tell thee who I am.
My name, dear saint, is hateful to myself 55
Because it is an enemy to thee.
Had I it written, I would tear the word.

JULIET My ears have yet not drunk a hundred words
Of thy tongue's uttering, yet I know the sound.
Art thou not Romeo, and a Montague? 60

ROMEO Neither, fair maid, if either thee dislike.

JULIET How camest thou hither, tell me, and wherefore?
The orchard walls are high and hard to climb,
And the place death, considering who thou art,
If any of my kinsmen find thee here. 65

ROMEO With love's light wings did I o'erperch these walls,
For stony limits cannot hold love out;

2.2 Inside Capulet's garden

Juliet is embarrassed that her private declaration of love has been overheard, but is anxious to know whether Romeo returns her love.

Activities

Character review: Juliet (2)

Juliet is worried (85–106) about having revealed her feelings to Romeo too early in their relationship.

A Why might it be unwise for a young girl in Juliet's position to let a man know that she loves him? Discuss your ideas in pairs.

B Follow Juliet's train of thought by expressing the main points of her speech in your own words, using the following as a structure:
- 85–87: If it weren't dark . . .
- 88–89: I ought to take back what I said . . .
- 90–94: Do you truly love me . . .?
- 95–97: Perhaps you think I have been won over too quickly . . .
- 98–101: I might be foolish, but . . .
- 102–106: I ought never to have revealed my love to you, but . . .

C Which particular qualities of Juliet's character, background and upbringing are revealed in this speech?

73 **proof against** immune to; protected against

76 **but** unless; if you don't love me

78 **proroguèd** postponed, deferred

78 **wanting of** lacking

82 **pilot** seafarer, navigator

82 **wert thou** even if you were

84 **I should adventure . . .** I would run the risks at sea to gain goods (**merchandise**) like that

88 **Fain would I dwell on form** I would prefer to keep to a formal way of doing things

89 **farewell compliment!** Goodbye to polite, conventional speech!

92–93 **At lovers' perjuries . . .** *Jupiter (Jove), king of the gods and god of oaths, did not take lovers' lies seriously: they always break their promises.*

96 **perverse** stubborn, contrary

97 **So thou wilt woo** so that you will go on wooing me

98 **fond** infatuated, loving, foolishly tender

99 **. . . my 'haviour light** you might consider my behaviour to be too forward and immodest

101 **. . . cunning to be strange** cleverness in playing hard-to-get

101 **strange** reserved, distant

103 **But that** Had it not been for the fact that

103 **ere I was ware** before I was aware of it

And what love can do, that dares love attempt:
Therefore thy kinsmen are no stop to me.

JULIET   If they do see thee, they will murder thee.   70

ROMEO   Alack, there lies more peril in thine eye
          Than twenty of their swords. Look thou but sweet
          And I am proof against their enmity.

JULIET   I would not for the world they saw thee here.

ROMEO   I have night's cloak to hide me from their eyes.   75
          And but thou love me, let them find me here;
          My life were better ended by their hate
          Than death proroguèd, wanting of thy love.

JULIET   By whose direction found'st thou out this place?

ROMEO   By love, that first did prompt me to inquire;   80
          He lent me counsel, and I lent him eyes.
          I am no pilot, yet wert thou as far
          As that vast shore washed with the farthest sea,
          I should adventure for such merchandise.

JULIET   Thou knowest the mask of night is on my face,   85
          Else would a maiden blush bepaint my cheek,
          For that which thou hast heard me speak tonight.
          Fain would I dwell on form; fain, fain deny
          What I have spoke: but farewell compliment!
          Dost thou love me? I know thou wilt say "Ay",   90
          And I will take thy word; yet if thou swear'st
          Thou mayst prove false. At lovers' perjuries
          They say Jove laughs. O gentle Romeo,
          If thou dost love, pronounce it faithfully;
          Or if thou think I am too quickly won,   95
          I'll frown, and be perverse, and say thee nay,
          So thou wilt woo; but else, not for the world.
          In truth, fair Montague, I am too fond,
          And therefore thou mayst think my 'haviour light.
          But trust me, gentleman, I'll prove more true   100
          Than those that have more cunning to be strange.
          I should have been more strange, I must confess,
          But that thou overheard'st, ere I was ware,
          My true-love passion; therefore pardon me,

2.2 Inside Capulet's garden

Romeo and Juliet declare their love for each other, but Juliet is anxious about the suddenness of it all

Activities

Themes: love

Because *Romeo and Juliet* explores so many different features of love, the images used are themselves extremely varied. On the opposite page, for example, love can be:
- as changeable as the moon (109–111)
- too sudden, like lightning (118–120)
- capable of growing, like a flower (121–122)
- like a gift or a possession (130–132)
- as deep as the sea (133–134).

Perform their dialogue (107–135) and try to feel the power of their emotions.

A Draw one of these pictures, to bring out the meaning.

B Look again at each of the five images above and discuss how accurately you think it represents (a) Romeo's love for Juliet at this moment; and (b) her love for him. How different are Romeo's emotions here from the feelings he had for Rosaline?

C Invent your own image, which, in your opinion, represents (a) Romeo's love for Juliet at this moment; and (b) her love for him.

105 **And not impute . . .** Don't judge my giving in to be a sign of lightweight (or immodest) love

106 **discoverèd** revealed

109 **inconstant** changeable *(and therefore a symbol of unfaithfulness)*

110 **circled orb** *the imagined sphere in which the moon moves (see line 17)*

111 **likewise variable** similarly changeable and inconstant

114 **idolatry** idol-worship

117 **I have no joy of** I cannot enjoy; I am not happy about our lovers' agreement (**contract**)

118 **unadvised** carelessly thought through; lacking careful consideration

129 **I would it were** I wish I still had it

130 **Would'st thou withdraw it?** Do you want to take it back?

131 **frank** generous

133 **bounty** (1) gifts; (2) generosity

133 **boundless** limitless, infinite

And not impute this yielding to light love,   105
Which the dark night hath so discoverèd.

ROMEO   Lady, by yonder blessèd moon I vow,
That tips with silver all these fruit-tree tops –

JULIET   O swear not by the moon, th' inconstant moon,
That monthly changes in her circled orb,   110
Lest that thy love prove likewise variable.

ROMEO   What shall I swear by?

JULIET   Do not swear at all;
Or if thou wilt, swear by thy gracious self,
Which is the god of my idolatry,
And I'll believe thee.

ROMEO   If my heart's dear love –   115

JULIET   Well, do not swear. Although I joy in thee,
I have no joy of this contract tonight:
It is too rash, too unadvised, too sudden,
Too like the lightning, which doth cease to be
Ere one can say "It lightens." Sweet, good night.   120
This bud of love, by summer's ripening breath,
May prove a beauteous flower when next we meet.
Good night, good night. As sweet repose and rest
Come to thy heart as that within my breast.

ROMEO   O wilt thou leave me so unsatisfied?   125

JULIET   What satisfaction canst thou have to-night?

ROMEO   Th' exchange of thy love's faithful vow for mine.

JULIET   I gave thee mine before thou didst request it;
And yet I would it were to give again.

ROMEO   Would'st thou withdraw it? For what purpose, love? 130

JULIET   But to be frank and give it thee again:
And yet I wish but for the thing I have.
My bounty is as boundless as the sea,
My love as deep; the more I give to thee,
The more I have, for both are infinite.   135

2.2 Inside Capulet's garden

Juliet hears the Nurse calling her, but before she leaves the window, asks Romeo to send her a message the following day telling her when and where they can be married.

Activities

Character review: Juliet (3)

1. Discuss why, when Juliet returns to the window (142), she immediately talks of marriage. Has something happened indoors to prompt her, for example?
2. Why does Juliet feel that she should marry Romeo as a matter of urgency? Give as many reasons as you can.

Actors' interpretations (11)

In threes perform lines 130–154.

NURSE: Don't wait for Juliet to end her speeches before calling offstage, but interrupt the last few words each time. Make each call more urgent than the last.

JULIET: Think about the reaction you want to have each time you hear the Nurse calling (impatience, anxiety, desperation . . . ?).

136 **adieu** ggodbye *(from French à dieu = to God)*

137 **Anon** I'm coming

138 **Stay but . . .** Just stay a little while; I'll come back.

141 **Too flattering . . .** too wonderfully delightful to be real (**substantial**)

143 **bent** intentions

145 **procure** arrange

146 **rite** marriage ceremony

151 **beseech** beg

151 **By and by** straightaway

152 **cease thy suit** give up your courtship of me

153 **So thrive my soul** May my soul prosper

155 **want** lack

The NURSE calls.

> I hear some noise within. Dear love, adieu.
> (*To the* NURSE) Anon, good Nurse! (*To* ROMEO) Sweet
>   Montague, be true.
> Stay but a little; I will come again.

JULIET leaves the window and goes in.

ROMEO   O blessed, blessed night! I am afeard,
Being in night, all this is but a dream,   140
Too flattering-sweet to be substantial.

JULIET returns to the window.

JULIET   Three words, dear Romeo, and good night indeed.
If that thy bent of love be honourable,
Thy purpose marriage, send me word to-morrow
By one that I'll procure to come to thee,   145
Where and what time thou wilt perform the rite;
And all my fortunes at thy foot I'll lay,
And follow thee, my lord, throughout the world.

NURSE   (*From inside the house*) Madam!

JULIET   (*To the* NURSE) I come, anon. (*To* ROMEO) But if thou
      mean'st not well,   150
I do beseech thee –

NURSE   (*Calling again from within*) Madam!

JULIET   By and by, I come –
(*Continuing, to* ROMEO) To cease thy suit, and leave me
      to my grief,
Tomorrow will I send.

ROMEO   So thrive my soul, –

JULIET   A thousand times good night!

JULIET goes in.

ROMEO   A thousand times the worse, to want thy light!   155
Love goes toward love as schoolboys from their books,
But love from love, toward school with heavy looks.

ROMEO is walking away as JULIET returns.

2.2 Inside Capulet's garden

Juliet returns to the window and arranges to send someone at nine o'clock for Romeo's message. The lovers are reluctant to part.

Activities

Character review: Romeo (9)

Look back at Romeo's replies to Juliet throughout the scene and his comments to himself.

1. Does he actually give a direct answer to Juliet's question 'By whose direction . . .?' (79)?
2. Does he succeed in giving an answer to 'Dost thou love me?' (90)?
3. Why is Juliet dissatisfied with his attempt to prove that he loves her (107–115)?
4. What has happened which might cause him to wonder if it had all been a dream (139–141)?

Write down Romeo's thoughts as he leaves Juliet. What does he feel about their love and what does he now plan to do?

158 **Hist . . .** Psst! *(She wants the voice of a falconer who can call the bird back.)*

159 **tassel-gentle** *male falcon*

160 **Bondage . . .** *because she is 'imprisoned' in the house, she has to whisper and so makes herself hoarse*

161 **Else would I** *otherwise I would*

161 **Echo** *was a nymph in classical mythology who pined away for love in a cave.*

162 **airy tongue** *All that was left of Echo was her voice in the air.*

166 **attending** *listening*

167 **Madam?** *In some editions, Romeo says 'My nyas?', a nyas (eyas) being a young hawk, just taken from its nest for training*

172, 174 **still** *always*

177 **wanton** *irresponsible woman (or spoilt child)*

179 **gyves** *shackles*

182 **I would** *I wish*

JULIET	Hist, Romeo, hist! O for a falconer's voice,
	To lure this tassel-gentle back again.
	Bondage is hoarse, and may not speak aloud,
	Else would I tear the cave where Echo lies,
	And make her airy tongue more hoarse than mine
	With repetition of my "Romeo!"

160

ROMEO	It is my soul that calls upon my name.
	How silver-sweet sound lovers' tongues by night,
	Like softest music to attending ears.

165

| JULIET | Romeo! |

| ROMEO | Madam? |

| JULIET | What o'clock tomorrow |
| | Shall I send to thee? |

| ROMEO | By the hour of nine. |

| JULIET | I will not fail. 'T is twenty years till then. |
| | I have forgot why I did call thee back. |

170

| ROMEO | Let me stand here till thou remember it. |

| JULIET | I shall forget, to have thee still stand there, |
| | Remembering how I love thy company. |

| ROMEO | And I'll still stay, to have thee still forget, |
| | Forgetting any other home but this. |

175

JULIET	'T is almost morning. I would have thee gone,
	And yet no farther than a wanton's bird,
	Who lets it hop a little from her hand,
	Like a poor prisoner in his twisted gyves,
	And with a silk thread plucks it back again,
	So loving-jealous of his liberty.

180

| ROMEO | I would I were thy bird. |

JULIET	Sweet, so would I,
	Yet I should kill thee with much cherishing.
	Good night, good night. Parting is such sweet sorrow,
	That I shall say "good night" till it be morrow.

185

2.3 Friar Lawrence's cell

Juliet goes in and Romeo leaves, planning to seek advice and help from Friar Lawrence. When Romeo arrives at the Friar's cell early in the morning, he is collecting herbs which have healing properties.

Activities

Shakespeare's language: antithesis and oxymoron

The Friar's first speech is notable for the kinds of oppositions (antitheses and oxymorons) that we have heard earlier in the play (see page 16). Pick out the oppositions to do with:
- morning and day – night and darkness
- sunshine – clouds
- poisons – precious juices
- mother and birth – grave and death
- vileness – goodness
- proper use – abuse
- virtue – vice
- poison – medicine
- stimulating the senses – deadening them
- virtue derived from God – physical passions.

1. Draw a picture to illustrate one of these oppositions and write a sentence underneath to explain the point that the Friar is making.
2. Discuss natural substances that you know of which can be used for good ends or misused, as the Friar observes (19–20). (Think, for example, about atomic power or drugs.)

---

188 **ghostly sire's close cell** spiritual father's private room *(in the friary)*

189 **His help . . .** to ask for his help and tell him of my good fortune

3 **fleckled** dappled with spots of light

4 **From forth** away from

5 **advance** pushes forward (rising in the sky)

7 **osier cage** willow basket

8 **baleful** harmful

9–10 **The earth . . . womb** The earth is both the mother of all natural things and their grave.

11 **divers kind** various species

13 **for many virtues excellent** with many beneficial natural properties

14 **None but . . .** there are no plants which do not have some good qualities

17 **For nought so vile** for there is nothing, however lowly

19–20 **Nor aught . . .** nor is there anything, however naturally good, which cannot be misused

21–22 **Virtue itself . . . dignified** If good things are misused, they become evil; and an evil quality can become good if it is used in the right way.

23 **infant rind** tender young skin

25 **each part** every part of the body

ROMEO	Sleep dwell upon thine eyes, peace in thy breast. Would I were sleep and peace, so sweet to rest.

JULIET goes in.

Hence will I to my ghostly sire's close cell,
His help to crave, and my dear hap to tell.

Exit.

Scene 3

Friar Lawrence's cell.

Enter FRIAR LAWRENCE with a basket.

FRIAR LAWRENCE	The grey-eyed morn smiles on the frowning night, Check'ring the eastern clouds with streaks of light; And fleckled darkness like a drunkard reels From forth day's path and Titan's fiery wheels. Now, ere the sun advance his burning eye The day to cheer and night's dank dew to dry, I must upfill this osier cage of ours With baleful weeds and precious-juicèd flowers. The earth that's nature's mother is her tomb: What is her burying grave, that is her womb, And from her womb children of divers kind We sucking on her natural bosom find: Many for many virtues excellent, None but for some, and yet all different. O mickle is the powerful grace that lies In plants, herbs, stones, and their true qualities: For nought so vile that on the earth doth live But to the earth some special good doth give; Nor aught so good but, strained from that fair use, Revolts from true birth, stumbling on abuse. Virtue itself turns vice, being misapplied, And vice sometime by action dignified.	5 10 15 20

Enter ROMEO, unseen by the FRIAR.

Within the infant rind of this weak flower
Poison hath residence and medicine power:
For this, being smelt, with that part cheers each
    part;   25

2.3 Friar Lawrence's cell

The Friar thinks about the fact that plants are like people, containing both good and evil qualities. As Romeo is up so early, he assumes that he has been with Rosaline, but Romeo begins to explain what has happened.

Activities

Leo McKern as the Friar in the 1954 production at the shakespeare Memorial Theatre

Shakespeare's language: imagery

1. What does Romeo say he has been doing? Why does he choose to describe the events in this way? Remember what Romeo knows about the Friar:
   - that he is a holy man
   - that he is interested in medicines
   - that he must be keen to make peace between the feuding families.
2. Sketch a series of cartoons to illustrate the image Romeo uses when describing what he has been up to (49–54).
3. What is the Friar's reaction to Romeo's imagery (55–56)?

26 **stays** ... stops the heart and the senses too

27 **still** always

28 **grace and rude will** *the ability to receive God's goodness; and the tendency to give in to physical desires*

30 **canker** cankerworm *(that eats up the plant from inside)*

31 **Benedicite** *Latin for* 'Bless you'

33 **it argues** ... it proves that you are not in perfect health

35 **Care keeps** ... Old men are kept awake by worries.

37 **unbruisèd youth** ... Young men who have not been damaged by the world and have brains which are not full of worries **(unstuffed)**

40 **uproused** ... forced to get up early because you are not well

46 **that name's woe** the unhappiness that name caused me

51–52 **Both** ... Your help and holy medicine can be the remedy for both of us.

54 **My intercession** ... My request will benefit my enemy too.

55 **Be** ... **homely in thy drift** Give me your meaning in a plain, straightforward way.

56 **Riddling confession** ... If you confess your sins to me in riddles, the absolution I give you will be difficult to understand too.

Being tasted, stays all senses with the heart.
Two such opposèd kings encamp them still
In man as well as herbs, grace and rude will;
And where the worser is predominant,
Full soon the canker death eats up that plant.   30

ROMEO   Good morrow, father.

FRIAR   Benedicite.
LAWRENCE   What early tongue so sweet saluteth me?
Young son, it argues a distempered head
So soon to bid good morrow to thy bed.
Care keeps his watch in every old man's eye,   35
And where care lodges, sleep will never lie;
But where unbruisèd youth with unstuffed brain
Doth couch his limbs, there golden sleep doth reign.
Therefore thy earliness doth me assure
Thou art uproused with some distemperature;   40
Or if not so, then here I hit it right,
Our Romeo hath not been in bed to-night.

ROMEO   That last is true: the sweeter rest was mine.

FRIAR   God pardon sin! Wast thou with Rosaline?
LAWRENCE

ROMEO   With Rosaline, my ghostly father? No.   45
I have forgot that name, and that name's woe.

FRIAR   That's my good son. But where hast thou been then?
LAWRENCE

ROMEO   I'll tell thee ere thou ask it me again:
I have been feasting with mine enemy,
Where on a sudden one hath wounded me   50
That's by me wounded. Both our remedies
Within thy help and holy physic lies.
I bear no hatred, blessed man, for lo,
My intercession likewise steads my foe.

FRIAR   Be plain, good son, and homely in thy drift;   55
LAWRENCE   Riddling confession finds but riddling shrift.

ROMEO   Then plainly know, my heart's dear love is set

2.3 Friar Lawrence's cell

Romeo explains that he has fallen in love with Juliet and asks the Friar to marry them. The Friar chides Romeo for being fickle in love, but agrees to help him.

Activities

Themes: love

Discuss the Friar's comments on Romeo's change of heart (65–88), including the distinction that he draws between 'loving' and 'doting' (82). Use his ideas to write a letter to a teenage magazine from Rosaline, pointing out how immature young men can be, citing Romeo's behaviour as an example.

Character review: the Friar (1)

What is your impression of the Friar?
1. The character can be interpreted in many different ways. What can you learn from these photographs about the actors' approach?

Continued on page 78

63 **pass** walk along together

67 **forsaken** abandoned

67–68 **Young men's ... eyes** Young men's love is not deeply felt; they are only interested in a girl's beauty.

69 **brine** salt water *(tears: see line 71)*

70 **sallow** pale

72 **season** (1) give a flavour to; (2) preserve (as salt does to food)

79 **Pronounce this sentence** Repeat this proverb

80 **fall** commit sins *(if men are weak, women can be excused for being sinful)*

81 **chid'st** told me off; rebuked me

82 **doting** being excessively infatuated

86 **Doth grace ...** Juliet is willing to exchange love's goodness with me.

88 **read by rote ...** *Rosaline knew that it was not a genuine love: it was like somebody who could recite words learnt by heart, without actually being able to read from the book.*

90 **In one respect** on account of one thing; for one reason

The Friar played by Milo O'Shea in the 1968 film (above) and Julian Glover in the 1995 Royal Shakespeare Company production

On the fair daughter of rich Capulet:
As mine on hers, so hers is set on mine,
And all combined, save what thou must combine   60
By holy marriage. When and where and how
We met, we wooed, and made exchange of vow,
I'll tell thee as we pass, but this I pray,
That thou consent to marry us to-day.

FRIAR   Holy Saint Francis, what a change is here!   65
LAWRENCE   Is Rosaline that thou didst love so dear
So soon forsaken? Young men's love then lies
Not truly in their hearts, but in their eyes.
Jesu Maria, what a deal of brine
Hath washed thy sallow cheeks for Rosaline!   70
How much salt water thrown away in waste
To season love, that of it doth not taste!
The sun not yet thy sighs from heaven clears,
Thy old groans ring yet in mine ancient ears;
Lo, here upon thy cheek the stain doth sit   75
Of an old tear that is not washed off yet.
If e'er thou wast thyself, and these woes thine,
Thou and these woes were all for Rosaline.
And art thou changed? Pronounce this sentence
    then:
Women may fall, when there's no strength in men. 80

ROMEO   Thou chid'st me oft for loving Rosaline.

FRIAR   For doting, not for loving, pupil mine.
LAWRENCE

ROMEO   And bad'st me bury love.

FRIAR   Not in a grave
LAWRENCE   To lay one in, another out to have.

ROMEO   I pray thee chide me not. Her I love now   85
Doth grace for grace and love for love allow:
The other did not so.

FRIAR   O she knew well
LAWRENCE   Thy love did read by rote that could not spell.
But come, young waverer, come go with me;
In one respect I'll thy assistant be,   90

2.4 A street

The Friar believes that a marriage between Romeo and Juliet will help to end their families' feuding. Meanwhile Mercutio and Benvolio speculate on what has become of Romeo; Tybalt has sent Romeo a challenge.

Activities

2. What is the relationship between the Friar and Romeo? What kind of things does Romeo tell him? Do you think Romeo tells the Friar more about his love life than he would reveal to his parents or to his friends (see 1.1)?

Character review: Mercutio (2)

Romeo and Tybalt are the targets for Mercutio's wit in the opening of this scene.

Use the notes to help you find examples of Mercutio's use of: bawdy innuendo; references to medieval literature; classical references; alliteration; foreign languages.

(a) Perform the speech and discuss how he uses these features to mock Romeo.

(b) Nearly all Mercutio's examples of lovers came to tragic ends or caused tragedy. Discuss whether Mercutio has chosen the examples deliberately to make a point to Romeo (if so, what point is Mercutio making?); or whether he has chosen them unconsciously (in which case, what point is Shakespeare making?).

92   **rancour** bitter hatred

93   **I stand on ...** I insist upon doing this quickly.

1   **should** can

2   **to-night** last night

10   **answer it** accept the challenge

12–13   **how he dares, being dared** by saying that, having been challenged, he accepts the dare

15   **white ... black** *Rosaline has fair skin and dark eyes.*

16   **very pin ... cleft** the central peg of the bull's eye, pierced

17   **blind bowboy's butt shaft** Cupid's arrow *(see note to 1.1.169–170)*

19   **Why, what ...** And who does Tybalt think he is!

20   **Prince of Cats** *Tybalt was the cat's name in many old stories.*

For this alliance may so happy prove
To turn your households' rancour to pure love.

ROMEO   O let us hence. I stand on sudden haste.

FRIAR   Wisely and slow. They stumble that run fast.
LAWRENCE

Exeunt.

Scene 4

A street.

Enter MERCUTIO and BENVOLIO.

MERCUTIO   Where the devil should this Romeo be? Came he
not home to-night?

BENVOLIO   Not to his father's; I spoke with his man.

MERCUTIO   Why, that same pale hard-hearted wench, that
Rosaline, torments him so, that he will sure run   5
mad.

BENVOLIO   Tybalt, the kinsman to old Capulet, hath sent a
letter to his father's house.

MERCUTIO   A challenge, on my life.

BENVOLIO   Romeo will answer it.   10

MERCUTIO   Any man that can write may answer a letter.

BENVOLIO   Nay, he will answer the letter's master, how he
dares, being dared.

MERCUTIO   Alas, poor Romeo, he is already dead – stabbed
with a white wench's black eye, run through the   15
ear with a love song, the very pin of his heart cleft
with the blind bowboy's butt shaft. And is he a
man to encounter Tybalt?

BENVOLIO   Why, what is Tybalt?

MERCUTIO   More than Prince of Cats. O, he's the courageous   20

2.4 A street

Mercutio comments on Tybalt's skills as a fencer and mocks current fashions. When Romeo arrives, Mercutio teases him (assuming that he still loves Rosaline) and complains that Romeo gave them the slip after the Capulet feast.

21 **compliments** conventions *(of duelling)*

21–22 **... as you sing pricksong** *Tybalt fights like somebody singing off sheet music, strictly following the notes.*

25 **butcher of ...** He is so accurate, he can slice an opponent's silk button.

26 **... of the very first house ...** from the finest school *(of duelling)*

26–27 **... of the first and second cause** *Duelling was considered acceptable if the fighter could give one of the numbered 'causes', or reasons. Tybalt's reason is that the Capulet house has been dishonoured.*

27–28 **passado, punto reverso** *and* **hai** *were fashionable terms in fencing*

30–31 **antic ... affecting fantasticoes** grotesque, posing weirdos

31 **new tuners of accent** people using trendy language. *(Words such as 'duellist' were just entering the language and many people objected to them.)*

32 **blade** *literally* sword, *but beginning to be used to mean a 'gallant' (a man of fashion)*

32 **tall** brave, elegant, fine

35 **strange flies** foreign parasites

36–38 **... who stand so much ...** People who insist so much on the new ways of doing things that they are not comfortable with the old ways.

40 **Without his roe** *Wordplay:* (1) roe = female deer *(Romeo is without his girlfriend)*; (2) take 'Ro' from his name (and he is only 'half himself'); (3) roe = fish eggs *(Romeo is like a fish that has spawned – which leads to the 'fish' jokes in 40–41).*

42 **numbers** poetry

42 **Petrarch** *(1304–74) wrote sonnets to express his love for* **Laura**.

42–43 **to his lady** compared to Romeo's lady *(Rosaline)*

44–46 **Dido ...** *Dido, Cleopatra, Hero and Thisbe were all women from classical myth or history who lost their lovers and committed suicide.*

44 **dowdy** plain-looking woman, shabbily dressed

45–46 **hildings and harlots** sluts and prostitutes

46–47 **a grey eye or so ...** quite attractive, but that doesn't matter

48 **French slop** *style of baggy trousers*

48–49 **gave us the counterfeit** deceived us; cheated us

52 **conceive** use your imagination

54–55 **strain courtesy** forget good manners

captain of compliments. He fights as you sing
pricksong, – keeps time, distance, and
proportion: he rests me his minim rests – one,
two, and the third in your bosom. The very
butcher of a silk button, a duellist, a duellist, a   25
gentleman of the very first house of the first and
second cause. Ah, the immortal passado, the
punto reverso, the hai!

BENVOLIO   The what?
MERCUTIO   The pox of such antic, lisping, affecting   30
            fantasticoes, these new tuners of accent! "By Jesu,
            a very good blade! a very tall man! a very good
            whore!" Why, is not this a lamentable thing,
            grandsire, that we would be thus afflicted with
            these strange flies, these fashion-mongers, these   35
            "pardon-me's" who stand so much on the new
            form that they cannot sit at ease on the old
            bench? O, their bones, their bones!

        Enter ROMEO.

BENVOLIO   Here comes Romeo, here comes Romeo.

MERCUTIO   Without his roe, like a dried herring. O flesh,   40
            flesh, how art thou fishified! Now is he for the
            numbers that Petrarch flowed in! Laura to his
            lady was a kitchen wench – marry, she had a
            better love to berhyme her – Dido a dowdy,
            Cleopatra a gipsy, Helen and Hero hildings and   45
            harlots, Thisbe a grey eye or so, but not to the
            purpose. Signior Romeo, bonjour! There's a
            French salutation to your French slop. You gave
            us the counterfeit fairly last night.

ROMEO   Good morrow to you both. What counterfeit did I   50
            give you?

MERCUTIO   The slip, sir, the slip. Can you not conceive?

ROMEO   Pardon, good Mercutio. My business was great,
            and in such a case as mine a man may strain
            courtesy.   55

 **A street**

Mercutio and Romeo have fun with some complicated word-play, trying to outdo each other with clever puns.

57 **constrains a man ...** forces a man to bend his legs: (1) to bow; (2) to make love

59 **... most kindly hit it** You have got the right meaning.

58–69 *Romeo and Mercutio engage in continuous wordplay:* **curtsy** *(58) leads to* **pink of courtesy** (61); **pink** (61) = (1) perfection; (2) a small flower; (3) a hole-pattern in material) *leads to the pinking pattern on Romeo's shoe or* **pump** (64); *this leads to sole* (66) = (1) sole of a shoe; (2) alone), *which sounds like 'soul'.*

69 **single-soled** thin and poor

71–72 **Switch ... match** Make your horse go faster with whip (**switch**) and spurs, or I'll declare myself the winner.

71–88 *More wordplay. The idea of horse-racing leads to wild-goose chases, which lead to a sequence of plays on 'goose'.*

73 **wild-goose chase** *(in which you have to follow wherever the leader takes you)*

74 **wild-goose** stupid person

76 **Was I with you ...?** Did I get even with you ...?

78 **there for the goose** playing the fool

79 **I will bite** ... *Biting someone's ear was a sign of affection, but Mercutio is possibly being ironic.*

84 **cheveril** fine kid leather, easily stretched from an inch to 45 inches (**ell**) (2.5 to 110 cm)

2.4

MERCUTIO	That's as much as to say, such a case as yours constrains a man to bow in the hams.
ROMEO	Meaning to curtsy?
MERCUTIO	Thou hast most kindly hit it.
ROMEO	A most courteous exposition.

A most courteous exposition.   60

MERCUTIO   Nay, I am the very pink of courtesy.

ROMEO   Pink for flower?

MERCUTIO   Right.

ROMEO   Why, then is my pump well-flowered.

MERCUTIO   Sure wit! Follow me this jest now till thou hast   65
worn out thy pump, that when the single sole of
it is worn, the jest may remain, after the wearing,
solely singular.

ROMEO   O single-soled jest, solely singular for the singleness!

MERCUTIO   Come between us, good Benvolio; my wits faints.   70

ROMEO   Switch and spurs, switch and spurs! or I'll cry a
match.

MERCUTIO   Nay, if our wits run the wild-goose chase, I am
done, for thou hast more of the wild-goose in one
of thy wits than, I am sure, I have in my whole   75
five. Was I with you there for the goose?

ROMEO   Thou wast never with me for anything when thou
wast not there for the goose.

MERCUTIO   I will bite thee by the ear for that jest.

ROMEO   Nay, good goose, bite not.   80

MERCUTIO   Thy wit is a very bitter sweeting; it is a most sharp
sauce.

ROMEO   And is it not well served in to a sweet goose?

MERCUTIO   O here's a wit of cheveril, that stretches from an
inch narrow to an ell broad!   85

2.4 A street

The wordplay is at its most sexual when the Nurse arrives with her servant, Peter.

Activities

Actors' interpretations (12): the Nurse's costume

1. What do you make of Romeo's cry of 'A sail, a sail!'? What does it suggest about the Nurse's dress and movements?

2. How would the Nurse be dressed in your production of the play? Sketch out your ideas and compare them with other people's.

3. Brenda Bruce, who played the Nurse with the Royal Shakespeare Company in a modern-dress production in 1980, wore 'an outrageous purple and silver cloak and long glass earrings for the street scene' with 'red bubble curls for my hair'. Study the photograph below and compare it with your image of the Nurse.

Judy Buxton as Juliet and Brenda Bruce as the Nurse in the 1980 RSC production

86–88 *Wordplay:* **broad** *can also mean 'crude' (as in 'broad humour') and* **goose** *a prostitute.*

91 **by art** by using your skill (with words)

93 **natural** born idiot

94 **bauble** (1) jester's stick; (2) penis *(which is also a slang meaning of 'tail', see the pun 'tale', line 97)*

96 **against the hair** (1) against the grain (when I don't want to); (2) pubic hair; (3) 'hare' *was a slang term for prostitute.*

97 **large** (1) crude (like 'broad', line 88); (2) erect *(if we take the slang meaning of 'tail', a bawdy joke continued in 98–100)*

100 **occupy** *nearly always had a sexual meaning in Shakespeare's plays.*

101 **goodly gear** a sight for sore eyes

101 **A sail!** *The cry of sailors when a ship was sighted.*

102 **shirt ... smock** a man and a woman

111 **bawdy** sexually vulgar *(see the activity on page 6)*

112 **prick** exact point *(but with an obvious bawdy meaning)*

113 **Out upon you!** Get away with you!

ROMEO   I stretch it out for that word "broad", which, added
             to the "goose", proves thee far and wide a broad
             goose.

MERCUTIO   Why, is not this better now than groaning for
             love? Now art thou sociable; now art thou   90
             Romeo; now art thou what thou art, by art as well
             as by nature. For this drivelling love is like a great
             natural that runs lolling up and down to hide his
             bauble in a hole.

BENVOLIO   Stop there, stop there.   95

MERCUTIO   Thou desirest me to stop in my tale against the hair.

BENVOLIO   Thou wouldst else have made thy tale large.

MERCUTIO   O thou art deceived. I would have made it short,
             for I was come to the whole depth of my tale, and
             meant indeed to occupy the argument no longer.   100

             Enter NURSE and her man PETER.

ROMEO   Here's goodly gear! A sail, a sail!

MERCUTIO   Two, two! a shirt and a smock.

NURSE   Peter!

PETER   Anon.

NURSE   My fan, Peter.   105

MERCUTIO   Good Peter, to hide her face, for her fan's the fairer
             face.

NURSE   God ye good morrow, gentlemen.

MERCUTIO   God ye good e'en, fair gentlewoman.

NURSE   Is it good e'en?   110

MERCUTIO   'T is no less, I tell ye, for the bawdy hand of the
             dial is now upon the prick of noon.

NURSE   Out upon you! What a man are you?

2.4 A street

The boys mock the Nurse with more sexual jokes, before Mercutio and Benvolio leave, still teasing her.

Activities

Character review: Mercutio (3)

'for the bawdy hand of the dial is now upon the prick of noon' (111–112)

1. How would you respond to the person who said: 'I'm bored by Mercutio: he can't even tell someone the time without making a dirty joke out of it'?

2. Look also at the song he sings and the way he introduces it (130–137) and, using the notes, work out (a) the surface meaning, and (b) the underlying sexual meaning. Again, how would you answer the allegation that it is extremely offensive and simply not funny?

3. What is the Nurse's opinion of Mercutio?

115 **mar** ruin

117 **quoth 'a?** did he say?

122 **for fault of** in the absence of

124 **Very well took** well understood

126 **confidence** a discussion in confidence; *or perhaps she means 'conference' (talk), a mistake mocked by Benvolio, who deliberately uses* **endite** *(127) for 'invite'*

128 **bawd** *someone who arranges customers for prostitutes*

128 **So ho!** *a hunter's cry (like 'tally ho!')*

129 **found** got the scent of a quarry

130 **hare** *See note to line 96.*

130 **lenten pie** *one served without meat (in Lent); Mercutio implies that the Nurse is old and unappetising*

132 **hoar** (1) stale; (2) *pronounced the same as 'whore'*

136 **too much for a score** not worth paying for

137 **When it hoars** When it: (1) gets stale; (2) spends time with whores.

137 **ere it be spent** before it is finished up

ROMEO   One, gentlewoman, that God hath made, for
        himself to mar.   115

NURSE   By my troth, it is well said. "For himself to mar,"
        quoth 'a? Gentlemen, can any of you tell me where
        I may find the young Romeo?

ROMEO   I can tell you, but young Romeo will be older
        when you have found him than he was when you   120
        sought him. I am the youngest of that name, for
        fault of a worse.

NURSE   You say well.

MERCUTIO Yea, is the worst well? Very well took, i' faith;
        wisely wisely.   125

NURSE   If you be he, sir, I desire some confidence with you.

BENVOLIO She will endite him to some supper.

MERCUTIO A bawd, a bawd, a bawd! So ho!

ROMEO   What, hast thou found?

MERCUTIO No hare, sir, unless a hare, sir, in a lenten pie that   130
        is something stale and hoar ere it be spent.

        He sings.
                    An old hare hoar,
                    And an old hare hoar,
                    Is very good meat in Lent:
                    But a hare that is hoar   135
                    Is too much for a score,
                    When it hoars ere it be spent.

        Romeo will you come to your father's? We'll to
        dinner thither.

ROMEO   I will follow you.   140

MERCUTIO Farewell, ancient lady; farewell, lady, lady, lady.

                                Exeunt MERCUTIO and BENVOLIO.

2.4 A street

The Nurse complains about Mercutio's behaviour and then warns Romeo not to deceive Juliet and take advantage of her innocence.

Activities

Character review: Romeo (10)

1. Discuss whether you think Romeo ought to have stopped Mercutio from treating the Nurse in this way.
2. What does it reveal about Romeo, that he seems prepared to go along with Mercutio's behaviour?
3. Is there any way of acting the scene to show that Romeo does not approve of it?

---

142 **saucy merchant** insolent character

143 **ropery** rude jokes

146 **stand to** (1) live up to; (2) be sexually aroused

147–148 **take him down** sort him out; deal with him *(with an unintended sexual meaning)*

148 **and 'a were lustier** even if he were livelier

149 **Jacks** rogues

150 **Scurvy** rotten

150 **flirt-gills** 'fast' women

151 **skainsmates** brawling friends *(skain = long knife)*

152 **suffer** permit

154 **use you at his pleasure** *Peter takes the sexual meaning and continues it with*: **my weapon should quickly have been out** (154–155).

159 **vexed** angered, irritated

164–165 **lead her into a fool's paradise** lead her on with deceitful promises; take advantage of her

168 **deal double** double-cross

170 **weak dealing** contemptible behaviour

171 **commend me to** give my regards to *(a warmer greeting than today)*

172 **I protest** I swear *(but the Nurse understands a different meaning: I declare my love)*

176 **mark me** take notice of what I say

NURSE	I pray you, sir, what saucy merchant was this that was so full of his ropery?	
ROMEO	A gentleman, Nurse, that loves to hear himself talk, and will speak more in a minute than he will stand to in a month.	145
NURSE	And 'a stand to anything against me, I'll take him down and 'a were lustier than he is, and twenty such Jacks; and if I cannot, I'll find those that shall. Scurvy knave! I am none of his flirt-gills, I am none of his skainsmates. (*To* PETER) And thou must stand by, too, and suffer every knave to use me at his pleasure!	150
PETER	I saw no man use you at his pleasure. If I had, my weapon should quickly have been out. I warrant you, I dare draw as soon as another man if I see occasion in a good quarrel, and the law on my side.	155
NURSE	Now, afore God, I am so vexed that every part about me quivers. (*Referring to* MERCUTIO) Scurvy knave! (*To* ROMEO) Pray you, sir, a word. And, as I told you, my young lady bid me inquire you out. What she bid me say I will keep to myself; but first let me tell ye, if ye should lead her into a fool's paradise, as they say, it were a very gross kind of behaviour, as they say; for the gentlewoman is young, and therefore, if you should deal double with her, truly it were an ill thing to be offered to any gentlewoman, and very weak dealing.	160 165 170
ROMEO	Nurse, commend me to thy lady and mistress. I protest unto thee –	
NURSE	Good heart! and i' faith I will tell her as much. Lord, Lord, she will be a joyful woman!	
ROMEO	What wilt thou tell her, Nurse? Thou dost not mark me.	175

2.4 A street

Romeo instructs the Nurse to tell Juliet to meet him at Friar Lawrence's cell that afternoon, where they will be married; meanwhile his servant will take her a rope-ladder so that Romeo can climb to Juliet's room that night.

Activities

Character review: the Nurse (2)

Write the Nurse's diary entry to cover the events of the morning. Include sections on:

- the conversation she had with Juliet before leaving the house (which presumably included Juliet's instructions about what to tell Romeo)
- her account of her meeting with Romeo, including her treatment by Mercutio
- her anxieties about the way Romeo might behave (164–170)
- the plans for Romeo and Juliet to meet and get married.

Conclude the entry with an expression of her feelings for Juliet and her reasons for helping her to marry Romeo.

Plot review (6)

1. What has to happen between now (noon) and midnight in order to ensure Romeo and Juliet's happiness?
2. What part has to be played by: (a) the Friar; (b) the Nurse; (c) Romeo's man?
3. What could go wrong?

179	**shrift** confession *(a visit to the Friar to confess sins and be forgiven, or **shrived**, line 181)*
181	**for thy pains** for your trouble
187	**tackled stair** rope-ladder
188	**high topgallant** highest point *(in a ship)*
189	**convoy** means of access
190	**quit thy pains** reward you for your trouble
194	**secret** trustworthy
195	**"Two may keep ..."** Two people can keep a secret, but not three.
196	**warrant** assure
198	**when 't was ...** when she was a little chattering (**prating**) thing
199–200	**would fain lay knife aboard** would very much like to stake a claim for her *(people invited to a meal used to bring their own knives and place them on the table to make sure they were served)*
200	**as lief** as soon
202	**properer** more handsome
204	**any clout ...** any sheet in the entire (**versal** = universal) world
205–206	**Doth not ... letter?** *Rosemary is the herb of remembrance used at Elizabethan weddings and funerals.*

Nurse	I will tell her, sir, that you do protest, which, as I take it, is a gentlemanlike offer.
Romeo	Bid her devise some means to come to shrift this afternoon.
	And there she shall, at Friar Lawrence's cell, 180
	Be shrived and married. (*He offers her money*) Here is for thy pains.
Nurse	No, truly, sir; not a penny.
Romeo	Go to, I say you shall.
Nurse	(*Taking the money*) This afternoon, sir? Well, she shall be there.
Romeo	And stay, good Nurse, behind the abbey wall: 185
	Within this hour my man shall be with thee,
	And bring thee cords made like a tackled stair,
	Which to the high topgallant of my joy
	Must be my convoy in the secret night.
	Farewell. Be trusty, and I'll quit thy pains. 190
	Farewell. Commend me to thy mistress.
Nurse	Now God in heaven bless thee! Hark you, sir.
Romeo	What say'st thou, my dear Nurse?
Nurse	Is your man secret! Did you ne'er hear say,
	"Two may keep counsel, putting one away"? 195
Romeo	I warrant thee my man's as true as a steel.
Nurse	Well, sir. My mistress is the sweetest lady. Lord, Lord! when 't was a little prating thing – O, there is a nobleman in town, one Paris, that would fain lay knife aboard, but she, good soul, had as lief 200 see a toad, a very toad, as see him. I anger her, sometimes, and tell her that Paris is the properer man, but I'll warrant you, when I say so, she looks as pale as any clout in the versal world. Doth not "rosemarry" and "Romeo" begin with a 205 letter?
Romeo	Ay, Nurse, what of that? Both with an R.

2.5 The Capulets' house

Juliet waits at home, impatient for the return for the Nurse who finally arrives.

208 **the dog-name** *R was called the dog's letter, possibly because it sounds like a dog growling. The Nurse does not finish 'R is for the . . .', remembering that the word she is thinking of begins with a different letter.*

210 **sententious** *She probably means 'sentences' (witty sayings).*

215 **and apace** and get a move on

3 **Perchance** perhaps

4 **heralds** messengers

6 **louring** gloomy and threatening

7 **nimble-pinioned** swift-winged

7 **draw Love** pull Venus' chariot

12 **affections** feelings

14 **bandy** strike *(with a tennis racket)*

16 **feign as they were** pretend to be

| NURSE | Ah, mocker, that's the dog-name. R is for the – No, I know it begins with some other letter; and she hath the prettiest sententious of it, of you and rosemary, that it would do you good to hear it. | 210 |

ROMEO   Commend me to thy lady.

NURSE   Ay, a thousand times. Peter!

PETER   Anon.

NURSE   Before, and apace.   215

Exeunt.

Scene 5

The Capulets' garden.

Enter JULIET.

JULIET   The clock struck nine when I did send the Nurse;
In half an hour she promised to return.
Perchance she cannot meet him – that's not so.
O, she is lame! Love's heralds should be thoughts,
Which ten times faster glides than the sun's beams   5
Driving back shadows over louring hills.
Therefore do nimble-pinioned doves draw Love,
And therefore hath the wind-swift Cupid wings.
Now is the sun upon the highmost hill
Of this day's journey, and from nine to twelve   10
Is three long hours, yet she is not come.
Had she affections and warm youthful blood,
She would be as swift in motion as a ball:
My words would bandy her to my sweet love,
And his to me.   15
But old folks – many feign as they were dead:
Unwieldy, slow, heavy, and pale as lead.

Enter PETER followed by NURSE.

O God, she comes! – O honey Nurse, what news?
Hast thou met with him? Send thy man away.

93

2.5 The Capulets' house

The Nurse frustratingly delays her report of the discussion with Romeo, complaining of head aches and back pains after her long trudge around Verona.

Activities

Character review: the Nurse (3)

In pairs, act out lines 21–65, first as though the Nurse really is exhausted, then as though she is deliberately teasing Juliet. Compare your two versions with other people and discuss which you consider to be more convincing.

The Nurse seems to be criticising Romeo when she says:

Well, you have made a simple choice: you know
Not how to choose a man. (38–39)

What does the rest of her speech (39–44) reveal about her true opinions? Why doesn't she tell Juliet what she thinks of Romeo in a more straightforward way?

Actors' interpretations (13): Juliet's behaviour

What do you think Juliet should be doing in this part of the scene (1–55)? If you were directing the scene, what notice would you take of line 51?

25 **give me leave** leave me alone

26 **What a jaunce ...!** What a merry dance I've had!

27 **I would thou hadst** I wish you had

29 **stay** wait

34 **excuse** make excuses for not telling

36 **I'll stay the circumstance** I'll wait for the details

38 **simple** foolish

42 **be not to be talked on** are not worth talking about

45 **Go thy ways, wench ...** Off you go, girl. Be good.

51 **a' t' other** on the other

94

NURSE	Peter, stay at the gate.	20

Exit PETER.

JULIET	Now good sweet Nurse – O Lord, why lookest thou sad? Though news be sad, yet tell them merrily: If good, thou shamest the music of sweet news By playing it to me with so sour a face.	
NURSE	I am aweary; give me leave a while. Fie, how my bones ache! What a jaunce have I!	25
JULIET	I would thou hadst my bones, and I thy news. Nay, come, I pray thee, speak; good, good Nurse, speak,	
NURSE	Jesu, what haste! Can you not stay a while? Do you not see that I am out of breath?	30
JULIET	How art thou out of breath, when thou hast breath To say to me that thou art out of breath? The excuse that thou dost make in this delay Is longer than the tale thou dost excuse. Is thy news good or bad? Answer to that. Say either, and I'll stay the circumstance. Let me be satisfied; is 't good or bad?	35
NURSE	Well, you have made a simple choice; you know not how to choose a man. Romeo? No, not he. Though his face be better than any man's, yet his leg excels all men's; and for a hand and a foot and a body, though they be not to be talked on, yet they are past compare. He is not the flower of courtesy, but, I'll warrant him, as gentle as a lamb. Go thy ways, wench; serve God. What, have you dined at home?	40 45
JULIET	No, no. But all this did I know before. What says he of our marriage? What of that ?	
NURSE	Lord, how my head aches! What a head have I! It beats as it would fall in twenty pieces. My back a' t' other side; ah, my back, my back!	50

2.5 The Capulets' house

The Nurse finally tells Juliet that she is to meet Romeo at Friar Lawrence's cell and be married. She meanwhile will fetch a rope-ladder.

Activities

Character review: Juliet (5)

How does Juliet feel during these exchanges with the Nurse? Look again at lines 21–65 and write notes to help the actress playing Juliet. First decide how you interpret the Nurse's behaviour (see the activity on page 92) and then give advice on:

- movements and actions
- how to speak the lines (impatiently, shouting, cajoling . . .)
- where to pause
- facial expressions
- how she is feeling at different points in the scene.

Actors' interpretations (14): Juliet and the Nurse

Use what you have learned from the activities on the Nurse and Juliet (on this page and page 92) to act out their scene. Discuss your ideas first and try to use everything that you have discovered about the characters to make the scene as lively and interesting as you can.

52 **Beshrew** Curse

54 **I' faith** I promise you (In faith)

56 **honest** honourable

59 **within** indoors

63 **hot** impatient (*perhaps also*: eager for Romeo)

63 **Marry, come up, I trow** *The Nurse is impatient.*

64 **poultice** cure (*like a warm cloth placed on the spot*)

66 **coil** fuss, deal of trouble

69 **hie you hence** hurry off

71 **wanton** playful (*a word often linked with sex*)

72 **They'll be in scarlet straight** They blush very readily

76 **the drudge, and toil ...** the servant and labour for your pleasure

77 **bear the burden** carry the weight (*another bawdy joke*)

Beshrew your heart for sending me about
To catch my death with jauncing up and down.

JULIET   I' faith, I am sorry that thou art not well.
Sweet, sweet, sweet Nurse, tell me, what says my
     love?   55

NURSE   Your love says, like an honest gentleman, and a
courteous, and a kind, and a handsome, and, I
warrant, a virtuous – Where is your mother?

JULIET   Where is my mother? Why, she is within.
Where should she be? How oddly thou repliest: 60
"Your love says, like an honest gentleman,
'Where is your mother?' "

NURSE   O God's Lady dear!
Are you so hot? Marry, come up, I trow.
Is this the poultice for my aching bones?
Henceforth do your messages yourself.   65

JULIET   Here's such a coil! Come, what says Romeo?

NURSE   Have you got leave to go to shrift to-day?

JULIET   I have.

NURSE   Then hie you hence to Friar Lawrence' cell;
There stays a husband to make you a wife.   70
Now comes the wanton blood up in your cheeks:
They'll be in scarlet straight at any news.
Hie you to church; I must another way,
To fetch a ladder, by the which your love
Must climb a bird's nest soon when it is dark.   75
I am the drudge, and toil in your delight,
But you shall bear the burden soon at night.
Go. I'll to dinner; hie you to the cell.

JULIET   Hie to high fortune! Honest Nurse, farewell.

Exeunt.

2.6 Friar Lawrence's cell

The Friar warns Romeo about the suddenness and violence of his passion and then Juliet arrives.

Niamh Cusack (Juliet), Sean Bean (Romeo) and Robert Demeger (the Friar) in the 1986 RSC production

1 **So smile ...** So may the heavens approve of

2 **That after-hours ...** and not send us unhappiness in the future to tell us that we have done wrong

3–4 **But come what ...** I don't care what sorrow comes, it cannot outweigh (**countervail**) the joy

6 **Do thou but close ...** Simply join our hands

11–13 **The sweetest ...** The most delicious honey can become sickly and disgusting, and its taste can make you lose your appetite.

15 **Too swift ...** 'More haste, less speed.'

16–17 **so light a foot ... flint** Her feet are barely touching the ground!

18 **bestride the gossamers** ride on spiders' threads

19 **wanton** playful

20 **so light is vanity** The delights of this world are lightweight and trivial *(compared with those of his religion).*

23 **As much ...** I must give him the same (*a kiss*); otherwise he will have thanked me too much.

24–29 **if the measure ... encounter** If you are feeling as much happiness as I am, and you are better at expressing it, then utter your sweet words and let your musical voice describe the joy we are sharing because of this meeting.

Scene 6

Friar Lawrence's cell.

Enter FRIAR LAWRENCE and ROMEO.

FRIAR
LAWRENCE
So smile the heavens upon this holy act
That after-hours with sorrow chide us not.

ROMEO
Amen, amen. But come what sorrow can,
It cannot countervail the exchange of joy
That one short minute gives me in her sight.   5
Do thou but close our hands with holy words,
Then love-devouring death do what he dare;
It is enough I may but call her mine.

FRIAR
LAWRENCE
These violent delights have violent ends,
And in their triumph die like fire and powder,   10
Which, as they kiss, consume. The sweetest honey
Is loathsome in his own deliciousness,
And in the taste confounds the appetite.
Therefore love moderately; long love doth so:
Too swift arrives as tardy as too slow.   15

Enter JULIET.

Here comes the lady. O, so light a foot
Will ne'er wear out the everlasting flint.
A lover may bestride the gossamers
That idles in the wanton summer air,
And yet not fall, so light is vanity.   20

JULIET
Good even to my ghostly confessor.

FRIAR
LAWRENCE
Romeo shall thank thee, daughter, for us both.

ROMEO kisses her.

JULIET
As much to him, else is his thanks too much.

She returns his kiss.

ROMEO
Ah, Juliet, if the measure of thy joy
Be heaped like mine, and that thy skill be more   25
To blazon it, then sweeten with thy breath

2.6 Friar Lawrence's cell

Romeo and Juliet express their love for each other and Friar Lawrence ushers them off to be married.

Activities

Themes: love

'These violent delights ...'. The Friar's advice to Romeo is extremely important. In the 1997 film, his words (9–15) are spoken as part of his sermon to Romeo and Juliet at their wedding.

A Why do you think the Friar feels it necessary to advise the young couple to 'love moderately' (14)? What is the connection with his advice to Romeo at 2.3.94)?

B In giving his advice to 'love moderately' (14), the Friar uses three images to illustrate the dangers of falling in love too quickly and too passionately; they are to do with gunpowder (10–11), honey (11–13) and travelling (15).

1. Create a collage which includes pictures to represent all three images and display it with the heading 'These violent delights have violent ends'.

2. Create a parallel collage which represents Romeo's images of happiness – heaping it up like treasure (24–25), displaying it in a coat-of-arms (25–26), hearing it in music (27–29).

C Discuss the differences between the two sets of images and what they reveal about the different views of love held by the Friar and Romeo.

30–31 **Conceit ... ornament** Imagination, when it is richer in substance than in mere words, boasts of the reality of feelings, not of the outward appearances.

32 **They are but beggars ...** If you can say how much money you've got, you're not really rich.

34 **I cannot sum up sum of** I cannot calculate

36 **by your leaves** with your permission

This neighbour air, and let rich music's tongue
Unfold the imagined happiness that both
Receive in either, by this dear encounter.

JULIET   Conceit more rich in matter than in words   30
Brags of his substance, not of ornament.
They are but beggars that can count their worth,
But my true love is grown to such excess
I cannot sum up sum of half my wealth.

FRIAR   Come, come with me, and we will make short
LAWRENCE   work;   35
For, by your leaves, you shall not stay alone
Till Holy Church incorporate two in one.

Exeunt.

Exam practice

Shakespeare's language: bawdy innuendo

After the beauty of the scene between the lovers, Shakespeare takes us back to lads' talk about sex in 2.1. Mercutio's language in this short scene is full of sexual puns.

In pairs, discuss why Mercutio should use so much sexual language at this point, grading each of the following suggestions from I (very unlikely) to 5 (very likely) and then comparing your judgements with other people's. Of course, all of these might be true to some extent:

(a) Mercutio doesn't yet know about Juliet and he is trying to make the point that Romeo's obsession with Rosaline is purely sexual and has nothing to do with love.

(b) He does know about Juliet and is taunting Romeo by reminding him of his earlier passion for Rosaline.

(c) He is jealous because he sees that he is losing his close friend.

(d) He is simply obsessed with sex all the time.

(e) Shakespeare wanted to show how pure and genuine Romeo's love for Juliet was, by contrasting it with this very sexual description of his feelings for Rosaline.

(f) Shakespeare knew that his audience enjoyed bawdy puns and saw this as a good opportunity to include some old favourites.

Character review: the Nurse (4)

 How would you describe the Nurse's:
- feelings for Juliet
- attitude towards Juliet's mother
- role and position in the Capulet household?

B Imagine that Juliet were writing her autobiography. Write the section in which she describes the part that the Nurse has played in her life and the feelings she has for her. Juliet could also compare the relationships she has with the Nurse and with her mother.

C Discuss these descriptions of the Nurse by the actress Brenda Bruce and try to find at least one quotation to support (or contradict) each one:

(a) The Nurse's philosophy is it's a man's world and it's a young world.

(b) She takes the view that very young girls must prepare for love, especially the physical aspect of love.

(c) She believes in romantic love and happiness.

(d) She is a religious woman.

(e) Her position in the Capulet family is that of servant who, once her position as a wet-nurse is over and Juliet is weaned, is kept in their employ.

(f) She brought up Juliet as a child.

(g) She runs the domestic side of the household.

(h) She is Juliet's confidante (the person in whom Juliet confides).

(i) She is not a deep-thinking woman: she has learned to live with the inevitable happenings of a life such as hers.

(j) Her infant dead, her husband dead, she dedicates her life to Juliet.

(k) She feels that, if Juliet really loves Romeo, she will do everything in her power to see them married.

(l) She doesn't let the Capulet–Montague feud affect her actions.

What has been left out of this list?

Actors' interpretations (15): the set

Although there is no mention of a balcony anywhere in the script, the famous moment in 2.2 has come to be known as 'the balcony scene'. There are a number of reasons why this moment presents a challenge to a set designer:

- Juliet has to appear through 'yonder window' (2)
- although Romeo hears Juliet's first words (25–49), she does not hear his comments
- after he makes himself known to her (49), they have a long conversation, and it is difficult to keep up the emotions if they are not able to touch each other.

Study the photographs below and, using the stage plan on page 242, discuss in pairs how each set might be used: (a) to allow Juliet to appear from an upper window; (b) to conceal Romeo until he speaks; (c) to allow the lovers to touch.

3.1 A street

Benvolio is anxious about walking the streets when the Capulets are likely to be around, but Mercutio mockingly accuses him of being a quarreller himself.

Activities

Actors' interpretations (16)

1. Benvolio's name means something like 'well-wishing'.

   What does Benvolio say here which suggests that he is a peacemaker? Where else in the play has he shown that quality?

2. Pick one of the examples of quarrelling that Mercutio describes and either (a) draw a sequence of cartoons to represent what happens; or (b) improvise the situation. Try to make your representation as exaggerated as Mercutio's account.

3. How does Shakespeare create tension in the opening of this scene? In the 1968 film, you can almost feel the heat coming off the screen as this scene opens; Baz Luhrmann's 1997 film shows the boys on the beach, with Mercutio shooting his gun into the waves. If you were filming this moment, how would you convey the mounting tension and sense of danger?

2   **the Capels ...** the Capulets are out and about

3   **scape** avoid

6   **claps me his sword** bangs his sword down

8   **by the operation of ...** by the time his second glass of wine has taken effect

9   **draws him on the drawer** draws his sword on the barman

12 **Jack** fellow (*see 2.4.149*)

13 **as soon ... moved** as quickly moved to anger and as angry at being provoked

16 **two such** two people like you

22 **hazel** (1) a nut; (2) an eye colour

24 **meat** food

25 **addle** rotten

30 **doublet** jacket

30 **before Easter** *Easter was traditionally the time for bringing out new fashions; the argument arises because the tailor should not have been wearing them before his customers did.*

31 **riband** laces

32 **tutor me from quarrelling** teach me not to quarrel

33 **And** If

Act 3

Scene 1

A street.

Enter MERCUTIO, his page, BENVOLIO and SERVANTS.

BENVOLIO   I pray thee, good Mercutio, let's retire:
The day is hot, the Capels are abroad,
And if we meet we shall not scape a brawl,
For now, these hot days, is the mad blood stirring.

MERCUTIO   Thou art like one of these fellows that, when he   5
enters the confines of a tavern, claps me his sword
upon the table and says, "God send me no need
of thee"; and by the operation of the second cup
draws him on the drawer, when indeed there is
no need.   10

BENVOLIO   Am I like such a fellow?

MERCUTIO   Come, come; thou art as hot a Jack in thy mood
as any in Italy, and as soon moved to be moody,
and as soon moody to be moved.

BENVOLIO   And what to?   15

MERCUTIO   Nay, and there were two such, we should have
none shortly, for one would kill the other. Thou?
Why, thou wilt quarrel with a man that hath a
hair more or a hair less in his beard than thou
hast. Thou wilt quarrel with a man for cracking   20
nuts, having no other reason but because thou
hast hazel eyes. What eye but such an eye would
spy out such a quarrel? Thy head is as full of
quarrels as an egg is full of meat, and yet thy head
hath been beaten as addle as an egg for   25
quarrelling. Thou last quarrelled with a man for
coughing in the street because he hath wakened
thy dog that hath lain asleep in the sun. Didst
thou not fall out with a tailor for wearing his new
doublet before Easter? With another for tying his   30
new shoes with old riband? And yet thou wilt
tutor me from quarrelling!

BENVOLIO   And I were so apt to quarrel as thou art, any man

3.1 A street

Tybalt arrives. Mercutio provokes Tybalt, but Tybalt's real interest is in Romeo, who soon appears.

Activities

Character review: Mercutio (4)

Chook Sibtain, who played Mercutio with the Royal Shakespeare Company in 1998, said, 'Mercutio loves to fight. I think he loves anything that gives him an adrenalin* kick. So when he encounters Tybalt I think he gets a tremendous rush form fighting the best fighter in town.' (*Adrenalin is a substance produced by the body in moments of action or excitement.)

A Re-read the exchange between Tybalt and Mercutio (41–59).
1. Why has Tybalt approached Mercutio? What does he actually want?
2. Is Mercutio trying to provoke a fight with Tybalt?
3. What is Benvolio trying to do?

B Discuss what evidence you can find, from this scene or from earlier in the play, which supports Sibtain's views that Mercutio seems to use excitement as a kind of drug.

C Imagine that the roles were reversed at the beginning of the scene, and Benvolio were accusing Mercutio of being a quarreller. Use Mercutio's behaviour in his exchange with Tybalt as a basis for a description that Benvolio might write, beginning 'Thou wilt quarrel with a man for . . .'.

---

34 **. . . buy the fee-simple . . .** *legal terms*: anybody would be able to buy the permanent lease on my life *(it would be cheap, because it would only last an hour and a quarter)*

36 **O, simple!** Stupid!

37 **By my head** *a common oath; Mercutio invents his own version (line 38), suggesting that he won't 'take to his heels' = run away.*

44 **apt . . . to** ready for

45 **occasion** reason

48–52 **thou consortest . . .** you are often in the company of; you hang around with. *But a* **consort** *(49) is a group of musicians and Mercutio takes offence, as* **minstrels** *(49) are no better than servants. Keeping up the language of music, he describes his sword as a* **fiddlestick** *(51), and threatens to make Tybalt dance (52).*

53 **the public haunt . . .** a place frequented by the public

55 **reason coldly** discuss your differences (**grievances**) calmly and rationally

56 **depart** go your separate ways

58 **for no man's pleasure** to suit anybody

59 **my man** the man I'm looking for. *Mercutio (line 60) takes 'man' to mean 'servant'.*

60 **livery** servant's uniform

should buy the fee-simple of my life for an hour
and a quarter.   35

MERCUTIO   The fee-simple? O, simple!

Enter TYBALT and his followers.

BENVOLIO   By my head, here come the Capulets!

MERCUTIO   By my heel, I care not.

TYBALT   (*To his followers*) Follow me close, for I will speak
to them.
(*To* MERCUTIO *and* BENVOLIO)   40
Gentlemen, good e'en; a word with one of you.

MERCUTIO   And but one word with one of us? Couple it with
something: make it a word and a blow.

TYBALT   You shall find me apt enough to that, sir, and you
will give me occasion.   45

MERCUTIO   Could you not take some occasion without
giving?

TYBALT   Mercutio, thou consortest with Romeo –

MERCUTIO   Consort? What, dost thou make us minstrels?
And thou make minstrels of us, look to hear   50
nothing but discords. Here's my fiddlestick; here's
that shall make you dance. Zounds, consort!

BENVOLIO   We talk here in the public haunt of men.
Either withdraw unto some private place,
Or reason coldly of your grievances,   55
Or else depart. Here, all eyes gaze on us.

MERCUTIO   Men's eyes were made to look, and let them gaze.
I will not budge for no man's pleasure, I.

Enter ROMEO.

TYBALT   (*To* MERCUTIO) Well, peace be with you, sir; here
comes my man.

MERCUTIO   But I'll be hanged, sir, if he wear your livery.   60

3.1 A street

Romeo replies calmly to Tybalt's insults and tries to make peace with him. Mercutio disapproves of Romeo's attitude; he challenges Tybalt and they fight.

Activities

Actors' interpretations (17): Tybalt and Romeo

Where has Romeo just come from, when he enters on line 59?

A In groups of four, freeze-frame the moment just before Mercutio steps in after Romeo has said, 'be satisfied' (75). The people playing Benvolio, Mercutio, Romeo and Tybalt then say what their character is thinking and feeling at that moment.

B In pairs, act out the exchange between Romeo and Tybalt (63–75). Discuss what you think each character's one overriding emotion is. Then act out their confrontation again, using only one word from each line.

C In the 1983 Royal Shakespeare production, the director John Caird deliberately made it as hard as possible for Romeo to resist taking up Tybalt's challenge, by having Tybalt slap him brutally and spit in his face. John Leguizamo (Tybalt in the 1997 film) kicks Romeo to the ground and injures him quite badly. How could this be done differently? Write directors' notes to lines 63–75, giving advice to the two actors on how they should behave, stating precisely what Tybalt does to provoke Romeo and how Romeo reacts.

---

61 **go before to field** walk in front of him to the duelling field

66 **"man"** (1) servant *(Mercutio's earlier interpretation)*; (2) man of honour *(willing to fight a duel)*

64 **thou art a villain** This is the classic insult.

66–67 **Doth much excuse the appertaining rage . . .** excuses me for not displaying the anger appropriate to your greeting

69 **Boy** *a further insult*

72 **devise** imagine

74 **tender** regard

77 **"Alla stoccata"** *Mercutio's mocking name for Tybalt, a jibe at the affected fencing terms that he thinks Tybalt would employ (see 2.4.20–28):* 'The trendy fencer has won (**carries it away**)!' *Next he calls him a* **rat-catcher** *(78), because he is* **King of Cats** *(80).*

78 **will you walk?** *This is a challenge to a duel.*

80–83 **. . . make bold withal . . .** I only want one of your lives to do what I want with; and then, depending on how you behave to me afterwards, I'll beat up the other eight.

82 **dry-beat** beat without drawing blood

84 **pilcher** scabbard

85 **about your ears** attacking you

90 **forbear** stop

	Marry, go before to field, he'll be your follower:	
	Your worship in that sense may call him "man".	

TYBALT Romeo, the love I bear thee can afford
No better term than this: thou art a villain.

ROMEO Tybalt, the reason that I have to love thee   65
Doth much excuse the appertaining rage
To such a greeting. Villain am I none;
Therefore, farewell; I see thou know'st me not.

TYBALT Boy, this shall not excuse the injuries
That thou hast done me; therefore turn and draw.   70

ROMEO I do protest I never injured thee,
But love thee better than thou can'st devise
Till thou shalt know the reason of my love.
And so, good Capulet, which name I tender
As dearly as mine own, be satisfied.   75

MERCUTIO O calm, dishonourable, vile submission!
"Alla stoccata" carries it away.
(*He draws his sword*) Tybalt, you rat-catcher, will you
          walk?

TYBALT What would'st thou have with me?

MERCUTIO Good King of Cats, nothing but one of your nine   80
lives that I mean to make bold withal, and, as you
shall use me hereafter, dry-beat the rest of the
eight. Will you pluck your sword out of his
pilcher by the ears? Make haste, lest mine be
about your ears ere it be out.   85

TYBALT (*Drawing his sword*) I am for you.

ROMEO Gentle Mercutio, put thy rapier up.

MERCUTIO (*To* TYBALT) Come, sir, your passado.

MERCUTIO and TYBALT fight.

ROMEO Draw, Benvolio; beat down their weapons.
Gentlemen, for shame, forbear this outrage!   90
Tybalt! Mercutio! the Prince expressly hath

3.1 A street

In his attempts to break up the fight, Romeo accidently causes Mercutio to be fatally wounded. Cursing the Capulet-Montague feud, the dying Mercutio is carried out. Left alone, Romeo feels ashamed.

Activities

Actors' interpretations (18): Mercutio's realisation

1. In threes, re-read lines 93–112 and discuss where you think Mercutio actually realises that his wound is a fatal one.

Harold Perrineau in the 1997 film keeps joking until 'grave man' (101–102) and then suddenly notices his wound; Roger Allam in the 1983 production at Stratford did not realise that he had been seriously wounded until he coughed up blood after 'arithmetic!' (106). Try acting out the sequence in different ways and decide which works best.

2. Look again at Mercutio's final lines (99–112). Who or what does he seem to blame most for his death: Romeo? Tybalt? the ancient grudge between the two houses? Where does the blame lie most in your opinion?

3. Re-read lines 93–112 and find examples of (a) wordplay; (b) vivid images; and (c) insults. Find examples from earlier in the play to show that Mercutio's dying words are typical of his language throughout.

92 **bandying** brawling

94 **A plague o' both your houses** *Mercutio delivers a dying man's curse on both families.*

94 **sped** finished, mortally wounded

95 **and hath nothing** without being wounded in return

96 **a scratch** *(perhaps because it was inflicted by the 'King of Cats', see line 104)*

100 **'t will serve** it'll do; it will be enough (to kill me)

101 **grave** (1) serious *(unusual for him)*; (2) buried in a grave

102 **peppered** finished off

103 **Zounds!** God's wounds!

105 **braggart** boaster

105–106 **by the book ...** by the rule book *(see 2.4.20–28)*

111 **worms' meat** a corpse, only fit to be devoured by worms

111–112 **I have it, And soundly too** I am wounded, and fatally.

113 **near ally** close relative

116 **slander** insulting words

118 **effeminate** lacking manly virtues

119 **temper** mood *(with a play on 'to temper' = to harden steel)*

119 **... in my temper softened** ... Juliet's beauty has weakened my courage.

3.1

Forbid this bandying in Verona streets.
Hold, Tybalt! Good Mercutio!

ROMEO comes between them. TYBALT wounds MERCUTIO from behind
ROMEO, then runs away, followed by his men.

MERCUTIO   I am hurt.
A plague o' both your houses! I am sped.
Is he gone, and hath nothing?

BENVOLIO   What, art thou hurt? 95

MERCUTIO   Ay, ay, a scratch, a scratch; marry, 't is enough.
Where is my page? Go, villain, fetch a surgeon.

Exit page.

ROMEO   Courage, man; the hurt cannot be much.

MERCUTIO   No, 't is not so deep as a well, nor so wide as a   100
church door, but 't is enough, 't will serve. Ask for
me to-morrow and you shall find me a grave man.
I am peppered, I warrant, for this world. A plague,
o' both your houses! Zounds! a dog, a rat, a
mouse, a cat, to scratch a man to death! A
braggart, a rogue, a villain that fights by the book   105
of arithmetic! Why the devil came you between
us? I was hurt under your arm.

ROMEO   I thought all for the best.

MERCUTIO   Help me into some house, Benvolio,
Or I shall faint. A plague o' both your houses!   110
They have made worms' meat of me. I have it,
And soundly too. Your houses!

BENVOLIO helps him out.

ROMEO   This gentlemen, the Prince's near ally,
My very friend, hath got this mortal hurt
In my behalf, my reputation stained   115
With Tybalt's slander – Tybalt that an hour
Hath been my cousin. O sweet Juliet,
Thy beauty hath made me effeminate,
And in my temper softened valour's steel.

Benvolio returns to report Mercutio's death. Romeo furiously pursues Tybalt, kills him and flees before the officers arrive.

Activities

Actors' interpretations (19): the fight between Romeo and Tybalt

Make a list of the ways in which this fight ought to be different from the earlier one between Mercutio and Tybalt, discussing the following possibilities, among others that you can think of, and giving reasons for your responses. Should the Romeo–Tybalt fight be:
- more violent?
- faster?
- more passionate?

What are the main differences between the two conflicts as they are presented in the 1997 film? Look at (a) what leads up to each fight; (b) where they take place; (c) how Mercutio and Tybalt die; (d) the different reactions of the killers, Tybalt and then Romeo.

Character review: Romeo (11)

At the moment of Tybalt's death, Romeo's only spoken reaction is 'O, I am fortune's fool' (140). Try to imagine what Romeo is feeling at this moment. List the kinds of emotions that he might be experiencing and discuss which ones might be uppermost in his mind, in your opinion.

Michael York as Tybalt in the 1968 film

121 **aspired** soared up to

122 **untimely** early

123 **on more . . . depend** threatens the future (with more unhappiness)

127 **respective lenity** gentleness which comes from respect *(perhaps for the Prince's laws, or his new relationship with Tybalt)*

128 **be my conduct** guide my actions

132 **Staying** waiting

134 **consort** accompany *(the word that angered Mercutio; see 48–52)*

137 **up** roused up and in arms

138–139 **Stand not amazed . . . taken** Don't stand there in a daze. The Prince will sentence you to death if you are arrested.

140 **. . . fortune's fool** I am like a household fool, kept by Fortune *(or Fate)* for its amusement.

BENVOLIO returns.

BENVOLIO	O Romeo, Romeo, brave Mercutio is dead.	120
	That gallant spirit hath aspired the clouds,	
	Which too untimely here did scorn the earth.	

ROMEO   This day's black fate on more days doth depend;
This but begins the woe others must end.

TYBALT returns.

BENVOLIO   Here comes the furious Tybalt back again.   125

ROMEO   Alive, in triumph! And Mercutio slain!
Away to heaven, respective lenity,
And fire-eyed fury be my conduct now!
Now, Tybalt, take the "villain" back again
That late thou gavest me, for Mercutio's soul   130
Is but a little way above our heads,
Staying for thine to keep him company.
Either thou or I, or both, must go with him.

TYBALT   Thou, wretched boy, that did consort him here,
Shalt with him hence.

ROMEO   (*Drawing his sword*)   This shall determine that.   135

They fight, and ROMEO kills TYBALT.

BENVOLIO   Romeo, away, be gone!
The citizens are up, and Tybalt slain.
Stand not amazed: the Prince will doom thee death
If thou art taken. Hence, be gone, away!

ROMEO   O, I am fortune's fool.

BENVOLIO   Why dost thou stay?   140

Exit ROMEO.

Enter an OFFICER and citizens.

OFFICER   Which way ran he that killed Mercutio?
Tybalt, that murderer, which way ran he?

BENVOLIO   There lies that Tybalt.

3.1 A street

Lady Capulet calls upon the Prince to punish Tybalt's death and Benvolio reports how Mercutio and Tybalt came to die.

Activities

Plot review (7)

(A) Write out Benvolio's account of the fight in the form of brief notes in your own words: 1. Tybalt started it. 2. Romeo . . . etc.

(B) Turn Benvolio's account into a newspaper report for the following day's *Verona Independent*. Make it an eyewitness account (from 'our correspondent on the spot', Benvolio Montague), written mainly in your own words, but including some of Benvolio's more vivid expressions.

(C) Write a brief analysis of Benvolio's account (156–179). Comment on (a) the differences between Benvolio's account and what actually happened according to the script; (b) his use of vivid metaphors to describe the fighting; and (c) how far Benvolio's report might be thought to be biased in favour of the Montagues.

144 **charge** order

146 **discover** reveal, explain

147 **manage** sequence of events

152 **true** fair and just

157–158 **spoke him fair . . .** spoke politely to him and asked him to consider (**bethink**) how trivial (**nice**) the argument was, and in addition stressed (**urged withal**)

161 **Could not take truce with . . .** was not enough to pacify Tybalt's uncontrolled temper (**unruly spleen**)

164 **all as hot** just as angry

165 **martial scorn** aggressive contempt

165–167 **with one hand . . . with the other . . .** They were fighting with swords and daggers.

167–168 **whose dexterity Retorts it** whose skill turns it back

172 **envious** hostile

173 **stout** brave

174 **by and by** immediately

175 **but newly entertained** just at that moment thought about

Act 3 Scene 1

OFFICER	Up, sir, go with me:	
	I charge thee in the Prince's name, obey.	

Enter PRINCE ESCALUS, MONTAGUE, CAPULET, their wives and servants.

PRINCE   Where are the vile beginners of this fray?   145

BENVOLIO   O noble Prince, I can discover all
                     The unlucky manage of this fatal brawl.
                     There lies the man, slain by young Romeo,
                     That slew thy kinsman, brave Mercutio.

LADY   Tybalt, my cousin! O my brother's child!   150
CAPULET   O Prince! O cousin! husband! O the blood is spilled
                     Of my dear kinsman. Prince, as thou art true,
                     For blood of ours, shed blood of Montague.
                     O cousin, cousin!

PRINCE   Benvolio, who began this bloody fray?   155

BENVOLIO   Tybalt, here slain, whom Romeo's hand did slay.
                     Romeo, that spoke him fair, bid him bethink
                     How nice the quarrel was, and urged withal
                     Your high displeasure. All this, utterèd
                     With gentle breath, calm look, knees humbly
                          bowed,   160
                     Could not take truce with the unruly spleen
                     Of Tybalt, deaf to peace, but that he tilts
                     With piercing steel at bold Mercutio's breast,
                     Who, all as hot, turns deadly point to point,
                     And, with a martial scorn, with one hand beats   165
                     Cold death aside, and with the other sends
                     It back to Tybalt, whose dexterity
                     Retorts it. Romeo – he cries aloud,
                     "Hold, friends! friends part!" and, swifter than his
                          tongue,
                     His agile arm beats down their fatal points,   170
                     And 'twixt them rushes, underneath whose arm
                     An envious thrust from Tybalt hit the life
                     Of stout Mercutio, and then Tybalt fled,
                     But by and by comes back to Romeo,
                     Who had but newly entertained revenge,   175
                     And to 't they go like lightning, for, ere I
                     Could draw to part them, was stout Tybalt slain,

3.2 Juliet's room

Lady Capulet demands Romeo's death as punishment for killing Tybalt, but instead the Prince exiles him from Verona. Meanwhile Juliet is longing for night, when Romeo will be with her.

187 **Who now . . .?** Who is now to pay for shedding Mercutio's precious blood?

189–190 **His fault . . .** Although Romeo has done wrong, his crime has simply put into effect what the law would have demanded: the death of Tybalt. *(Romeo has killed the man that the law would have condemned to death anyway.)*

191 **exile** banish (from Verona)

192 **have an interest** am personally concerned

193 **My blood** my family's blood *(Mercutio's)*

194 **amerce** punish

197 **Nor tears, nor . . .** neither tears nor prayers will be able to buy a pardon for (**purchase out**) your wrongs (**abuses**)

198 **Let Romeo hence** Romeo must leave here

200 **attend our will** come with me to hear what I intend to do

201 **Mercy but murders . . .** If you pardon killers, you will cause more murders.

1 **apace** quickly

1–3 **steeds** horses, which draw the chariot of the sun god, **Phoebus**

5 **love-performing** when acts of love take place

6 **runaway's** possibly: the sun's (in his chariot)

6 **wink** close

And as he fell, did Romeo turn and fly.
This is the truth, or let Benvolio die.

LADY　　He is a kinsman to the Montague.　　　　　　180
CAPULET　Affection makes him false; he speaks not true.
Some twenty of them fought in this black strife,
And all those twenty could but kill one life.
I beg for justice, which thou, Prince, must give:
Romeo slew Tybalt; Romeo must not live.　　　185

PRINCE　Romeo slew him; he slew Mercutio.
Who now the price of his dear blood doth owe?

MONTAGUE　Not Romeo, Prince; he was Mercutio's friend.
His fault concludes but what the law should end –
The life of Tybalt.

PRINCE　　　　　　　　　　And for that offence　　190
Immediately we do exile him hence.
I have an interest in your hate's proceedings:
My blood for your rude brawls doth lie a-bleeding.
But I'll amerce you with so strong a fine
That you shall all repent the loss of mine.　　195
I will be deaf to pleading and excuses;
Nor tears, nor prayers shall purchase out abuses.
Therefore use none. Let Romeo hence in haste,
Else when he is found, that hour is his last.
Bear hence this body, and attend our will.　　200
Mercy but murders, pardoning those that kill.

Exeunt.

Scene 2

Juliet's room.

Enter JULIET.

JULIET　Gallop apace, you fiery-footed steeds,
Towards Phoebus' lodging! Such a waggoner
As Phaeton would whip you to the west,
And bring in cloudy night immediately.
Spread thy close curtain, love-performing night;　　5
That runaway's eyes may wink, and Romeo

3.2 Juliet's room

Juliet is thinking excitedly about Romeo when the Nurse arrives, grieving over Tybalt's death.

Activities

Character review: Juliet (6)

(A) Juliet is impatiently waiting for night, when Romeo will be with her.
1. Pick out the words which are to do with (a) night; and (b) light.
2. Pick out all the commands.
3. Discuss how far you can gain an idea of Juliet's mood and emotions from this combination of (a) 'night' words; (b) 'light' words; and (c) commands.

(B) Work in pairs to express the main points of her train of thought, using the following key words as a structure:
- 1–4: sun
- 5–7: night
- 8–10: night and lovers
- 10–13: virginity
- 14–16: blushing
- 17–19: Romeo and night
- 20–25: stars
- 26–28: possessing Romeo
- 28–31: impatient

(C) Much of Juliet's language in this speech is sexual. Pick out the sexual references and, bearing in mind the earlier exchanges between Romeo and her, discuss how significant a part sexual attraction is playing in their relationship.

8 **amorous rites** the religious acts of love

10 **agrees with** suits

10 **civil** respectable

12 **learn me ...** teach me how to lose my virginity but win a husband

13 **stainless maidenhoods** They will both lose their spotless virginity.

14 **Hood ...** Cover up my blushes. *Juliet sees herself as a falcon, kept hooded because it is unused to men (***unmanned***) and fluttering its wings in excitement (***bating***).*

15 **black mantle** the dark covering of night

15 **strange** (1) new to me; (2) bashful

15–16 *Night will help her to overcome her shyness about lovemaking.*

21 **die** *In Elizabethan love poetry, 'die' could mean to experience an orgasm.*

25 **garish** crudely bright

26–28 **O, I have bought ...** *The language of buying and selling houses: Juliet and Romeo are married but have not enjoyed each other physically.*

34 **cords** rope-ladder

37, 39 **well-a-day! ... Alack the day** *expressions of grief (and line 72)*

38 **undone** ruined

Leap to these arms untalked of and unseen.
Lovers can see to do their amorous rites
By their own beauties; or, if love be blind
It best agrees with night. Come, civil night,   10
Thou sober-suited matron all in black,
And learn me how to lose a winning match,
Played for a pair of stainless maidenhoods.
Hood my unmanned blood, bating in my cheeks,
With thy black mantle, till strange love, grown
    bold,   15
Think true love acted simple modesty.
Come, night; come, Romeo; come, thou day in night,
For thou wilt lie upon the wings of night,
Whiter than new snow upon a raven's back.
Come, gentle night; come, loving, black-browed
    night,   20
Give me my Romeo; and when I shall die,
Take him and cut him out in little stars,
And he will make the face of heaven so fine
That all the world will be in love with night
And pay no worship to the garish sun.   25
O, I have bought the mansion of a love,
But not possessed it; and though I am sold,
Not yet enjoyed. So tedious is this day
As is the night before some festival
To an impatient child that hath new robes   30
And may not wear them. O here comes my Nurse,

Enter NURSE with the rope ladder.

And she brings news; and every tongue that speaks
But Romeo' s name, speaks heavenly eloquence.
Now, Nurse, what news? What hast thou there? The
    cords
That Romeo bid thee fetch?

NURSE   Ay, ay, the cords.   35

JULIET   Ay me, what news? Why dost thou wring thy hands?

NURSE   Ah, well-a-day! He's dead, he's dead, he's dead!
We are undone, lady, we are undone.
Alack the day, he's gone, he's killed, he's dead!

3.2 Juliet's room

Juliet is desperate, thinking at first that it is Romeo who has died. Then she is unable to believe the truth: that Romeo has killed Tybalt.

Activities

Character review: the Nurse (5)

Why do you think the Nurse does not tell Juliet straight away that it is Tybalt who has died (35–70)? In pairs discuss each of the following suggestions, finding evidence from earlier in the play, as well as from this scene, to support your views:

- she is angry with Romeo and is deliberately tormenting Juliet by not telling her all the facts
- she always rambles before coming to the point
- she is genuinely grief-stricken about Tybalt and simply does not think about Juliet's feelings for Romeo
- she has difficulty expressing herself
- she is worried about her own position, if Capulet finds out that she helped Juliet to marry Romeo.

40 **envious** cruel

45 **"Ay"** *wordplay on: (1) Ay = yes; (2) the letter i; (3) the pronoun I; (4) eye*

47 **cockatrice** *mythical creature which could kill by looking at you*

51 **Brief sounds . . .** A few words will decide my happiness or misery.

53 **God save the mark!** *a common expression:* 'forgive me for saying it'

54 **corse** corpse

56 **gore** clotted

57–58 **bankrupt . . .** *someone who has lost all their money and must be ruined (**break**) and go to prison for their debts*

59 **Vile earth** *her physical body*

59 **to earth resign** surrender to death (the grave) and end all activity (**motion**)

60 **And thou . . .** both you, death, and Romeo lie on the same sad (**heavy**) funeral carriage (**bier**)

67 **dreadful trumpet . . .** *the trumpet which will signal (**sound**) the end of the world and Judgement Day (**the general doom**)*

73 **O serpent heart . . .** What wicked emotions were hidden behind a handsome face! *(Romeo is compared with the serpent which tempted Eve in the Bible.)*

JULIET	Can heaven be so envious?	
NURSE	Romeo can,	40

JULIET   Can heaven be so envious?

NURSE   Romeo can,   40
Though heaven cannot. O Romeo, Romeo!
Whoever would have thought it? Romeo!

JULIET   What devil art thou dost torment me thus?
This torture should be roared in dismal hell.
Hath Romeo slain himself? Say thou but "Ay",   45
And that bare vowel "I" shall poison more
Than the death-darting eye of cockatrice.
I am not I, if there be such an "I",
Or those eyes shut that makes thee answer "Ay".
If he be slain, say "Ay", or if not, "No".   50
Brief sounds determine my weal or woe.

NURSE   I saw the wound, I saw it with mine eyes –
God save the mark! – here on his manly breast;
A piteous corse, a bloody, piteous corse;
Pale, pale as ashes, all bedaubed in blood,   55
All in gore blood; I swounded at the sight.

JULIET   O break, my heart! poor bankrupt, break at once!
To prison, eyes; ne'er look on liberty!
Vile earth, to earth resign, end motion here,
And thou and Romeo press one heavy bier!   60

NURSE   O Tybalt, Tybalt, the best friend I had!
O courteous Tybalt, honest gentleman,
That ever I should live to see thee dead!

JULIET   What storm is this that blows so contrary?
Is Romeo slaughtered, and is Tybalt dead?   65
My dearest cousin, and my dearer lord?
Then, dreadful trumpet, sound the general doom,
For who is living if those two are gone?

NURSE   Tybalt is gone and Romeo banishèd;
Romeo that killed him, he is banishèd.   70

JULIET   O God! did Romeo's hand shed Tybalt's blood?

NURSE   It did, it did! alas the day, it did!

JULIET   O serpent heart, hid with a flowering face!

3.2 Juliet's room

Juliet bitterly accuses Romeo of hiding his evil behind a beautiful exterior, but angrily defends her new husband when the Nurse criticises him. In her confusion she tries to sort out her true feelings.

Activities

Character review: Juliet (7)

When she realises that Romeo has killed Tybalt, Juliet experiences terrible conflicting emotions.

1. What are her divided loyalties here? Where do her loyalties in fact lie?
2. To show her conflicts, Juliet's language is full of oxymorons (73–85). (Look back at page 16 to remind yourself about antithesis and oxymoron.) Pick out three oxymorons which, in your opinion, best capture the conflicting feelings that Juliet is trying to express about Romeo, and draw sketches to represent them.

Judy Buxton as Juliet and Brenda Bruce as the Nurse in the 1980 RSC production

74   **... so fair a cave** *the reverse of line 73; an ugly outside guarding the beautiful treasure within*

75–85   **Beautiful tyrant ...** *All examples of badness being concealed behind an attractive cover.*

76   **wolvish-ravening** ravenous as a wolf

77   **Despisèd substance ...** *anything which appears virtuous but is in reality bad*

78   **Just** exact

81   **bower** beautifully enclose

86–87   **all perjured, All forsworn ...** they all lie and break their promises, they're all wicked (**naught**), all cheats (**dissemblers**)

88   **aqua-vitae** *spirits (e.g. brandy) to revive her (literally 'water of life')*

95   **chide at** speak harshly of

98   **smooth** speak pleasantly about

100   **wherefore** why

102   **your native spring** your source

103–104   **Your tributary drops ... joy** Your tears were a tribute offered up to sadness; but, realising your mistake, you now offer them up to joy.

109   **I would ... fain** I would gladly

Did ever dragon keep so fair a cave?
Beautiful tyrant, fiend angelical,   75
Dove-feathered raven, wolvish-ravening lamb,
Despisèd substance of divinest show,
Just opposite to what thou justly seem'st,
A damnèd saint, an honourable villain!
O nature, what hadst thou to do in hell   80
When thou didst bower the spirit of a fiend
In mortal paradise of such sweet flesh?
Was ever book containing such vile matter
So fairly bound? O that deceit should dwell
In such a gorgeous palace!

NURSE   There's no trust,   85
No faith, no honesty in men; all perjured,
All forsworn, all naught, all dissemblers.
Ah, where's my man? Give me some aqua-vitae.
These griefs, these woes, these sorrows make me old.
Shame come to Romeo!

JULIET   Blistered be thy tongue   90
For such a wish! He was not born to shame.
Upon his brow shame is ashamed to sit,
For 't is a throne where honour may be crowned
Sole monarch of the universal earth.
O what a beast was I to chide at him!   95

NURSE   Will you speak well of him that killed your cousin?

JULIET   Shall I speak ill of him that is my husband?
Ah, poor my lord, what tongue shall smooth thy
    name,
When I, thy three-hours' wife, have mangled it?
But wherefore, villain, didst thou kill my cousin?   100
That villain cousin would have killed my husband.
Back, foolish tears, back to your native spring;
Your tributary drops belong to woe,
Which you, mistaking, offer up to joy.
My husband lives, that Tybalt would have slain,   105
And Tybalt's dead that would have slain my husband.
All this is comfort. Wherefore weep I then?
Some word there was, worser than Tybalt's death,
That murdered me. I would forget it fain,

3.2 Juliet's room

Juliet is horrified, as it gradually sinks in that Romeo has been banished. The Nurse knows that Romeo is hiding at Friar Lawrence's cell and promises to bring him to Juliet that night.

Activities

Character review: Juliet (8)

A Juliet experiences some dramatic changes of emotion in this scene. Look back through the scene and note down emotions that you think she might be experiencing (e.g. impatience, grief, anger . . .) at the following points: lines 1, 31, 36, 43, 57, 64, 71, 73, 90, 100–101, 106, 113, 142–143.

B Re-read the scene from line 102, in which the full horror of Romeo's banishment hits her. Then write directors' notes for an actress playing Juliet, giving advice on:
• movements and actions
• how to speak the lines (e.g. whispering, sobbing . . .)
• where to pause
• facial expressions
• how the character is feeling.

C Write a response to Niamh Cusack's opinion that: 'This scene is where Juliet really grows up: she understands what commitment and depth of love are in this scene; as she makes herself face up to the fact that being married to someone means that you stand by him even if he has killed someone you love . . . This scene is the turning point for Juliet, the realisation that a wife's love must come on top of all other loves.'

116 **delights in fellowship** likes company

117 **needly will be ranked** has to be accompanied by

120 **Which modern lamentation . . .** which might have caused the usual kind of grief

121 **with a rearward** with a rearguard *(following up behind, causing more destruction)*

125 **bound** limit

126 **sound** (1) give expression to; (2) measure the depth of

130 **spent** used up

132 **beguiled** cheated

138 **Hie** hurry

139 **wot** know

But O, it presses to my memory   110
Like damnèd guilty deeds to sinners' minds:
"Tybalt is dead, and Romeo banishèd."
That "banishèd", that one word "banishèd",
Hath slain ten thousand Tybalts. Tybalt's death
Was woe enough if it had ended there;   115
Or, if sour woe delights in fellowship
And needly will be ranked with other griefs,
Why followed not, when she said, "Tybalt's dead",
"Thy father", or "thy mother", nay, or both,
Which modern lamentation might have moved?   120
But with a rearward following Tybalt's death,
"Romeo is banishèd"! To speak that word
Is father, mother, Tybalt, Romeo, Juliet,
All slain, all dead. "Romeo is banishèd".
There is no end, no limit, measure, bound,   125
In that word's death; no words can that woe sound.
Where is my father and my mother, Nurse?

NURSE   Weeping and wàiling over Tybalt's corse.
            Will you go to them? I will bring you thither.

JULIET   Wash they his wounds with tears? Mine shall be
                spent   130
            When theirs are dry, for Romeo's banishment.
            Take up those cords. Poor ropes, you are beguiled,
            Both you and I, for Romeo is exiled.
            He made you for a highway to my bed,
            But I, a maid, die maiden-widowèd.   135
            Come, cords; come Nurse; I'll to my wedding bed,
            And death, not Romeo, take my maidenhead.

NURSE   Hie to your chamber. I'll find Romeo
            To comfort you; I wot well where he is.
            Hark ye, your Romeo will be here at night: 140
            I'll to him; he is hid at Lawrence' cell.

JULIET   O find him! Give this ring to my true knight,
            And bid him come to take his last farewell.

                                                    Exeunt.

3.3 Friar Lawrence's cell

The Friar returns to his cell and reports the Prince's sentence. He rebukes Romeo for not being grateful for having received a sentence of banishment rather than death.

1 **fearful** frightened

2–3 **Affliction . . .** Suffering is in love with (**enamoured of**) your qualities (**parts**) and you have married misfortune (**calamity**).

4 **doom** judgement

5 **craves acquaintance . . .** wants to be introduced to me

6–7 **Too familiar . . . company** You already know it too well.

9 **doomsday** Judgement Day *(in other words, death)*

10 **vanished** was uttered

18 **purgatory** *the place where souls had to wait and suffer for their sins before being allowed into heaven*

21 **mis-termed** given the wrong name

24 **O deadly sin!** *Romeo's ungratefulness is a sin which will lead to damnation.*

25 **fault** crime

25 **calls death** requires the death penalty

26 **rushed** swept

28 **dear** unusual and precious

Scene 3

Friar Lawrence's cell.

Enter FRIAR LAWRENCE.

FRIAR LAWRENCE	Romeo, come forth; come forth, thou fearful man.
	Affliction is enamoured of thy parts,
	And thou art wedded to calamity.

ROMEO comes forward from the inner room.

ROMEO	Father, what news? What is the Prince's doom?	
	What sorrow craves acquaintance at my hand	5
	That I yet know not?	
FRIAR LAWRENCE	Too familiar	
	Is my dear son with such sour company:	
	I bring thee tidings of the Prince's doom.	
ROMEO	What less than doomsday is the Prince's doom?	
FRIAR LAWRENCE	A gentler judgement vanished from his lips:	10
	Not body's death, but body's banishment.	
ROMEO	Ha, banishment? Be merciful, say "death",	
	For exile hath more terror in his look,	
	Much more, than death; do not say "banishment".	
FRIAR LAWRENCE	Hence from Verona art thou banishèd.	15
	Be patient, for the world is broad and wide.	
ROMEO	There is no world without Verona walls,	
	But purgatory, torture, hell itself.	
	Hence "banishèd" is banished from the world,	
	And world's exile is death. Then "banishèd"	20
	Is death mis-termed. Calling death "banishèd",	
	Thou cut'st my head off with a golden axe,	
	And smilest upon the stroke that murders me.	
FRIAR LAWRENCE	O deadly sin! O rude unthankfulness!	
	Thy fault our law calls death, but the kind Prince,	25
	Taking thy part, hath rushed aside the law,	
	And turned that black word "death" to	
	"banishment".	
	This is dear mercy, and thou seest it not.	

3.3 CT

Romeo is devastated that, because he is banished, he will not be able to be with Juliet, and refuses to listen to the Friar's words of comfort.

Activities

Actors' interpretations (20): Romeo the 'fond madman'

This is a difficult scene for actors to play successfully, as Romeo is highly emotional. Write some directors' notes to help the actors in their approach to lines 29–70. Give advice on:

- movements and actions: does Romeo actually try to find some poison (44), for example? Should you take into account Romeo's own description in lines 68–70?
- how to speak the lines (it does not work if Romeo shouts everything, or displays the same emotion throughout)
- where to pause
- facial expressions
- how the characters are feeling.

33 **validity** value

34 **courtship** (1) courtly behaviour; (2) wooing

35 **carrion flies** flies which live off rotting flesh

38 **vestal** virginal

43 **And say'st thou yet** And do you still say

45 **sudden mean ... though ...** quick method ... however dishonourable (**mean**)

48 **attends** accompanies

49 **a divine ...** a holy man, a spiritual (**ghostly**) confessor

50 **my friend professed** someone who claims to be my friend

51 **mangle** destroy

52 **fond** foolish

55 **Adversity** misfortune

55 **philosophy** *the ability to understand why things happen and to accept them*

59 **Displant** transplant; move to another place

60 **prevails not** has no effect; is no use

63 **dispute with thee ...** discuss your position (**estate**) with you

ROMEO 'T is torture and not mercy. Heaven is here
Where Juliet lives, and every cat and dog 30
And little mouse, every unworthy thing,
Live here in heaven and may look on her,
But Romeo may not. More validity,
More honourable state, more courtship, lives
In carrion flies than Romeo: they may seize 35
On the white wonder of dear Juliet's hand,
And steal immortal blessing from her lips,
Who even in pure and vestal modesty
Still blush, as thinking their own kisses sin,
But Romeo may not; he is banishèd. 40
Flies may do this, but I from this must fly;
They are free men, but I am banishèd.
And say'st thou yet that exile is not death?
Hadst thou no poison mixed, no sharp-ground knife,
No sudden mean of death, though ne'er so mean, 45
But "banishèd" to kill me? "Banishèd"!
O Friar, the damnèd use that word in hell;
Howling attends it. How hast thou the heart,
Being a divine, a ghostly confessor,
A sin-absolver, and my friend professed, 50
To mangle me with that word "banishèd"?

FRIAR Thou fond madman, hear me a little speak.
LAWRENCE

ROMEO O thou wilt speak again of banishment.

FRIAR I'll give thee armour to keep off that word:
LAWRENCE Adversity's sweet milk, philosophy, 55
To comfort thee though thou art banishèd.

ROMEO Yet "banishèd"? Hang up philosophy!
Unless philosophy can make a Juliet,
Displant a town, reverse a Prince's doom,
It helps not, it prevails not, talk no more. 60

FRIAR O, then I see that madmen have no ears.
LAWRENCE

ROMEO How should they, when that wise men have no eyes?

FRIAR Let me dispute with thee of thy estate.
LAWRENCE

3.3 Friar Lawrence's cell

Romeo flings himself emotionally onto the floor and refuses to move even when they hear someone knocking on the door. It is the Nurse, come with Juliet's message.

Activities

Actors' interpretations (21): the Nurse's arrival

In groups of three, plan a performance of lines 71–83. First think about:
(a) what the characters are thinking and feeling (how does the Friar react to the sudden knocking, for example?);
(b) where they should be positioned (where is Romeo lying?);
(c) what the moves are (where does the Nurse enter from?).

67 **Doting** being deeply in love
70 **Taking the measure of ...** measuring out ...
73 **infold** wrap me up and hide me
75 **taken** caught, arrested
76 **By and by!** I'm coming!
77 **simpleness** foolishness

ROMEO	Thou canst not speak of that thou dost not feel.
	Wert thou as young as I, Juliet thy love, 65
	An hour but married, Tybalt murderèd,
	Doting like me, and like me banishèd,
	Then mightst thou speak, then mightst thou tear
	thy hair,
	And fall upon the ground as I do now,
	Taking the measure of an unmade grave. 70

ROMEO flings himself on the floor. There is knocking at the door.

FRIAR LAWRENCE	Arise; one knocks. Good Romeo, hide thyself.
ROMEO	Not I, unless the breath of heartsick groans
	Mist-like infold me from the search of eyes.

More knocking.

FRIAR LAWRENCE	Hark, how they knock! – Who's there? – Romeo, arise;
	Thou wilt be taken. – (*He calls*) Stay a while! – (*To ROMEO*) Stand up! 75
	Run to my study. – (*He calls*) By and by! – (*To ROMEO*) God's will,
	What simpleness is this? – (*He calls*) I come, I come!

Louder knocking.

	Who knocks so hard? Whence come you? What's your will?
NURSE	(*From outside*) Let me come in, and you shall know my errand.
	I come from Lady Juliet.
FRIAR LAWRENCE	(*Opening the door*) Welcome then. 80
NURSE	(*Entering*) O holy Friar, O tell me, holy Friar,
	Where's my lady's lord? Where's Romeo?
FRIAR LAWRENCE	There on the ground, with his own tears made drunk.

3.3 Friar Lawrence's cell

Romeo asks the Nurse about Juliet, fearing that she must now hate him for killing her cousin Tybalt. Intent upon killing himself, he draws a dagger, but the Nurse snatches if from him. The Friar is furious with Romeo for his suicide attempt.

Activities

Character review: the Nurse (6)

Discuss the Nurse's use of bawdy language here: 'case' can mean pregnancy; 'stand' and 'rise' occur earlier (see page 102); 'O' represents the female sexual organs. Is it possible that she does not realise she is doing it?

84   **even … case** in exactly the same state as Juliet

85   **O woeful sympathy!** O, they're feeling the same grief!

88–89   **… rise and stand** *Even here, the Nurse unintentionally comes out with bawdy double meanings.*

99   **an O** the shape made by the mouth when uttering 'O!'

93   **old** hardened by experience *(though 'old' is often used as in the expression, 'a fair old problem')*

95   **removed but little** closely related *(Tybalt was her cousin)*

97   **concealed** hidden *(she is secretly his wife)*

99   **now** one minute

102   **level** aim

105   **anatomy** body

106   **sack** destroy

107   **mansion** the place where the name lives

108   **form** physical shape

109   **denote** are the sign of

110   **unreasonable** lacking human reason

112   **ill-beseeming** unnatural and wrong

114   **… thy disposition …** I thought your personality was more stable.

NURSE	O he is even in my mistress' case,

NURSE   O he is even in my mistress' case,
Just in her case. O woeful sympathy! 85
Piteous predicament! Even so lies she,
Blubbering and weeping, weeping and blubbering.
(*To ROMEO*) Stand up, stand up! Stand, and you
    be a man!
For Juliet's sake; for her sake rise and stand.
Why should you fall into so deep an O? 90

ROMEO   (*Rising*) Nurse!

NURSE   Ah sir! Ah sir! Death's the end of all.

ROMEO   Spak'st thou of Juliet? How is it with her?
Doth she not think me an old murderer,
Now I have stained the childhood of our joy
With blood removed but little from her own? 95
Where is she? and how doth she? and what says
My concealed lady to our cancelled love?

NURSE   O she says nothing, sir, but weeps and weeps,
And now falls on her bed, and then starts up,
And Tybalt calls, and then on Romeo cries, 100
And then down falls again.

ROMEO   As if that name,
Shot from the deadly level of a gun,
Did murder her as that name's cursèd hand
Murdered her kinsman. O tell me, Friar, tell me,
In what vile part of this anatomy 105
Doth my name lodge? Tell me, that I may sack
The hateful mansion.

He draws his dagger to kill himself, but the NURSE snatches it from him.

FRIAR   Hold thy desperate hand!
LAWRENCE   Art thou a man? Thy form cries out thou art:
Thy tears are womanish, thy wild acts denote
The unreasonable fury of a beast. 110
Unseemly woman in a seeming man,
And ill-beseeming beast in seeming both!
Thou hast amazed me. By my holy order,
I thought thy disposition better tempered.
Hast thou slain Tybalt? Wilt thou slay thyself? 115

3.3 Friar Lawrence's cell

Friar Lawrence angrily rebukes Romeo for bringing shame upon his manly appearance, his love for Juliet and his intelligence. He forces him to count his blessings and instructs him to visit Juliet as planned, but to leave at dawn for Mantua.

117 **damnèd hate** a hateful act that will damn you *(suicide)*

118 **rail'st** curse

121 **shape** *(manly)* physical appearance

121 **wit** intelligence

122–123 **Which like a usurer ... none** you who, like a money-lender, do not spend your wealth properly

124 **bedeck** be an ornament to

125–126 **... but a form of wax ...** Your manliness is nothing more than a wax model *(in other words, a poor copy)*, if it deviates (**digressing**) from manly courage (**valour**).

127 **hollow perjury** empty lies

129–133 **Thy wit ... defence** Your intelligence ... is like gunpowder stored in a clumsy soldier's container; it is ignited by your own ignorance and you are blown limb from limb (**dismembered**) by the very thing that should protect you.

140 **light** alight, land

141 **best array** finest clothes

147 **look thou ...** take care you don't stay until the watch go on duty

150 **blaze** publicise

156 **Which heavy sorrow ...** *Their grief at Tybalt's death should make them inclined to* (**apt unto**) *get to bed early.*

And slay thy lady, that in thy life lives,
But doing damnèd hate upon thyself?
Why rail'st thou on thy birth, the heaven, and earth,
Since birth, and heaven, and earth, all three, do meet
In thee at once, which thou at once would'st lose?   120
Fie, fie! Thou sham'st thy shape, thy love, thy wit,
Which like a usurer abound'st in all,
And usest none in that true use indeed
Which should bedeck thy shape, thy love, thy wit.
Thy noble shape is but a form of wax,   125
Digressing from the valour of a man;
Thy dear love sworn but hollow perjury,
Killing that love which thou hast vowed to cherish;
Thy wit, that ornament to shape and love,
Misshapen in the conduct of them both,   130
Like powder in a skilless soldier's flask,
Is set afire by thine own ignorance,
And thou dismembered with thine own defence.
What? Rouse thee, man! Thy Juliet is alive,
For whose dear sake thou wast but lately dead,   135
There art thou happy. Tybalt would kill thee,
But thou slew'st Tybalt; there art thou happy.
The law that threatened death becomes thy friend,
And turns it to exile; there art thou happy too.
A pack of blessings light upon thy back;   140
Happiness courts thee in her best array,
But like a misbehaved and sullen wench
Thou frown'st upon thy fortune and thy love.
Take heed, take heed, for such die miserable.
Go, get thee to thy love, as was decreed;   145
Ascend her chamber; hence, and comfort her,
But look thou stay not till the watch be set,
For then thou can'st not pass to Mantua,
Where thou shalt live till we can find a time
To blaze your marriage, reconcile your friends,   150
Beg pardon of the Prince, and call thee back
With twenty hundred thousand times more joy
Than thou went'st forth in lamentation.
Go before, Nurse. Commend me to thy lady,
And bid her hasten all the house to bed,   155
Which heavy sorrow makes them apt unto.
Romeo is coming.

3.4 Capulet's house

Romeo is cheered when the Nurse gives him Juliet's ring and the Friar promises to send messages to Romeo in Mantua. Meanwhile Capulet explains to Paris that Juliet cannot see him as she is mourning the death of her cousin Tybalt.

Activities

Part 3: suggesting a course of action
- 145–149: what Romeo must do . . .
- 149–153: what the Friar will do in the meantime . . .
- 154–157: what the Nurse must do now . . .

Character review: Paris (1)

1. As a class, discuss whether you have any sympathy for Paris and the situation he is in. Has he behaved badly, in your opinion? How far do you blame him for being an obstacle in the way of Romeo and Juliet's happiness?

2. Shakespeare does not give Paris many lines and it is difficult to see what kind of person he is. Look back at the scene in which he has appeared so far (1.2) and write his diary entry for this evening, after he leaves the Capulet house. Among other things, Paris might explain what he thinks of Capulet's concerns that Juliet might be too young to marry (1.2.8–15).

161 **chide** rebuke me, tell me off

165 **And here stands . . .** your future happiness depends on this *(following the Friar's instructions in lines 166–170)*

168 **Sojourn** Stay for the time being

169–170 **. . . signify . . . Every good hap** he will report to you every fortunate thing that happens here in Verona

172–173 **But that a joy . . .** I would be very sad to leave you in such a hurry, were not great happiness waiting for me.

1 **fallen out** happened

2 **move** persuade *(to marry Paris)*

3 **Look you** You have to understand that

8 **afford** allow

9 **commend me** give my regards to

NURSE	O Lord, I could have stayed here all the night
	To hear good counsel. O what learning is!
	My lord, I'll tell my lady you will come.	160

| ROMEO | Do so, and did my sweet prepare to chide. |

| NURSE | Here, sir, a ring she bid me give you, sir. |
| | Hie you, make haste, for it grows very late. |

| ROMEO | How well my comfort is revived by this. |

| FRIAR
LAWRENCE | Go hence; good night. |

Exit NURSE.

          And here stands all your state: 165
Either be gone before the watch be set,
Or by the break of day disguised from hence.
Sojourn in Mantua. I'll find out your man,
And he shall signify from time to time
Every good hap to you that chances here.   170
Give me thy hand. 'T is late; farewell, good night.

ROMEO	But that a joy past joy calls out on me,
	It were a grief so brief to part with thee.
	Farewell.

Exeunt.

Scene 4

Capulet's house.

Enter CAPULET, LADY CAPULET and PARIS.

CAPULET	Things have fallen out, sir, so unluckily
	That we have had no time to move our daughter.
	Look you, she loved her kinsman Tybalt dearly,
	And so did I. Well, we were born to die.
	'T is very late; she'll not come down tonight.	5
	I promise you, but for your company,
	I would have been a-bed an hour ago.

| PARIS | These times of woe afford no time to woo. |
| | Madam, good night; commend me to your daughter. |

3.4 Capulet's house

Capulet decides that Juliet will marry Paris in three days' time and tells his wife to inform her.

Activities

Character review: Capulet (2)

A What does this short scene tell us about Capulet as a father? How far is he concerned for his daughter's happiness? How much does he understand her feelings?

B Capulet seems to behave very oddly in this scene, constantly interrupting himself and changing the subject. In threes, take it in turn to improvise Capulet's dialogue, the other two acting as Lady Capulet and Paris.

C Discuss the possible reasons for Capulet's disjointed language.

10 **her mind** her views (about the marriage)

11 **mewed up** caged up (like a falcon)

11 **heaviness** sadness

12 **desperate tender** bold offer (bold because he has not had a chance to talk to her)

16 **son** Capulet already sees Paris as a son-in-law.

18 **soft** wait a minute

19 **ah ha** perhaps 'hmm', while he is turning things over in his mind

21 **earl** the English title for a count

23 **keep no great ado** won't make a great fuss

24 **so late** so recently

25–26 **It may be thought ... much** People might think we did not care about him (**held him carelessly**), given that he was our relative, if we have a big celebration (**revel much**).

29 **would that** wish

32 **against** for

34 **Afore me** A common mild oath: 'My goodness!'

35 **by and by** before long

| LADY CAPULET | I will, and know her mind early to-morrow; | 10 |
| | To-night she's mewed up to her heaviness. | |

CAPULET calls back PARIS who is leaving.

CAPULET Sir Paris! I will make a desperate tender
Of my child's love. I think she will be ruled
In all respects by me: nay, more I doubt it not.
Wife, go you to her ere you go to bed;   15
Acquaint her here of my son Paris' love,
And bid her, mark you me, on Wednesday next –
But soft, what day is this?

PARIS   Monday, my lord.

CAPULET Monday, ah ha; well, Wednesday is too soon;
O' Thursday let it be. O' Thursday, tell her,   20
She shall be married to this noble earl.
Will you be ready? Do you like this haste?
We'll keep no great ado; a friend or two;
For hark you, Tybalt being slain so late,
It may be thought we held him carelessly,   25
Being our kinsman, if we revel much.
Therefore we'll have some half a dozen friends,
And there an end. (*To* PARIS) But what say you to
    Thursday?

PARIS My lord, I would that Thursday were to-morrow.

CAPULET Well, get you gone; o' Thursday be it then.   30
(*To his wife*) Go you to Juliet ere you go to bed;
Prepare her, wife, against this wedding day.
Farewell, my lord. (*To his servant*) Light to my
    chamber, ho!
Afore me, 't is so very late that we
May call it early by and by. Good night.   35

Exeunt.

3.5 Juliet's bedroom

As their night together draws to a close, Juliet at first tries to persuade Romeo to stay longer, but then fears for his safety and reluctantly encourages him to go.

Activities

Actors' interpretations (22): 'It was the nightingale ...'

The lovers' dialogue goes something like this:
- Part 1: they disagree: J says N – R says L:
  J: Don't go: it was the N.
  R: I must. It wasn't the N: it was the L.
  J: I'm sure it was the N, because ...
- Part 2: now J says L – R says N:
  R: You're right: it was the N. And I don't care if I'm captured anyway ...
  J: No! You were right! It was the L! Go now!

Either (a) in pairs, improvise a similar friendly disagreement between two people, in which they both change sides halfway through; or (b) act out lines 1–28, using only one word per line.

2 **nightingale ...** *nightingales sing at night; larks at dawn*

3 **fearful** anxious

7 **envious** jealous and malicious

9 **Night's candles** *the stars*

9 **jocund** joyful, cheerful

13 **exhales** breathes out

17 **ta'en** arrested

18 **so thou ...** so long as that is what you want

20 **pale reflex ...** pale refleciton of the moon's forehead (**Cynthia** *was another name for Diana, the moon goddess.*)

22 **vaulty** arched

23 **care** concern, desire

28 **sharps** sharp notes

29 **division** (1) melody; (2) separation *(of the lovers)*

31 **... changed eyes** *a piece of folklore: the lark has dull eyes, the toad remarkable ones*

33 **arm from arm** the lark's song frightens us (**doth us affray**) out of each other's arms

34 **hunt's-up** *an early morning hunting call*

Scene 5

Juliet's bedroom.

ROMEO and JULIET stand at the window.

JULIET	Wilt thou be gone? It is not yet near day.
	It was the nightingale, and not the lark,
	That pierced the fearful hollow of thine ear.
	Nightly she sings on yond pomegranate tree.
	Believe me, love, it was the nightingale. 5
ROMEO	It was the lark, the herald of the morn,
	No nightingale. Look, love, what envious streaks
	Do lace the severing clouds in yonder east.
	Night's candles are burnt out, and jocund day
	Stands tiptoe on the misty mountain tops. 10
	I must be gone and live, or stay and die.
JULIET	Yond light is not daylight; I know it, I.
	It is some meteor that the sun exhales
	To be to thee this night a torchbearer
	And light thee on thy way to Mantua. 15
	Therefore stay yet; thou need'st not to be gone.
ROMEO	Let me be ta'en, let me be put to death:
	I am content, so thou wilt have it so.
	I'll say yon grey is not the morning's eye,
	'T is but the pale reflex of Cynthia's brow; 20
	Nor that is not the lark whose notes do beat
	The vaulty heaven so high above our heads.
	I have more care to stay than will to go.
	Come, death, and welcome! Juliet wills it so.
	How is 't, my soul? Let's talk; it is not day. 25
JULIET	It is, it is! Hie hence, be gone, away!
	It is the lark that sings so out of tune,
	Straining harsh discords and unpleasing sharps.
	Some say the lark makes sweet division:
	This doth not so, for she divideth us. 30
	Some say the lark and loathèd toad changed eyes;
	O now I would they had changed voices too,
	Since arm from arm that voice doth us affray,
	Hunting thee hence with hunt's-up to the day.
	O now be gone; more light and light it grows. 35

3.5 Juliet's bedroom

As the Nurse enters to report that Lady Capulet is on her way to speak to her daughter, Romeo climbs down the rope-ladder. Both the lovers experience feelings of heavy foreboding.

Activities

Shakespeare's language: imagery

Both Romeo and Juliet visualise their situation in very strong images. Create illustrations (either by drawing or painting them yourself, or by cutting images from magazines) to represent:

(a) Romeo's oxymoron:
More light and light, more dark and dark our woes (36)

(b) Juliet's premonition:
Methinks I see thee, now thou art so low,
As one dead in the bottom of a tomb (54–55).
(In the 1997 film, Juliet looked down to see Romeo's face beneath the surface of the swimming pool.)

36 **More light ...** The lighter it gets
40 **wary** careful
43 **ay** for ever
44 **in the hour** on the hour
46 **count** method of counting
46 **much in years** very old
52 **discourses** conversations
53 **ill-divining** prophesying bad things
58 **Dry** thirsty

Act 3 Scene 5

ROMEO   More light and light, more dark and dark our woes.

Enter NURSE, in a hurry.

NURSE   Madam!

JULIET   Nurse?

NURSE   Your lady mother is coming to your chamber.
The day is broke; be wary, look about.   40

Exit NURSE.

JULIET   Then, window, let day in, and let life out.

ROMEO   Farewell, farewell. One kiss and I'll descend.

He descends the ladder.

JULIET   Art thou gone so, love, lord, ay husband, friend?
I must hear from thee every day in the hour,
For in a minute there are many days.   45
O, by this count I shall be much in years
Ere I again behold my Romeo.

ROMEO   (*From the garden below*) Farewell. I will omit no
    opportunity
That may convey my greetings, love, to thee.

JULIET   O, think'st thou we shall ever meet again?   50

ROMEO   I doubt it not; and all these woes shall serve
For sweet discourses in our time to come.

JULIET   O God, I have an ill-divining soul!
Methinks I see thee, now thou art so low,
As one dead in the bottom of a tomb;   55
Either my eyesight fails, or thou look'st pale.

ROMEO   And trust me, love, in my eye so do you.
Dry sorrow drinks our blood. Adieu, adieu.

Exit ROMEO.

JULIET   O Fortune, Fortune, all men call thee fickle;
If thou art fickle, what dost thou with him   60

3.5 Juliet's bedroom

Lady Capulet misinterprets Juliet's weeping: she thinks her daughter is mourning Tybalt's death and is angry that his killer is still alive.

Activities

Actors' interpretations (23): staging the scene

How would you stage the opening of this scene (up to Lady Capulet's entrance, line 67)? Look at the illustration of Shakespeare's stage on page 240. Answer the following questions in pairs and give reasons for your decisions:

(a) Where would you place the scene: on the floor of the stage, or on an upper level?

(b) Have Romeo and Juliet been standing throughout the scene so far? Sitting down? Lying in bed?

(c) Is any furniture needed in the scene? If so, where would you put it?

(d) Where does the Nurse enter from (37)?

(e) The stage direction after 42 can be ignored or changed. What do you think Romeo ought to do at this point?

(f) Is he in the garden by line 48, in your opinion, or would you place him somewhere else?

(g) Where does Lady Capulet enter from (67)?

65 **Is she not down ...** Is she late going to bed or up early?

66 **procures** brings

67 **how now ...?** what's the matter?

71 **some** a moderate amount of

72 **still** always

72 **want of wit** lack of common sense

73 **feeling** deeply felt

76 **friend** *can mean 'lover' – which is Juliet's private meaning*

80 **asunder** apart

82 **like he** as much as he

That is renowned for faith? Be fickle, Fortune,
For then I hope thou wilt not keep him long,
But send him back.

LADY
CAPULET
(*Outside* JULIET's *door*) Ho, daughter, are you up?

JULIET
Who is 't that calls? It is my lady mother.
Is she not down so late, or up so early?   65
What unaccustomed cause procures her hither?

Enter LADY CAPULET.

LADY
CAPULET
Why, how now, Juliet?

JULIET
                                        Madam, I am not well.

LADY
CAPULET
Evermore weeping for your cousin's death?
What, wilt thou wash him from his grave with tears?
And if thou could'st, thou could'st not make him
     live;   70
Therefore have done: some grief shows much of love,
But much of grief shows still some want of wit.

JULIET
Yet let me weep for such a feeling loss.

LADY
CAPULET
So shall you feel the loss, but not the friend
Which you weep for.

JULIET
                                 Feeling so the loss,   75
I cannot choose but ever weep the friend.

LADY
CAPULET
Well, girl, thou weep'st not so much for his death
As that the villain lives which slaughtered him.

JULIET
What villain, madam?

LADY
CAPULET
                              That same villain, Romeo.

JULIET
(*Aside*) Villain and he be many miles asunder. –   80
(*To her mother*) God pardon him; I do, with all my
     heart;
And yet no man like he doth grieve my heart.

3.5 Juliet's bedroom

Juliet deceives her mother into believing that she hates Romeo and pretends to approve when Lady Capulet promises to send a man to Mantua to poison Romeo; but, when Lady Capulet tells Juliet that she is to marry Paris in three days' time, she forcefully refuses.

Activities

Character review: Juliet (9) and her mother

By the end of this scene, Juliet has cut off all emotional contact with her mother. In pairs, re-read the exchange (67–124).

1. Then, for each of the following lines, write down (a) what Lady Capulet thinks Juliet means; and (b) what Juliet actually means: 67, 73, 75–76, 81, 82, 84, 85, 92–93, 98–99.
2. Act out the dialogue in a way that will bring out Juliet's real meaning and which shows that this is the moment at which Juliet totally cuts herself off from her mother.

Diane Venora as Lady Capulet in the 1997 film

85   **venge** avenge, get revenge for

88   **runagate** fugitive

89   **unaccustomed dram** strange dose *(of poison)*

94   **vexed** angered

96   **temper** (1) mix; (2) weaken, dilute

98   **abhors** hates

100   **wreak the love ...** (1) avenge her love *(for Tybalt)*; (2) physically express her love *(for Romeo)*

104   **in such a needy time** now, when we most need it

106   **careful** considerate, caring

107   **heaviness** sadness

108   **sorted out ...** arranged

      sudden unexpected

109   **nor I looked not for** and which I did not expect either

110   **in happy time** it has come just at the right time

LADY CAPULET	That is because the traitor murderer lives.	
JULIET	Ay, madam, from the reach of these my hands.	
	Would none but I might venge my cousin's death!	85
LADY CAPULET	We will have vengeance for it, fear thou not.	
	Then weep no more. I'll send to one in Mantua,	
	Where that same banished runagate doth live,	
	Shall give him such an unaccustomed dram	
	That he shall soon keep Tybalt company;	90
	And then I hope thou wilt be satisfied.	
JULIET	Indeed, I never shall be satisfied	
	With Romeo till I behold him– dead –	
	Is my poor heart, so for a kinsman vexed.	
	Madam, if you could find out but a man	95
	To bear a poison, I would temper it	
	That Romeo should upon receipt thereof	
	Soon sleep in quiet. O how my heart abhors	
	To hear him named and cannot come to him	
	To wreak the love I bore my cousin	100
	Upon his body that hath slaughtered him.	
LADY CAPULET	Find thou the means, and I'll find such a man.	
	But now I'll tell thee joyful tidings, girl.	
JULIET	And joy comes well in such a needy time.	
	What are they, beseech your ladyship?	105
LADY CAPULET	Well, well, thou hast a careful father, child;	
	One who, to put thee from thy heaviness,	
	Hath sorted out a sudden day of joy	
	That thou expects not, nor I looked not for.	
JULIET	Madam, in happy time! What day is that?	110
LADY CAPULET	Marry, my child, early next Thursday morn,	
	The gallant, young, and noble gentleman,	
	The County Paris, at Saint Peter's Church,	
	Shall happily make thee there a joyful bride.	
JULIET	Now, by Saint Peter's Church, and Peter too,	115
	He shall not make me there a joyful bride.	

3.5 Juliet's bedroom

Capulet enters to find his daughter in tears, but explodes with anger when he is told that she has refused to marry Paris.

Activities

Character review: Juliet (10) and her father

Seeing Juliet's grief as he comes into the room, Capulet compares her mood and her weeping to a ship at sea in stormy weather.

1. In pairs discuss each part of his developing imagery. What comparisons are being made in each of these sections of his speech?
   • When the sun sets . . . downright (125–127)
   • . . . . a conduit, girl? (128)
   • Evermore showering? (129)
   • In one little body . . . tempest-tossèd body (129–136).

2. Draw a picture or create a collage to illustrate this imagery in its four sections.

3. Discuss what the language reveals about Capulet here. Some actors perform the lines as though he is genuinely upset by Juliet's weeping; others feel that the imagery is overdone and shows that Capulet's feelings are false and that he is really only thinking of himself and getting Juliet married off to Paris. If you were acting the part, which interpretation would you follow and why?

117 **I wonder at** I am amazed at

118 **should be** wants to be

124 **at your hands** from you yourself

128 **conduit** street fountain

130 **Thou counterfeits a bark** you're giving an impression of a ship

135–136 **Without a sudden calm . . .** Unless there comes a sudden calm in the winds, your tempest-tossed body will capsize (**overset**).

137 **decree** decision

138 **she will none** she refuses; she will have none of it

140 **Soft, take me with you . . .** Wait a minute, I don't understand, say that again.

142 **count her** consider herself

143 **wrought** arranged

144 **bride** bridegroom *(Bride could be used for bride or groom in Shakespeare's time.)*

147 **hate that is meant love** a hateful action which was intended to be a loving one

148 **. . . how, chop-logic!** What do you mean, arguing like this?

150 **minion** spoilt brat

152 **fettle your fine joints** get yourself ready (language usually employed about horses)

152 **'gainst . . .** for next Thursday

I wonder at this haste, that I must wed
Ere he that should be my husband comes to woo.
I pray you tell my lord and father, madam,
I will not marry yet; and when I do, I swear   120
It shall be Romeo, whom you know I hate,
Rather than Paris. These are news indeed!

LADY   Here comes your father; tell him so yourself,
CAPULET   And see how he will take it at your hands.

Enter CAPULET and NURSE.

CAPULET   When the sun sets, the earth doth drizzle dew;   125
              But for the sunset of my brother's son
              It rains downright.
              How now, a conduit, girl? What, still in tears?
              Evermore showering? In one little body
              Thou counterfeits a bark, a sea, a wind;   130
              For still thy eyes, which I may call the sea,
              Do ebb and flow with tears; the bark thy body is,
              Sailing in this salt flood; the winds thy sighs,
              Who raging with thy tears, and they with them,
              Without a sudden calm will overset   135
              Thy tempest-tossèd body. How now, wife?
              Have you delivered to her our decree?

LADY   Ay, sir but she will none, she gives you thanks.
CAPULET   I would the fool were married to her grave!

CAPULET   Soft, take me with you, take me with you, wife.   140
              How will she none? Doth she not give us thanks?
              Is she not proud? Doth she not count her blest,
              Unworthy as she is, that we have wrought
              So worthy a gentleman to be her bride?

JULIET   Not proud you have, but thankful that you have.   145
              Pround can I never be of what I hate,
              But thankful even for hate that is meant love.

CAPULET   How, how! how, how, chop-logic! What is this?
              "Proud", and "I thank you", and "I thank you not",
              And yet "Not proud", mistress minion you?   150
              Thank me no thankings, nor proud me no prouds,
              But fettle your fine joints 'gainst Thursday next,

3.5 Juliet's bedroom

Capulet, maddened with rage at his daughter's disobedience, threatens and insults her. He ignores the attempts of his wife and the Nurse to calm him down.

Activities

Character review: Capulet (3)

In fours, re-read the section of the scene in which Capulet verbally abuses Juliet (140–186).

1. Using the notes, discuss exactly what Capulet means by each of his insults:
   - Is she not proud? (142)
   - Unworthy as she is (143)
   - mistress minion you (150)
   - you green-sickness carrion (155)
   - baggage (155 and 159)
   - You tallow-face (156)
   - disobedient wretch (159)
   - hilding (167)
   - wretched puling fool (183)
   - whining mammet (184).

2. When you are sure of the modern meanings, improvise the exchange between Capulet and his daughter, using your own words (you might need to refer to the checklist of abuse above so as not to miss anything out).

3. Finally act out the exchange in its original language, but keeping in mind the meanings which lie behind Capulet's words.

154 **hurdle** wooden rack used for dragging traitors to their execution

155 **green-sickness carrion** pale-looking corpse (**green-sickness** = anaemia)

156 **tallow-face** another reference to her paleness: she is as white as candle-wax

163 **My fingers itch** I'm tempted to hit you.

167 **Out on her, hilding!** Away with her, the worthless creature!

168 **rate** verbally attack

170 **Good Prudence ...** Madam Wisdom, go and natter (**Smatter**) with your women friends (**gossips**).

171 **O God gi' good e'en!** And good day to you!

173 **Utter ...** Save your serious words for when you're having a drink with your women friends.

174 **hot** angry

175 **God's bread!** a powerful oath (referring to the consecrated Communion bread)

177–178 **still my care hath been ...** the one thing I have always been concerned about has been to provide her with a husband (**have her matched**)

150

To go with Paris to Saint Peter's Church,
Or I will drag thee on a hurdle thither.
Out, you green-sickness carrion! out, you baggage!   155
You tallow-face.

LADY CAPULET   (*To her husband*) Fie, fie! What, are you mad?

JULIET   Good father, I beseech you on my knees,
Hear me with patience but to speak a word.

CAPULET   Hang thee, young baggage! disobedient wretch!
I tell thee what: get thee to church o' Thursday,   160
Or never after look me in the face.
Speak not, reply not, do not answer me.
My fingers itch. Wife, we scarce thought us blest
That God had lent us but this only child,
But now I see this one is one too much,   165
And that we have a curse in having her.
Out on her, hilding!

NURSE   God in heaven bless her!
You are to blame, my lord, to rate her so.

CAPULET   And why, my Lady Wisdom? Hold your tongue,
Good Prudence. Smatter with your gossips, go.   170

NURSE   I speak no treason.

CAPULET   O God gi' good e'en!

NURSE   May not one speak?

CAPULET   Peace, you mumbling fool!
Utter your gravity o'er a gossip's bowl,
For here we need it not.

LADY CAPULET   You are too hot.

CAPULET   God's bread! it makes me mad.   175
Day, night, hour, tide, time, work, play,
Alone, in company, still my care hath been
To have her matched; and having now provided
A gentleman of noble parentage,

3.5 Juliet's bedroom

Capulet storms out, threatening to throw Juliet out of the house unless she agrees to marry Paris. When her mother rejects her too, Juliet turns to the Nurse for comfort and advice.

180 **fair demesnes** good estates

181 **parts** qualities

182 **Proportioned ...** as well made as you could hope for

183 **puling** whimpering, whingeing

184 **whining mammet** crying doll

184 **in her fortune's tender** when she has had this fortunate offer *(of marriage)*

187 **and** if *(also in line 191)*

188 **house with me** live in my house

189 **I do not use to jest** I'm not in the habit of making jokes.

190 **advise** give it some careful thought

194 **Nor what is mine ...** *Juliet will inherit none of his wealth.*

195 **... forsworn** I will not break my word *(to Paris).*

205–208 **my faith ... earth?** I have made my wedding vows before God. How can I take them back unless my husband dies and sends them back to me from heaven?

209–210 **practise stratagems Upon** devise plots against

210 **soft** easy

213–214 **all the world to nothing ...** you can bet the world that he will never dare return to claim you as his wife (**challenge you**)

Of fair demesnes, youthful and nobly trained,   180
Stuffed, as they say, with honourable parts,
Proportioned as one's thought would wish a man,
And then to have a wretched puling fool,
A whining mammet, in her fortune's tender,
To answer "I'll not wed, I cannot love,   185
I am too young, I pray you pardon me"!
But and you will not wed I'll pardon you:
Graze where you will, you shall not house with me.
Look to 't, think on 't; I do not use to jest.
Thursday is near; lay hand on heart, advise.   190
And you be mine, I'll give you to my friend:
And you be not, hang, beg, starve, die in the streets,
For, by my soul, I'll ne'er acknowledge thee,
Nor what is mine shall never do thee good.
Trust to 't, bethink you; I'll not be forsworn.   195

Exit CAPULET.

JULIET   Is there no pity sitting in the clouds
That sees into the bottom of my grief?
O sweet my mother, cast me not away!
Delay this marriage for a month, a week;
Or, if you do not, make the bridal bed   200
In that dim monument where Tybalt lies.

LADY CAPULET   Talk not to me, for I'll not speak a word.
Do as thou wilt, for I have done with thee.

Exit LADY CAPULET.

JULIET   O God! O Nurse, how shall this be prevented?
My husband is on earth, my faith in heaven;   205
How shall that faith return again to earth,
Unless that husband send it me from heaven
By leaving earth? Comfort me, counsel me.
Alack, alack, that heaven should practise stratagems
Upon so soft a subject as myself?   210
What say'st thou? Hast thou not a word of joy?
Some comfort, Nurse.

NURSE   Faith, here it is: Romeo
Is banishèd; and all the world to nothing
That he dares ne'er come back to challenge you;

3.5 Juliet's bedroom

The Nurse advises Juliet to marry Paris, since Romeo will never be able to claim her as his wife. Juliet is appalled, but hides her feelings and instructs the Nurse to say that she has gone to Friar Lawrence's cell, sorry that she has displeased her father. In reality she goes to seek his help.

Activities

Character review: the Nurse (7)

A What advice does the Nurse give to Juliet after her parents have left the room?

B Write an entry in Juliet's diary in which she expresses her feelings about the Nurse and the advice she has just been given. Try to show that Juliet now feels completely isolated, because she cannot share her true feelings with either her mother or the Nurse.

C Brenda Bruce said: 'If Nurse sounds as though she believed this [218–219], she will get a laugh from the audience. What I wanted was a reaction of shock . . . I would like the audience to feel let down by someone they trusted. Nurse carries on to the end of the speech with her advice, not believing a word of it, in her heart . . . In an attempt to make the advice acceptable. In pairs, act out the exchange in two ways, first following Brenda Bruce's directions, and then acting as though the Nurse were sincere. Then discuss which of the two interpretations (a) is 'better theatre' – more interesting for the audience to watch and react to; and (b) fits your interpretation of the character up to this point.

219 **dishclout** dishcloth

221 **Beshrew** curse

222 **match** marriage

224 **or 't were as good he were** or he might as well be

225 **no use of him** without being able to enjoy him as a husband

235 **Ancient damnation!** Damned old woman!

236 **wish me thus forsworn** want me to break my (*marriage*) vows

237 **dispraise** criticise' speak ill of

238 **with above compare** as being beyond comparison

240 **twain** separated

Or if he do, it needs must be by stealth. 215
Then since the case so stands as now it doth,
I think it best you married with the County.
O, he's a lovely gentleman!
Romeo's a dishclout to him. An eagle, madam,
Hath not so green, so quick, so fair an eye 220
As Paris hath. Beshrew my very heart,
I think you are happy in this second match,
For it excels your first; or if it did not,
Your first is dead, or 't were as good he were,
As living here, and you no use of him. 225

JULIET Speak'st thou from thy heart?

NURSE And from my soul too; else beshrew them both.

JULIET Amen!

NURSE What?

JULIET Well, thou hast comforted me marvellous much. 230
Go in and tell my lady I am gone,
Having displeased my father, to Lawrence' cell
To make confession and to be absolved.

NURSE Marry, I will; and this is wisely done.

Exit NURSE.

JULIET Ancient damnation! O most wicked fiend! 235
Is it more sin to wish me thus forsworn,
Or to dispraise my lord with that same tongue
Which she hath praised him with above compare
So many thousand times? Go, counsellor,
Thou and my bosom henceforth shall be twain. 240
I'll to the Friar, to know his remedy.
If all else fail, myself have power to die.

Exit JULIET.

Exam practice

Themes: fate

In the Prologue, Shakespeare tells us that the play will be about two 'star-crossed' lovers. After Tybalt has killed Mercutio, Romeo recognises that today's action will have repercussions in the future (123–124). A few moments later, having avenged Mercutio's death, he realises the full implications of his actions and cries: 'O, I am fortune's fool'. (140)

With a partner, look back at the following moments in Romeo's story so far and, for each one, decide how much control he had over events and how much seemed to be determined by fate. Grade them from I (Romeo in control) to 5 (fate in control), bearing in mind that this is all a matter of opinion. Then compare your gradings with another pair's and discuss your reasoning.

- 1.2: Romeo is talking in the street with Benvolio when Peter happens to come along and ask him if he can read the invitation list to the Capulet party.
- 1.4: Romeo is not happy about going to the Capulets: he has had an unsettling dream and has an uneasy feeling that something is going to happen.
- 1.5: He attends the party and meets Juliet.
- 2.2: Juliet happens to come out on to the balcony.
- 2.3: The Friar is keen to find a way to stop the feud between the families.
- 3.1: Mercutio insists on walking the streets even though Benvolio has warned him that the Capulets are about.
- 3.1: Mercutio is accidentally killed when Romeo tries to stop the fight.
- 3.1: Romeo despises himself and feels he has to avenge his friend's death as well as redeem his own reputation.

Plot review (9)

Using the following headings, make notes on what you have learned about the society in which Romeo and Juliet live:
- the family (including the position of the father, the wife, children and servants)
- the church (including people's religious beliefs and their attitude towards priests and friars)
- the law (including the power of leaders such as the Prince)
- communications (including travel and the effects on someone who was banished).

Themes: violence

Act 3 contains some of the worst examples of violence in *Romeo and Juliet*. It is a theme that runs through the play.

Look back through the play and, starting with the riot in 1.1, note down the occasions where

(a) physical violence takes place on stage;
(b) physical violence is threatened, but does not actually take place;
(c) other kinds of violence occur (such as people abusing each other verbally).

Save your notes and add to them as you work through Acts 4 and 5, in preparation for an assignment on the theme of violence.

Character review: the Nurse (8)

This is the moment at which the Nurse advises Juliet to commit bigamy (marrying more than one person, which was not only illegal, but – in the eyes of the church at that time – an act which would condemn Juliet's soul to damnation).

A In pairs, discuss whether you think it is good advice or not.

B In pairs re-read lines 204–234 and write down what the Nurse is thinking and feeling as she speaks. Why do you think the Nurse is giving this advice? Does she really feel that it is in Juliet's best interest? Or is she perhaps fearing for her own safety if the truth about Juliet's marriage with Romeo becomes known?

C Brenda Bruce, who played the Nurse in the 1980 Royal Shakespeare Company production, described her approach to this scene in this way: 'Capulet's anger with Juliet ["Graze where you will ... die in the streets ..."]: 188–194] served as my sub-text. Nurse could advise Juliet to: (a) run away with her to Friar Lawrence; (b) seek refuge in a nunnery; (c) follow Romeo to Mantua; (d) call her mother and father, confess to them, pray for their understanding and forgiveness, and with their help plead with the Prince to forgive Romeo.
But Nurse has only one answer and it is immoral and against the law.'

Why might Capulet's words (188–194) have affected the Nurse and influenced her in the advice she gives Juliet? Why might the Nurse reject all the other options (a, b, c and d) that Brenda Bruce lists? How practical would each one be?

Character review: Capulet (4)

Re-read Capulet's words to Juliet in 3.5

1. Discuss the following views of Capulet, stating which you agree with and why (or arriving at an interpretation of your own):
   (a) Capulet does not mean any of this: he is understandably upset that his daughter is turning down the chance of a happy and successful marriage with an attractive and wealthy husband.
   (b) This shows that Capulet does not really love his daughter, but thinks of her as a possession; he is not interested in her feelings, only in getting his own way and exercising his power over her.
2. What do you feel about Capulet's behaviour here? Why do you think he reacts so violently?

4.1 Friar Lawrence's cell

Juliet arrives at Friar Lawrence's cell just as Paris is discussing arrangements for their wedding.

Activities

Character review: Paris (2)

A Paris has come to see the Friar to arrange to marry Juliet the following Thursday (and today is Tuesday – see line 90).

1. Discuss in pairs what the Friar means by his aside (16).
2. Improvise a conversation between Paris and the Friar from the point where Paris arrives at the Friar's cell and starts talking about the wedding (before Shakespeare's scene begins), through to the moment when Juliet enters (line 17).

B Write another entry in Paris's diary, commenting on his visit to the Friar. He might wonder about the Friar's lack of enthusiasm for the wedding (1; 4–5) and Juliet's reactions on meeting him.

C Re-read the conversation between Paris and Juliet (18–43) and then discuss Niamh Cusack's interpretation of the scene: 'The emotional strain of having to exchange courtesies with this flirtatious young man when all she wants is to get on with her appeal to the Friar, makes this a difficult moment for her. To be close to him, then to be kissed by him, is repulsive, and the feeling of being caged in is made even

Continued on page 160

2 **father Capulet** *Paris is already thinking of Capulet as his father-in-law (see 3.4.16).*

3 **nothing slow . . .** I am not showing any reluctance which might slow him down.

5 **Uneven is the course** This is an irregular way of going about things.

8 **Venus smiles not . . .** People in mourning do not want to discuss love.

9 **counts** considers

10 **give her sorrow . . . sway** gives way to her sorrow so much

12 **inundation** flood

13 **too much minded . . .** having brooded alone for too long

14 **society** company

16 **I would I knew not** I wish I didn't know

21 **a certain text** a true saying

158

Act 4

Scene 1

Friar Lawrence's cell.

Enter FRIAR LAWRENCE and PARIS.

FRIAR LAWRENCE	On Thursday, sir? The time is very short.
PARIS	My father Capulet will have it so,
	And I am nothing slow to slack his haste.
FRIAR LAWRENCE	You say you do not know the lady's mind?
	Uneven is the course; I like it not. 5
PARIS	Immoderately she weeps for Tybalt's death,
	And therefore have I little talked of love,
	For Venus smiles not in a house of tears.
	Now, sir, her father counts it dangerous
	That she do give her sorrow so much sway, 10
	And in his wisdom hastes our marriage,
	To stop the inundation of her tears,
	Which, too much minded by herself alone,
	May be put from her by society.
	Now do you know the reason of this haste. 15
FRIAR LAWRENCE	(*Aside*) I would I knew not why it should be slowed. –
	Look, sir, here comes the lady toward my cell.

Enter JULIET.

PARIS	Happily met, my lady and my wife!
JULIET	That may be, sir, when I may be a wife.
PARIS	That "may be" must be, love, on Thursday next. 20
JULIET	What must be shall be.
FRIAR LAWRENCE	That's a certain text.
PARIS	Come you to make confession to this father?
JULIET	To answer that, I should confess to you.

4.1 Friar Lawrence's cell

Juliet responds coldly and ambiguously to Paris's words of love and, as soon as he is gone, begs the Friar's help.

Activities

stronger by the meeting . . . Everything he says is possessive of her at the moment when she is desperately trying to escape from the nightmare of the world she has been brought up in and lives in.' In pairs, act out the exchange in this way, with Paris 'flirtatious' and 'possessive', Juliet feeling 'caged in'. Then try it differently, with a courteous and gentle Paris. Which of the two interpretations seems more effective at this stage of the play, in your opinion?

Themes: fate

Discuss as a class what Juliet and the Friar mean by:
• 21: What must be shall be.
              That's a certain text.
What do you think is going through their minds? How do thier words tie in with the theme of fate running through the play?

27 **price** value

29 **abused** spoiled

31 **spite** malice, spitefulness

34 **to my face** (1) about my face; (2) openly

39 **My leisure serves me** I am free

39 **pensive** anxious, sorrowful

40 **entreat** ask for

41 **God shield** God forbid

47 **It strains me . . . wits** I have racked my brains – without success.

48 **prorogue** postpone

Act 4 Scene 1   **4.1**

PARIS	Do not deny to him that you love me.
JULIET	I will confess to you that I love him. 25
PARIS	So will ye, I am sure, that you love me.
JULIET	If I do so, it will be of more price, Being spoke behind your back, than to your face.
PARIS	Poor soul, thy face is much abused with tears.
JULIET	The tears have got small victory by that, 30 For it was bad enough before their spite.
PARIS	Thou wrong'st it more than tears with that report.
JULIET	That is no slander, sir, which is a truth, And what I spake, I spake it to my face.
PARIS	Thy face is mine, and thou hast slandered it. 35
JULIET	It may be so, for it is not mine own. – Are you at leisure, holy Father, now, Or shall I come to you at evening Mass?
FRIAR LAWRENCE	My leisure serves me, pensive daughter, now. My lord, we must entreat the time alone. 40
PARIS	God shield I should disturb devotion. Juliet, on Thursday early will I rouse ye; Till then, adieu, and keep this holy kiss.

He kisses her and leaves.

JULIET	O shut the door, and when thou hast done so, Come weep with me, past hope, past care, past help. 45
FRIAR LAWRENCE	O Juliet, I already know thy grief; It strains me past the compass of my wits. I hear thou must, and nothing may prorogue it, On Thursday next be married to this County.
JULIET	Tell me not, Friar, that thou hearest of this, 50 Unless thou tell me how I may prevent it. If in thy wisdom thou can'st give no help,

4.1 Friar Lawrence's cell

Producing a dagger, Juliet threatens to kill herself rather than marry Paris and declares she will comply with any plan of the Friar's, however desperate.

Activities

Actors' interpretations (24): 'this bloody knife ...'

Write directors' notes to lines 44–88, giving advice on:

• what actions the actress playing Juliet should perform (in particular, what she should do at line 62)
• what thoughts are going through the Friar's head as Juliet speaks (in particular, how he arrives at the suggestion of a plan after line 88).

Character review: Juliet (11)

Produce an illustration of Juliet's desperate statement of the things she is prepared to do rather than marry Paris (77–85). Write out her speech carefully and draw the images around the margin, with a heading 'rather than marry Paris ...'.

57 **the label ...** the seal to another marriage contract

59 **this** She produces a knife. *(See line 62.)*

60 **time** life

61 **present counsel** immediate advice

62–65 **'Twixt my extremes ... bring** This knife will act as the final judge (**umpire**) between me and the terrible situation I am in (**my extremes**), making a decision (**arbitrating**) which the authority (**commission**) of your age and skill could not honourably end up with.

69–70 **Which craves ... prevent** which requires you to do something as desperate as the desperate act we are trying to prevent *(killing herself)*

75 **That cop'st ... from it** you who are prepared to face death itself, in order to escape from the disgrace *(of marrying Paris)*

79 **thievish ways** places where you find thieves

81 **charnel house** *building attached to a church in which old skulls and bones were stored when new graves were being dug in the churchyard*

83 **reeky shanks** stinking shin-bones

83 **chapless** with lower jaws missing

88 **unstained** pure, chaste

Do thou but call my resolution wise,
And with this knife I'll help it presently.
God joined my heart and Romeo's, thou our
    hands;   55
And ere this hand, by thee to Romeo's sealed,
Shall be the label to another deed,
Or my true heart with treacherous revolt
Turn to another, this shall slay them both.
Therefore, out of thy long-experienced time,   60
Give me some present counsel; or, behold,
'Twixt my extremes and me, this bloody knife
Shall play the umpire, arbitrating that
Which the commission of thy years and art
Could to no issue of true honour bring.   65
Be not so long to speak; I long to die
If what thou speak'st speak not of remedy.

FRIAR   Hold, daughter: I do spy a kind of hope,
LAWRENCE Which craves as desperate an execution
              As that is desperate which we would prevent.   70
              If, rather than to marry County Paris,
              Thou hast the strength of will to slay thyself,
              Then is it likely thou wilt undertake
              A thing like death to chide away this shame,
              That cop'st with death himself to scape from it;   75
              And, if thou darest, I'll give thee remedy.

JULIET   O bid me leap, rather than marry Paris,
              From off the battlements of any tower,
              Or walk in thievish ways, or bid me lurk
              Where serpents are; chain me with roaring bears,   80
              Or hide me nightly in a charnel house,
              O'ercovered quite with dead men's rattling bones,
              With reeky shanks and yellow chapless skulls;
              Or bid me go into a new-made grave,
              And hide me with a dead man in his shroud –   85
              Things that, to hear them told, have made me
                tremble –
              And I will do it without fear or doubt,
              To live an unstained wife to my sweet love.

FRIAR   Hold, then. Go home, be merry, give consent
LAWRENCE To marry Paris. Wednesday is to-morrow: 90

4.1 Friar Lawrence's cell

The Friar explains his plan. Juliet is to drink a potion which will cause her to seem dead. Romeo will be notified of the plan by letter, and, after Juliet is laid in the Capulet tomb, he will return secretly and they will escape to Mantua together.

Activities

Plot review (10)

1. The Friar's plan:
   (a) Discuss and note down the main points of the Friar's plan for Juliet.
   (b) Give your opinions on its strong points, and the potential weaknesses.
   (c) In his position, what would you have suggested?

2. The 'distillèd liquor' (94): imagine a scene in which two doctors are examining someone who has taken the Friar's potion. Improvise their discussion of the symptoms, based upon the Friar's account of the potion's workings ('no pulse ... like death': 96–103).

91 **look that thou lie ...** make sure you sleep alone
93 **vial** small flask
95 **presently** immediately
96 **humour** fluid
97 **native progress** natural rate
97 **surcease** stop
98 **testify** give evidence that
100 **wanny** pale
100 **windows** lids
102 **supple government** the power of movement
104 **borrowed likeness** imitation
108 **there art thou dead** they will find you *(apparently)* dead
109 **manner** custom
110 **uncovered** with your face uncovered
110 **bier** funeral carriage
113 **against** in preparation for the time when
114 **our drift** what we are doing
116 **watch thy waking** watch over you until you wake up
117 **bear thee hence** carry you off
119–120 **If no inconstant toy ... it** So long as no whim – making you change your mind – or womanish fear, lessen (**abate**) your courage to go through with it.
122 **prosperous** successful
125 **afford** provide

To-marrow night look that thou lie alone;
Let not the Nurse lie with thee in thy chamber.
Take thou this vial, being then in bed,
And this distillèd liquor drink thou off,
When presently through all thy veins shall run   95
A cold and drowsy humour, for no pulse
Shall keep his native progress, but surcease;
No warmth, no breath, shall testify thou livest;
The roses in thy lips and cheeks shall fade
To wanny ashes, thy eyes' windows fall   100
Like death when he shuts up the day of life.
Each part, deprived of supple government,
Shall, stiff and stark and cold, appear like death,
And in this borrowed likeness of shrunk death
Thou shalt continue two and forty hours,   105
And then awake as from a pleasant sleep.
Now, when the bridegroom in the morning comes
To rouse thee from thy bed, there art thou dead.
Then, as the manner of our country is,
In thy best robes, uncovered on the bier,   110
Thou shalt be borne to that same ancient vault
Where all the kindred of the Capulets lie.
In the meantime, against thou shalt awake,
Shall Romeo by my letters know our drift,
And hither shall he come; and he and I   115
Will watch thy waking, and that very night
Shall Romeo bear thee hence to Mantua.
And this shall free thee from this present shame,
If no inconstant toy nor womanish fear
Abate thy valour in the acting it.   120

JULIET   Give me, give me! O tell not me of fear!

FRIAR   Hold; get you gone. Be strong and prosperous
LAWRENCE   In this resolve. I'll send a friar with speed
To Mantua, with my letters to thy lord.

JULIET   Love give me strength! and strength shall help
afford.   125
Farewell, dear Father.

Exeunt.

4.2 Capulet's house

Juliet returns to the house to find her father organising preparations for the wedding. She says that, after speaking to the Friar, she wishes to ask forgiveness for her earlier disobedience.

Activities

Actors' interpretations (25): the servants

What does Capulet's dialogue with the servants add to the beginning of this scene? In productions it is often cut, with the scene beginning on line 11. In threes, act out the exchange several times, swapping roles each time, and then discuss what you think would be (a) gained, and (b) lost if the lines were cut.

2 **cunning** skilful

3 **none ill** no bad ones

3 **try** test

10 **much unfurnished** extremely underprepared

12 **Ay, forsooth** She certainly has.

14 **A peevish, self-willed harlotry it is** She is a moody, stubborn little hussy.

15 **shrift** confession

16 **gadding** running around enjoying yourself

19 **behests** wishes

20 **fall prostrate** get down on my knees

Scene 2

Capulet's house.

Enter CAPULET, LADY CAPULET, NURSE and SERVANTS.

CAPULET   (*Giving a paper to a servant*) So many guests invite
         as here are writ.

                                        Exit servant.

         (*To another* SERVANT) Sirrah, go hire me twenty
         cunning cooks.

SERVANT   You shall have none ill, sir, for I'll try if they can
         lick their fingers.

CAPULET   How can'st thou try them so?   5

SERVANT   Marry, sir, 't is an ill cook that cannot lick his own
         fingers. Therefore he that cannot lick his own
         fingers goes not with me.

CAPULET   Go, be gone.

                                        Exit SERVANT.

         We shall be much unfurnished for this time.   10
         What, is my daughter gone to Friar Lawrence?

NURSE   Ay, forsooth.

CAPULET   Well, he may chance to do some good on her.
         A peevish, self-willed harlotry it is.

      Enter JULIET.

NURSE   See where she comes from shrift with merry look.   15

CAPULET   How now, my headstrong? Where have you been
         gadding?

JULIET   Where I have learnt me to repent the sin
         Of disobedient opposition
         To you and your behests, and am enjoined
         By holy Lawrence to fall prostrate here   20

4.2 Capulet's house

Capulet is delighted that his daughter has submitted to his wishes and gives orders for the wedding to take place the next day, joyfully bustling off to inform Paris and look after the preparations himself.

Activities

Actors' interpertations (26): Juliet's 'repentance'

In groups of four rehearse the scene, paying particular attention to the ways in which:

- Capulet behaves with the servant (1–9: is he good-natured? bullying? absent-minded? . . .)
- Capulet refers to Juliet before she enters (11–14: is he bitter? optimistic? threatening? . . .)
- Capulet addresses Juliet when she enters (16: is he angry? affectionate? uncertain? . . .)
- Juliet addresses her father (17–22, 25–27: does she sound sincere? totally without emotion? what actions accompany her words?)
- Capulet reacts to Juliet's behaviour (23–24, 28–32, 37)
- Lady Capulet reacts (36, 38–39)

24 **this knot** *the 'marriage knot'*

26 **becomèd** appropriate

27 **not stepping . . .** not doing anything too forward

32 **bound** indebted

33 **closet** private room

34 **needful** necessary

35 **to furnish me** for me to wear

38 **We shall be short . . .** We will not have enough food ready.

39 **Tush, I will stir about** Nonsense, I'll stay up and get things done.

41 **deck up her** dress her

44 **They are all forth** They're all busy somewhere.

46 **Against** for

47 **reclaimed** obedient again

168

To beg your pardon. (*She kneels*) Pardon, I beseech you.
Henceforward I am ever ruled by you.

CAPULET   Send for the County; go, tell him of this.
I'll have this knot knit up to-morrow morning.

JULIET   I met the youthful lord at Lawrence' cell,   25
And gave him what becomèd love I might,
Not stepping o'er the bounds of modesty.

CAPULET   Why, I am glad on 't; this is well. Stand up.
This is as 't should be. Let me see the County:
Ay, marry, go, I say, and fetch him hither.   30
Now, afore God, this reverend holy Friar –
All our whole city is much bound to him.

JULIET   Nurse, will you go with me into my closet
To help me sort such needful ornaments
As you think fit to furnish me to-morrow?   35

LADY   No, not till Thursday; there is time enough.
CAPULET

CAPULET   Go, Nurse, go with her. We'll to church to-morrow.

Exeunt JULIET and NURSE.

LADY   We shall be short in our provision.
CAPULET   'T is now near night.

CAPULET   Tush, I will stir about,
And all things shall be well, I warrant thee, wife.   40
Go thou to Juliet: help to deck up her.
I'll not to bed to-night. Let me alone;
I'll play the housewife for this once. (*He calls the servants*) What ho!
They are all forth. Well, I will walk myself
To County Paris, to prepare up him   45
Against to-morrow. My heart is wondrous light
Since this same wayward girl is so reclaimed.

Exeunt CAPULET and LADY CAPULET.

4.3 Juliet's bedroom

Juliet says goodnight to her mother and the Nurse. She anxiously contemplates what might happen if the potion does not work and then fears that it might be the Friar's method of poisoning her to avoid being party to an illegal second marriage with Paris.

Activities

Actors' interpretations (27): the night before the wedding

Brenda Bruce wrote this about Juliet's opening speech in this scene (1–5): 'Nurse knows; it was Nurse's advice; she knows Juliet is married, and advised her to commit bigamy. At this moment Shakespeare does not give Nurse any lines. Lady Capulet kisses her child and goes happily to bed. Nurse can only search Juliet's face for a second and scurry off to prepare the wedding-breakfast.'

In pairs, write directors' notes to lines 1–13, giving advice to the actors on what they might be thinking and feeling. Among other things, discuss whether, if you were directing the scene, your Lady Capulet would kiss her daughter before leaving.

1 **attires** clothes

3 **orisons** prayers

4 **To move ... state** to persuade the heavens to look favourably upon my predicament

5 **cross** wrong

7 **culled such necessaries** got together what we need

8 **behoveful** suitable

8 **state** wedding ceremony

12 **sudden** unexpectedly quick

15 **thrills** trembles

18 **What should she ...?** What would be the point of her being here?

25 **Subtly hath ministered** cleverly prescribed for me

26 **Lest ... dishonoured** for fear of being disgraced by this wedding

Scene 3

Juliet's bedroom.

Enter JULIET and NURSE.

JULIET   Ay, those attires are best; but, gentle Nurse,
I pray thee leave me to myself to-night,
For I have need of many orisons
To move the heavens to smile upon my state,
Which well thou knowest is cross and full of sin.   5

Enter LADY CAPULET.

LADY
CAPULET   What, are you busy, ho? Need you my help?

JULIET   No, madam; we have culled such necessaries
As are behoveful for our state to-morrow:
So please you, let me now be left alone,
And let the Nurse this night sit up with you,   10
For I am sure you have your hands full all
In this so sudden business.

LADY   Good night.
CAPULET   Get thee to bed and rest, for thou hast need.

Exeunt LADY CAPULET and NURSE.

JULIET   Farewell. – God knows when we shall meet again.
I have a faint cold fear thrills through my veins,   15
That almost freezes up the heat of life.
I'll call them back again to comfort me.
(*She calls*) Nurse! – What should she do here?
My dismal scene I needs must act alone.
Come, vial.   20
What if this mixture do not work at all?
Shall I be married then to-morrow morning?
No, no. This shall forbid it. (*She lays down her knife*)
   Lie thou there.
What if it be a poison which the Friar
Subtly hath ministered to have me dead,   25
Lest in this marriage he should be dishonoured
Because he married me before to Romeo?
I fear it is; and yet methinks it should not,

171

4.4 The hall in Capulet's house

Juliet's fears about taking the potion continue. She thinks about suffocating in the tomb, or going mad with terror when she wakes to find herself surrounded by Capulet bones. Imagining Tybalt's ghost pursuing Romeo, she drinks the potion.

Activities

Character review: Juliet (12)

Juliet imagines what might happen if she takes the potion.

1. To gain a fuller understanding of her nightmare visions, work with a partner to express Juliet's soliloquy in your own words, using the following as a structure:

   What if ...?
   • 21
   • 22–23

   What if ...?
   • 24–27
   • 28–29

   How if ...?
   • 30–32
   • 33–35

   Or, if ...
   • 36–44
   • 45–54

   I have a vision of ...
   • 55–58

2. In groups of four, prepare Juliet's speech for performance as a radio play. Make notes on music and sound effects which you think might be helpful and how the actress ought to say particular lines. If you have the resources, try producing a recording of your own.

29 **still been tried** always proved to be

32 **redeem** rescue

33 **stifled** suffocated

34 **healthsome** fresh, wholesome

35 **strangled** suffocated

37 **conceit** thoughts

39 **receptacle** collecting place

42 **green in earth** freshly buried

44 **resort** meet

47 **mandrakes** *roots shaped like human beings. It was believed that, if someone pulled one out of the ground, it would scream and the person would go mad.*

49 **distraught** driven mad

50 **Environed with** surrounded by

53 **rage** madness

56 **spit** pierce *(as though spearing meat on a spit for roasting)*

57 **Stay** Stop!

2 **pastry** *section of the kitchen where bread and pastries were made*

For he hath still been tried a holy man.
How if, when I am laid into the tomb,   30
I wake before the time that Romeo
Come to redeem me? There's a fearful point!
Shall I not then be stifled in the vault,
To whose foul mouth no healthsome air breathes in,
And there die strangled ere my Romeo comes?   35
Or, if I live, is it not very like
The horrible conceit of death and night,
Together with the terror of the place –
As in a vault, an ancient receptacle,
Where, for this many hundred years, the bones   40
Of all my buried ancestors are packed;
Where bloody Tybalt yet but green in earth,
Lies festering in his shroud; where, as they say,
At some hours in the night spirits resort –
Alack, alack! is it not like that I,   45
So early waking, what with loathsome smells
And shrieks like mandrakes torn out of the earth,
That living mortals, hearing them run mad –
O, if I wake, shall I not be distraught,
Environed with all these hideous fears,   50
And madly play with my forefathers' joints,
And pluck the mangled Tybalt from his shroud,
And in this rage, with some great kinsman's bone,
As with a club, dash out my desperate brains?
O look! methinks I see my cousin's ghost,   55
Seeking out Romeo that did spit his body
Upon a rapier's point. Stay, Tybalt, stay!
Romeo, I come! this do I drink to thee.

She falls on her bed.

Scene 4

The hall in Capulet's house.

Enter LADY CAPULET and NURSE who carries herbs.

LADY CAPULET   Hold, take these keys and fetch more spices, Nurse.

NURSE   They call for dates and quinces in the pastry.

4.4 The hall in Capulet's house

Capulet bustles around, fussily supervising last-minute preparations for the wedding. Hearing Paris approaching with the musicians, he tells the Nurse to go and wake Juliet.

Activities

Actors' interpretations (28)

Very little actually happens in this scene, but Shakespeare must have had reasons for including it. In pairs, discuss each of the following possible reasons, grading each one from 1 (strongly disagree) to 5 (strongly agree). Then compare your gradings with another pair, giving reasons for your decisions. Shakespeare included this scene because:

(a) it gives the actors playing Romeo and Juliet a longer break before the difficult final scenes;

(b) its light-hearted bustle makes a striking contrast with the scenes preceding and following;

(c) it is ironic to see Capulet pointlessly rushing around with wedding preparations when we know what is going to happen;

(d) it provides a further picture of the Capulet household;

(e) it adds to our understanding of the relationship between Capulet and Lady Capulet;

(f) it builds tension for the discovery of the 'dead' Juliet;

(g) it acts as a 'buffer', to represent the passage of time between Juliet's going to bed and the next morning.

3 **stir!** get a move on!

4 **curfew** *early morning bell, rung when the watch (see 3.3.147) went off duty*

5 **baked meats** pies

6 **Spare not for cost** Don't think about the expense.

6 **cot-quean** *man who interferes with household matters (a woman's job in those days)*

8 **watching** staying up all night without sleeping

9 **not a whit** not at all

11 **mouse-hunt** woman-chaser

12 **watch you** keep an eye on you

13 **hood** woman

19 **Mass** *An oath:* By the mass *(the communion service)*

19 **whoreson** rogue *(less offensive than 'son of a whore' would be today)*

20 **loggerhead** blockhead *(with a pun on 'head' and 'logs', line 17)*

21 **straight** straightaway

24 **trim her up** get her ready

174

4.4

Enter CAPULET.

CAPULET   Come, stir, stir, stir! The second cock hath crowed,
The curfew bell hath rung, 't is three o'clock.
Look to the baked meats, good Angelica;   5
Spare not for cost.

NURSE   Go, ye cot-quean, go.
Get you to bed. Faith, you'll be sick to-morrow
For this night's watching.

CAPULET   No, not a whit. What! I have watched ere now
All night for lesser cause and ne'er been sick.   10

LADY   Ay, you have been a mouse-hunt in your time,
CAPULET   But I will watch you from such watching now.

Exeunt LADY CAPULET and NURSE.

CAPULET   A jealous hood, a jealous hood!

Enter SERVANTS with spits, logs, and baskets.

                Now, fellow, what is there?

SERVANT   Things for the cook, sir, but I know not what.

CAPULET   Make haste, make haste, sirrah. Fetch drier logs.   15
Call Peter; he will show thee where they are.

SERVANT   I have a head, sir, that will find out logs.
And never trouble Peter for the matter.

CAPULET   Mass, and well said; a merry whoreson, ha!
Thou shalt be loggerhead. – Good faith, 't is day!   20
The County will be here with music straight,
For so he said he would. (*Music sounds*) I hear him near.
Nurse! Wife! What ho! What, Nurse, I say!

Enter NURSE.

    Go waken Juliet; go, and trim her up.
I'll go and chat with Paris. Hie, make haste,   25
Make haste! The bridegroom he is come already.
Make haste, I say.

Exeunt all except NURSE.

4.5 Juliet's bedroom

The Nurse comes to wake Juliet, but the potion has worked and the Nurse thinks she is dead.

1 **Fast** fast asleep

4 **pennyworths** small quantities *(of sleep)*

6 **set up his rest** made up his mind

10 **take you** (1) find you; (2) take you sexually

11 **fright you up** frighten you into getting up

12 **down** lying down; back in bed

13 **I must needs** I'll have to

15 **well-a-day** *An expression of grief. (See 3.2.37.)*

Scene 5

Juliet's bedroom.

NURSE   (*Calling outside the bed-curtains*) Mistress! what,
              mistress! Fast, I warrant her, she.
         Why, lamb! why, lady! Fie, you slug-a-bed!
         Why, love, I say! madam! sweetheart! why, bride!
         What, not a word? You take your pennyworths now;
         Sleep for a week; for the next night, I warrant,   5
         The County Paris hath set up his rest
         That you shall rest but little. God forgive me!
         Marry, and amen! How sound is she asleep!
         I needs must wake her. Madam, madam, madam!
         Ay, let the County take you in your bed;   10
         He'll fright you up, i' faith. Will it not be?

         She opens the bed-curtains.

         What, dressed, and in your clothes, and down again?
         I must needs wake you. Lady, lady, lady!
         Alas, alas! Help, help! My lady's dead!
         O well-a-day that ever I was born!   15
         Some aqua-vitae, ho! My lord! my lady!

         Enter LADY CAPULET.

LADY   What noise is here?
CAPULET

NURSE   O lamentable day!

LADY   What is the matter?
CAPULET

NURSE   Look, look! O heavy day!

LADY   O me, O me! My child, my only life,
CAPULET   Revive, look up, or I will die with thee!   20
           Help, help! Call help!

         Enter CAPULET.

CAPULET   For shame, bring Juliet forth; her lord is come.

NURSE   She's dead, deceased; she's dead, alack the day!

4.5 Juliet's bedroom

Paris arrives with the Friar only to find Juliet's parents expressing their grief at their daughter's death.

Activities

Actors' interpretations (30): enter Friar Lawrence ...

1. In groups of five, freeze-frame the moment when the Friar enters with Paris. Then each person explains what they are thinking or feeling. (Think, for example, about the last time you saw Juliet, and what you said to her.)
2. Practise saying the Friar's opening line (33) in different tones of voice. Which tone works best and why?

Character review: Capulet (5)

Once again Capulet expresses his emotions very dramatically.

1. To gain an interesting perspective on the language he uses, draw a sketch to represent his image about death as Juliet's lover and his son-in-law (35–40).
2. Re-read two other speeches (59–64 and 84–90) and note down (a) what he actually says here; and (b) the subtext: what must be going through his head.

26 **is settled** is congealed; has ceased to flow

28 **untimely** too early

36 **lain with** had sex with

37 **deflowerèd by him** she has lost her virginity to him *(death)*

40 **living** means of living: property

45 **In lasting labour ...** in the unending toil of his journey through the ages

46 **But one** I had only one

47 **solace** find comfort and happiness

48 **catched** snatched

LADY **CAPULET**	Alack the day, she's dead, she's dead, she's dead!

CAPULET	Ha, let me see her. Out, alas! she's cold;	25
	Her blood is settled, and her joints are stiff.	
	Life and these lips have long been separated.	
	Death lies on her like an untimely frost	
	Upon the sweetest flower of all the field.	

NURSE	O lamentable day!

LADY **CAPULET**	O woeful time!	30

CAPULET	Death, that hath ta'en her hence to make me wail,
	Ties up my tongue and will not let me speak.

Enter FRIAR LAWRENCE and PARIS.

FRIAR **LAWRENCE**	Come, is the bride ready to go to church?

CAPULET	Ready to go, but never to return.	
	O son, the night before thy wedding day	35
	Hath Death lain with thy wife. There she lies,	
	Flower as she was, deflowerèd by him.	
	Death is my son-in-law, Death is my heir;	
	My daughter he hath wedded. I will die	
	And leave him all. Life, living, all is Death's.	40

PARIS	Have I thought long to see this morning's face,
	And doth it give me such a sight as this?

LADY **CAPULET**	Accursed, unhappy, wretched, hateful day!	
	Most miserable hour that e'er Time saw	
	In lasting labour of his pilgrimage.	45
	But one poor one, one poor and loving child;	
	But one thing to rejoice and solace in,	
	And cruel Death hath catched it from my sight.	

NURSE	O woe! O woeful, woeful, woeful day!	
	Most lamentable day, most woeful day	50
	That ever, ever I did yet behold!	
	O day, O day, O day, O hateful day!	

4.5 Juliet's bedroom

The Friar halts Paris's and Capulet's lamentations, offering the consolation that Juliet is now in heaven. They prepare themselves for the funeral.

Activities

Character review: the Friar (3)

The Friar knows that Juliet is not dead, but has to behave as though she were. To gain a fuller understanding of the arguments he puts to the Capulets, work in pairs to express his reasoning in your own words, using the following as a structure:

You won't put things right with this kind of behaviour ...
- 65–66

Heaven always has a share in human beings ...
- 66–68
- 69–70

You always wanted her to go to heaven when she died ...
- 71–74
- 75–76

As far as marriage is concerned ...
- 77–78

This is what you must do ...
- 79–81
- 82–83

55 **Beguiled** cheated

60 **Uncomfortable** bringing no comfort or consolation

61 **solemnity** ceremony *(the wedding)*

66 **confusions** disorderly behaviour

67 **Had part** had a share in *(she was created jointly by heaven and her parents)*

70 **his part** her soul

71 **her promotion** helping her to succeed in life *(by marrying Paris, for example)*

72 **your heaven** your greatest happiness

76 **well** happy *(a word often used of those who are dead – see 5.1.16–17)*

79 **rosemary** the herb associated with remembrance, used at weddings and funerals

80 **corse** corpse, body

82 **fond** (1) foolish; (2) too affectionate

82 **nature** natural feelings

83 **nature's tears ...** If we think about Juliet's death rationally, the idea of crying is laughable *(because she is now in heaven).*

84–85 **ordainèd festival ... funeral** Change the wedding plans into arrangements for the funeral.

85 **their office** their usual purpose

88 **sullen dirges** mournful funeral hymns

Never was seen so black a day as this.
O woeful day, O woeful day!

PARIS   Beguiled, divorcèd, wrongèd, spited, slain!   55
Most detestable Death, by thee beguiled;
By cruel, cruel thee quite overthrown!
O love! O life! Not life, but love in death!

CAPULET   Despised, distressed, hated, martyred, killed!
Uncomfortable Time, why cam'st thou now   60
To murder, murder our solemnity?
O child, O child! my soul, and not my child!
Dead art thou. Alack, my child is dead,
And with my child my joys are burièd.

FRIAR   Peace, ho, for shame! Confusion's cure lives not   65
LAWRENCE   In these confusions. Heaven and yourself
Had part in this fair maid: now Heaven hath all,
And all the better is it for the maid.
Your part in her you could not keep from Death,
But heaven keeps his part in eternal life.   70
The most you sought was her promotion,
For 't was your heaven she should be advanced;
And weep ye now, seeing she is advanced
Above the clouds, as high as heaven itself?
O, in this love you love your child so ill   75
That you run mad, seeing that she is well.
She's not well married that lives married long,
But she's best married that dies married young.
Dry up your tears, and stick your rosemary
On this fair corse, and as the custom is,   80
In all her best array bear her to church,
For though fond nature bids us all lament,
Yet nature's tears are reason's merriment.

CAPULET   All things that we ordainèd festival
Turn from their office to black funeral: 85
Our instruments to melancholy bells,
Our wedding cheer to a sad burial feast,
Our solemn hymns to sullen dirges change,
Our bridal flowers serve for a buried corse,
And all things change them to the contrary.   90

4.5 Juliet's bedroom

They all leave except for the musicians and Peter, who asks them to play a sad tune.

94 **lour** look angrily

94 **ill** sin

95 **Move** anger

95 **crossing** defying, going against

96 **we may put up** we might as well pack up our instruments *(the musicians are not necessarily pipers)*

98 **case** state of affairs

99 **the case may be amended** (1) things might get better; (2) my instrument case needs mending

100 **"Heart's ease"** *a popular song of the time*

101 **and** if

105 **dump** *sad song or tune*

107 **Not a dump, we** We're not playing a dump.

110 **give it you soundly** pay you out in full *(with a pun on 'soundly')*

| FRIAR LAWRENCE | Sir, go you in; and, madam, go with him; And go, Sir Paris. Everyone prepare To follow this fair corse unto her grave. The heavens do lour upon you for some ill: Move them no more by crossing their high will. | 95 |

They place rosemary on JULIET's body and close the bed-curtains.

Exeunt all except NURSE.

Enter MUSICIANS.

| FIRST MUSICIAN | Faith, we may put up our pipes and be gone. | |

| NURSE | Honest good fellow, ah, put up, put up, For well you know this is a pitiful case. | |

| FIRST MUSICIAN | Ay, by my troth, the case may be amended. | |

Exit NURSE.

Enter PETER.

| PETER | Musicians, O musicians, "Heart's ease", "Heart's ease"! O, and you will have me live, play "Heart's ease". | 100 |

| FIRST MUSICIAN | Why "Heart's ease"? | |

| PETER | O musicians, because my heart itself plays "My heart is full". O play me some merry dump to comfort me. | 105 |

| FIRST MUSICIAN | Not a dump, we. 'T is no time to play now. | |

| PETER | You will not then? | |

| FIRST MUSICIAN | No. | |

| PETER | I will then give it you soundly. | 110 |

| FIRST MUSICIAN | What will you give us? | |

4.5 Juliet's bedroom

Peter argues with the musicians, who are refusing to play, and tries to impress them with his wit.

Activities

Character review: Paris (3)

Write the final entry in his diary. Describe what happened on the day that should have been your wedding day, express your emotions about Juliet and say what you are proposing to do now.

---

112   **the gleek** *probably a gesture of contempt*

112–113   **give you the minstrel** call you minstrels *(an insult – see 3.1.49)*

116   **pate** head

116   **carry no crotchets** put up with any of your games *(with a pun on crotchets, the notes)*

116   **I'll re you** as in doh, re, mi, fa ... *(the scale of notes)*

118   **note us** (1) pay attention to us; (2) set us to music

119   **put out your wit** cut the clever jokes

120   **have at you** *an expression used when a fencer is about to attack*

120   **dry-beat** beat you up without drawing blood

121   **put up** put away, sheathe

127   **Catling** lute-string *(made of catgut)*

129   **Pretty!** Nice idea!

129   **Rebeck** *(pronounced ree-beck)* three-stringed fiddle

130–131   **sound for silver** play for money

132   **Soundpost** *the peg beneath the bridge of a stringed instrument*

136   **for sounding** (1) *as payment for playing;* (2) *to jingle in their purses*

138   **doth lend redress** puts things right

PETER	No money, on my faith, but the gleek. I will give you the minstrel.
FIRST MUSICIAN	Then will I give you the serving-creature.
PETER	Then will I lay the serving-creature's dagger on your pate. I will carry no crotchets. I'll re you, I'll fa you. Do you note me?
FIRST MUSICIAN	And you re us find fa us, you note us.
SECOND MUSICIAN	Pray you, put up your dagger, and put out your wit.

PETER	Then have at you with my wit! I will dry-beat you with an iron wit, and put up my iron dagger. Answer me like men:
	    When griping grief the heart doth wound,
	    And doleful dumps the mind oppress,
	    Then music with her silver sound –
	Why "silver sound"? Why "music with her silver sound"? What say you, Simon Catling?

FIRST MUSICIAN	Marry, sir, because silver hath a sweet sound.
PETER	Pretty! What say you, Hugh Rebeck?
SECOND MUSICIAN	I say "silver sound" because musicians sound for silver.
PETER	Pretty too! What say you, James Soundpost?
THIRD MUSICIAN	Faith, I know not what to say.

PETER	O, I cry you mercy! You are the singer. I will say for you. It is "music with her silver sound" because musicians have no gold for sounding.
	    Then music with her silver sound
	    With speedy help doth lend redress.

115

120

125

130

135

Exit PETER.

4.5 Juliet's bedroom

The musicians decide to wait for the mourners to return from the funeral and join them for dinner.

Activities

Actors' interpretations (32)

In many productions the sequence with the musicians (from line 96) is cut. Discuss why that might be, and what is
(a) gained, and
(b) lost by cutting it.

---

140 **Jack** rogue

140 **tarry** linger

141 **stay** wait for

FIRST
MUSICIAN   What a pestilent knave is this same!

SECOND   Hang him, Jack! Come, we'll in here, tarry for the   140
MUSICIAN   mourners, and stay dinner.

Exeunt.

Exam practice

Plot review (11)

In 4.1 (114) the Friar told Juliet that he would write to Romeo in Mantua, letting him know about the plan. Write his letter, explaining all about the potion, adding a report on how the Capulets had reacted to Juliet's apparent death and telling Romeo what he must now do.

Character review: the relationship between Capulet (6) and Lady Capulet (3)

1. Look back at earlier moments in the play (especially 3.5 and 4.2) and discuss the relationship between Juliet's parents.
   * What, roughly, is the difference in their ages? (See 1.2.3, 1.3.70–72 and 1.5.38–43.) Does this age difference seem to matter?
   * What does Capulet's comment to Paris suggest about the Capulet marriage (1.2.12–13)?
   * What does Lady Capulet think of her husband's treatment of Juliet? (See 3.5.156 and 174.)
   * What do you think lies behind Lady Capulet's comment to her husband at 4.4.11?
2. In the 1986 Royal Shakespeare Company production, Lady Capulet was clearly having an affair with Tybalt, and in the 1997 film she is seen kissing him passionately during the party. If you were directing the play, would you consider this interpretation? Which aspects of the Capulet–Lady Capulet relationship would it seem to tie in with, and what would be against it, in your opinion?

Character review: Juliet (13)

Look back through Act 4 and list the qualities that Juliet displays, in your opinion, supporting your ideas with evidence about her behaviour from the script. You should consider:
* 4.1: her behaviour with Paris
* 4.1: her reaction to the Friar's plan
* 4.3: her words to the Nurse and to her mother as she gets ready for bed (and what they show about her feelings about those two women by that stage)
* 4.3: her soliloquy before taking the potion.

Actors' interpretations (33)

This photograph shows Olivia Hussey as Juliet, Pat Heywood as the Nurse and
Natasha Parry as Lady Capulet in a scene from the 1968 film. Does it look as
though it comes from 4.3 or from the earlier conversation in 1.3? List the
evidence to support your view and try to find the actual moment which is
recorded in the photograph.

5.1 A street in Mantua

In Mantua, Romeo recalls a dream which has cheered him up. He is devastated when Balthasar arrives to report that Juliet is dead, her body lying in the Capulet tomb.

---

1 **flattering truth of sleep** *Romeo is aware that dreams often tell us what we want to believe.*

2 **presage** foretell

3 **My bosom's lord ...** *He imagines his heart, which feels light and happy, to be like a lord, sitting comfortably on his throne.*

4 **unaccustomed spirit** unusual feeling

7 **gives ... leave** permits

10–11 **how sweet is ... joy!** How sweet real, enjoyed love (**itself possessed**) must be, when dreams of it can make you so happy!

18 **monument** tomb

19 **immortal part** soul

20 **kindred's** family's

21 **presently took post** rode here straightaway *(post-horses, that is, hiring a series of horses from inns – see line 26 – were the fastest means of transport)*

23 **office** job, responsibility, duty

24 **Is it e'en so?** Is that how things are?

28–29 **import Some misadventure** suggest that some disaster is going to happen

29 **Tush ...** Nonsense, you're mistaken.

Act 5

Scene 1

A street in Mantua.

Enter ROMEO.

ROMEO   If I may trust the flattering truth of sleep,
           My dreams presage some joyful news at hand;
           My bosom's lord sits lightly in his throne,
           And all this day an unaccustomed spirit
           Lifts me above the ground with cheerful thoughts.   5
           I dreamt my lady came and found me dead –
           Strange dream, that gives a dead man leave to think! –
           And breathed such life with kisses in my lips
           That I revived and was an emperor.
           Ah me! how sweet is love itself possessed,   10
           When but love's shadows are so rich in joy!

Enter BALTHASAR.

           News from Verona! How now, Balthasar?
           Dost thou not bring me letters from the Friar?
           How doth my lady? Is my father well?
           How fares my Juliet? That I ask again,   15
           For nothing can be ill if she be well.

BALTHASAR Then she is well, and nothing can be ill.
           Her body sleeps in Capel's monument,
           And her immortal part with angels lives.
           I saw her laid low in her kindred's vault,   20
           And presently took post to tell it you.
           O pardon me for bringing these ill news,
           Since you did leave it for my office, sir.

ROMEO   Is it e'en so? Then I defy you, stars!
           Thou knowest my lodging. Get me ink and paper,   25
           And hire post-horses. I will hence to-night.

BALTHASAR I do beseech you, sir, have patience.
           Your looks are pale and wild, and do import
           Some misadventure.

ROMEO   Tush, thou art deceived.
           Leave me, and do the thing I bid thee do.   30
           Hast thou no letters to me from the Friar?

191

5.1 A street in Mantua

Balthasar leaves, having confirmed that he has not brought any letters from the Friar. Romeo is determined to lie with Juliet that night and calls on an apothecary who will sell him poison.

Activities

Actors' interpretations (34): the apothecary

1. If you were directing the play, what would your apothecary look like? Using Romeo's description (37–52), draw the apothecary and his shop.
2. What is there in the apothecary's appearance which made Romeo think that he would sell poisons?
3. Discuss what the apothecary and his shop might look like in a modern-dress production. The modern equivalent of an apothecary would be a chemist: how else could you represent him today so that the audience would immediately recognise a 'caitiff wretch' driven to selling illegal poisons?
4. Why do you think Shakespeare included such a detailed description at this point?

34 **lie with** (1) sleep beside; (2) sexually, as a lover

35 **Let's see for means** How am I going to accomplish this?

38 **hereabouts 'a dwells** he lives somewhere around here

38 **which late ...** who I recently spotted

39 **In tattered weeds ...** in ragged clothes and with overhanging eyebrows *(see 1.4.32)*

40 **Culling of simples** gathering herbs

45 **beggarly account** wretchedly small number

46 **bladders** *used as containers for liquids*

47 **remnants of packthread** bits of string

47 **cakes of roses** *compressed rose petals used as perfume*

51 **Whose sale is present death ...** the penalty for the sale of this poison in Mantua is immediate death

52 **caitiff wretch** wretched creature

53 **forerun my need** entered my head before I had need of it

56 **holiday** 'holy day'

59 **ducats** *forty ducats would be a very large sum*

60 **soon-speeding gear** fast-acting stuff

63 **the trunk ...** the body will stop breathing

BALTHASAR	No, my good lord.

ROMEO

               No matter; get thee gone,
And hire those horses. I'll be with thee straight.

Exit BALTHASAR.

Well, Juliet, I will lie with thee to-night.
Let's see for means. O mischief, thou art swift   35
To enter in the thoughts of desperate men!
I do remember an apothecary,
And hereabouts 'a dwells, which late I noted
In tattered weeds, with overwhelming brows,
Culling of simples. Meagre were his looks;   40
Sharp misery had worn him to the bones;
And in his needy shop a tortoise hung,
An alligator stuffed, and other skins
Of ill-shaped fishes; and about his shelves
A beggarly account of empty boxes,   45
Green earthen pots, bladders, and musty seeds,
Remnants of packthread, and old cakes of roses,
Were thinly scattered to make up a show.
Noting this penury, to myself I said:
"An if a man did need a poison now,   50
Whose sale is present death in Mantua,
Here lives a caitiff wretch would sell it him."
O this same thought did but forerun my need,
And this same needy man must sell it me.
As I remember, this should be the house.   55
Being holiday, the beggar's shop is shut.
What ho! apothecary!

Enter APOTHECARY.

APOTHECARY

               Who calls so loud?

ROMEO

Come hither, man. I see that thou art poor.
(*He shows him a bag of money*) Hold, there is forty
   ducats: let me have
A dram of poison, such soon-speeding gear   60
As will disperse itself through all the veins,
That the life-weary taker may fall dead,
And that the trunk may be discharged of breath

5.1 A street in Mantua

The apothecary is desperately poor and sells Romeo the deadly poison even though he knows that the penalty for doing so is death. Romeo leaves for Verona.

Activities

Character review: Romeo (13)

Once he has defied the stars and has made his plans to lie with Juliet that night, Romeo's speeches can be divided into four sections:
- 35–56: he gives a detailed description of the apothecary and his shop
- 57–65: he asks the apothecary for a deadly poison
- 68–84: he persuades the apothecary to sell him the poison
- 85–86 (concluding couplet): he sees the poison as a health-giving medicine and leaves for Verona and his death.

Look back at Romeo's appearances in Act 1 and compare the things he said then with his speeches here. What changes have taken place in his outlook on the world?

64 **hasty powder** explosive gunpowder

65 **womb** belly

66 **mortal** deadly, lethal

67 **to any he ...** to any man who sells (**utters**) them

68–69 **Art thou ... die?** Can anybody so poor ... be afraid to die?

70 **Need and ...** I can see your need, oppression and hunger in your eyes

71 **Contempt and ...** your clothes show your state of beggary and the way the world despises you

73 **affords** provides

74 **break it** (1) break the law; (2) break out of your poverty

79 **dispatch you straight** kill you instantly

82 **compounds** mixtures

84 **get thyself in flesh** fatten yourself up

85 **cordial** reviving medicine (*good for the heart*)

As violently as hasty powder fired
Doth hurry from the fatal cannon's womb.   65

APOTHECARY Such mortal drugs I have, but Mantua's law
Is death to any he that utters them.

ROMEO Art thou so bare and full of wretchedness,
And fear'st to die? Famine is in thy cheeks;
Need and oppression starveth in thy eyes,   70
Contempt and beggary hangs upon thy back.
The world is not thy friend, nor the world's law:
The world affords no law to make thee rich;
Then be not poor, but break it and take this.

APOTHECARY (*Taking the money*) My poverty, but not my will
consents.   75

ROMEO I pay thy poverty and not thy will.

APOTHECARY (*Giving him the poison*) Put this in any liquid thing
you will
And drink it off, and if you had the strength
Of twenty men, it would dispatch you straight.

ROMEO There is thy gold: worse poison to men's souls,   80
Doing more murder in this loathsome world,
Than these poor compounds that thou may'st not sell.
I sell thee poison: thou hast sold me none.
Farewell; buy food, and get thyself in flesh.

Exit APOTHECARY.

Come, cordial and not poison, go with me   85
To Juliet's grave, for there must I use thee.

Exit.

5.2 Friar Lawrence's cell

Friar John calls upon Friar Lawrence to report that he has been unable to deliver a letter to Romeo, as he has been confined in a house suspected of harbouring the plague. Friar Lawrence anxiously prepares to break into the Capulet monument, knowing that Juliet is about to awake.

Activities

Plot review (12)

1. In pairs, make sure that you know the story of Friar John and the letter by answering the following questions:
   - Who was sending the letter and to whom?
   - What was in it?
   - Which city did it have to go to (12)?
   - Why did he not leave with the letter immediately (5–7)?
   - What then delayed him (8–12)?
   - Why could he not let Friar Lawrence know that he had been delayed (15–16)?
   - What finally happened to the letter (14)?

2. Draw a series of storyboard frames to show what Friar John's experience would look like if represented in a film.

4 **if his mind be writ** if he has written down his thoughts

5 **barefoot brother** *Franciscan friars travelled barefoot*

6 **order** religious order, community

6 **associate** accompany

8 **searchers** city health inspectors, coroners

10 **pestilence** plague *(common in Shakespeare's England)*

11 **forth** out

12 **my speed ... stayed** so that I could not get to Mantua

13 **bare** delivered

14 **here it is again** you can have it back

18 **nice** trivial, unimportant

18–19 **full of charge ... import** full of serious matters and extremely important

20 **danger** serious harm

21 **crow** crowbar

26 **beshrew me much** curse me severely

27 **Hath had ... accidents** has received no report about what has happened

Scene 2

Friar Lawrence's cell.

Enter FRIAR JOHN.

FRIAR JOHN   Holy Franciscan! Friar! brother, ho!

Enter FRIAR LAWRENCE from his inner room.

FRIAR
LAWRENCE   This same should be the voice of Friar John.
Welcome from Mantua. What says Romeo?
Or, if his mind be writ, give me his letter.

FRIAR JOHN   Going to find a barefoot brother out,   5
One of our order, to associate me
Here in this city visiting the sick,
And finding him, the searchers of the town,
Suspecting that we both were in a house
Where the infectious pestilence did reign,   10
Sealed up the doors, and would not let us forth,
So that my speed to Mantua there was stayed.

FRIAR
LAWRENCE   Who bare my letter then to Romeo?

FRIAR JOHN   I could not send it – here it is again –
Nor get a messenger to bring it thee,   15
So fearful were they of infection.

FRIAR
LAWRENCE   Unhappy fortune! By my brotherhood,
The letter was not nice, but full of charge
Of dear import, and the neglecting it
May do much danger. Friar John, go hence;   20
Get me an iron crow, and bring it straight
Unto my cell.

FRIAR JOHN   Brother, I'll go and bring it thee.

Exit FRIAR JOHN.

FRIAR
LAWRENCE   Now must I to the monument alone.
Within this three hours will fair Juliet wake.   25
She will beshrew me much that Romeo
Hath had no notice of these accidents.

5.3 A churchyard containing the Capulet tomb

The Friar plans to write another letter to Romeo and to keep Juliet at his cell until Romeo can fetch her. Meanwhile Paris has arrived in the churchyard and, as he places flowers on the tomb, his page signals that someone is coming.

Activities

Actors' interpretations (35): staging the scene

Use the drawing on page 242 to show how you think these opening moments might have been staged in Shakespeare's theatre. Remember that:

- Paris's page has to hide somewhere (10) so that he is not seen by Romeo or Balthasar when they enter
- Paris also has to hide (21)
- Balthasar also 'withdraws and hides' somewhere (43)
- There will have to be space for Romeo and Paris to fight (71)
- Juliet is either already on stage or will have to be revealed asleep on the tomb inside the Capulet monument.

1   **aloof** some way off

3   **lay thee all along** lie flat on the ground

4   **hollow** because of the graves

5–7   **So shall ... hear it** In that way, no one will be able to enter the churchyard ... without you hearing them.

11   **adventure** take the risk

12   **strew** scatter

13   **canopy** *usually the 'ceiling' to a four-poster bed; here the covering to the tomb*

14   **sweet water** perfume

14   **dew** sprinkle like dew

15   **wanting** lacking: if I don't have any perfume

15   **distilled by** made out of *(like distilled spirits)*

16   **obsequies** funeral rituals

20   **cross** disturb

20   **rite** rituals

But I will write again to Mantua,
And keep her at my cell till Romeo come.
Poor living corse, closed in a dead man's tomb!　30

Exit.

Scene 3

The Capulets' vault.

Enter PARIS and his PAGE at the entrance.

PARIS　　Give me thy torch, boy. Hence, and stand aloof.
Yet put it out for I would not be seen.
Under yond yew trees lay thee all along,
Holding thy ear close to the hollow ground,
So shall no foot upon the churchyard tread,　5
Being loose, unfirm with digging up of graves,
But thou shalt hear it. Whistle then to me,
As signal that thou hear'st something approach.
Give me those flowers. Do as I bid thee, go.

PAGE　　(*Aside*) I am almost afraid to stand alone　10
Here in the churchyard, yet I will adventure.

He hides behind the trees.

PARIS　　(*To JULIET*) Sweet flower, with flowers thy bridal bed I
strew –
O woe, thy canopy is dust and stones –
Which with sweet water nightly I will dew,
Or, wanting that, with tears distilled by moans.　15
The obsequies that I for thee will keep,
Nightly shall be to strew thy grave and weep.

The PAGE whistles.

The boy gives warning; something doth approach.
What cursèd foot wanders this way to-night,
To cross my obsequies and true love's rite?　20
What, with a torch? Muffle me, night, a while.

He hides in the churchyard.

Enter ROMEO and BALTHASAR with a torch, mattock and crowbar.

199

5.3 A churchyard containing the Capulet tomb

Romeo approaches the tomb and orders Balthasar to leave him on pain of death, but the servant hides nearby. As Romeo tries to wrench open the tomb gate, Paris steps forward, determined to arrest him.

Activities

Character review: Romeo (14)

A Write the letter that Romeo asks Balthasar to give to his father, having first discussed in pairs what you think it might contain.

B Write notes to lines 22–44, showing (a) what is in Romeo's mind (and particularly explaining why he lies to Balthasar: 28–32); (b) what Balthasar is thinking (and particularly what he observes in Romeo's speech and actions which makes him suspicious: 43–44). Then use your notes to perform this part of the scene.

C Discuss Romeo's mixed emotions and unpredictable behaviour here, for example he is both aggressive and friendly to Balthasar (33–42). How significant are his words to Paris (61–67)?

22 **wrenching iron** crowbar

23 **Hold** wait

24 **See** make sure

25 **charge** order

27 **my course** what I am doing

28 **Why** the reason why

32 **In dear employment** for a very special purpose

33 **jealous** suspicious

36 **hungry** *because death has a great appetite*

38 **inexorable** relentless

39 **empty** hungry

44 **his intents I doubt** I am suspicious about his intentions

45–48 **Thou detestable ... food** *Death is seen here as a creature with a ravenous appetite. (see 36)*

45 **maw ... womb** *both can be used for stomach*

48 **more food** *his own body*

53 **apprehend** arrest

ROMEO	Give me that mattock and the wrenching iron.
	Hold, take this letter; early in the morning
	See thou deliver it to my lord and father.
	Give me the light. Upon thy life I charge thee, 25
	Whate'er thou hear'st or seest, stand all aloof,
	And do not interrupt me in my course.
	Why I descend into this bed of death
	Is partly to behold my lady's face,
	But chiefly to take thence from her dead finger 30
	A precious ring, a ring that I must use
	In dear employment. Therefore hence, be gone.
	But if thou, jealous, dost return to pry
	In what I farther shall intend to do,
	By heaven, I will tear thee joint by joint, 35
	And strew this hungry churchyard with thy limbs.
	The time and my intents are savage, wild,
	More fierce and more inexorable far
	Than empty tigers or the roaring sea.
BALTHASAR	I will be gone, sir, and not trouble ye. 40
ROMEO	So shalt thou show me friendship. (*Gives him money*)
	Take thou that.
	Live and be prosperous; and farewell, good fellow.
BALTHASAR	(*Aside*) For all this same, I'll hide me hereabout.
	His looks I fear, and his intents I doubt.

He withdraws and hides in the churchyard.

ROMEO	(*He smashes at the gate with the crowbar*) Thou
	detestable maw, thou womb of death 45
	Gorged with the dearest morsel of the earth;
	Thus I enforce thy rotten jaws to open,
	And in despite I'll cram thee with more food.
PARIS	This is that banished haughty Montague
	That murdered my love's cousin, with which grief 50
	It is supposed the fair creature died,
	And here is come to do some villainous shame
	To the dead bodies. I will apprehend him.

He comes forward.

5.3 A churchyard containing the Capulet tomb

Paris tries to stop Romeo, believing that he is attempting some vengeful vandalism on the Capulet tomb. They fight and Romeo kills him, not aware who he is. Shocked when he recognises the dead man, Romeo grants Paris's dying wish and lays his body next to Juliet's.

Activities

Character review: Paris (4)

Write directors' notes to help advise the actor playing Paris on how he should approach this scene. Think about:
- why he has come to the vault
- why he is so concerned not to be discovered (1–9)
- how sincere you think his words about Juliet are (12–17)
- why he seems so hostile to Romeo (49–51)
- why his hostility increases (52–57)
- what he intends to do to Romeo (69)
- how you interpret his dying words (72–73).

Juliet (Claire Danes) lying in the Capulet tomb in the 1997 film

54 **unhallowed** unholy, sacrilegious

58 **and therefore ...** and that's why I came here

59 **tempt** provoke, push

60 **these gone** the dead

65 **armed against myself** *with the poison for his suicide*

68 **I defy thy conjurations** I reject your prayers

69 **for a felon** as a criminal

74 **peruse** examine, look closely at

76 **betossèd soul** tormented mind

77 **attend** listen to

78 **should have** was supposed to have

84 **lantern** *a building with openings letting in light*

86 **a feasting presence** *a chamber for receiving guests, decorated as though for a celebration*

87 **interred** buried

	Stop thy unhallowed toil, vile Montague!	
	Can vengeance be pursued further than death?	55
	Condemnèd villain, I do apprehend thee.	
	Obey, and go with me, for thou must die.	

ROMEO   I must indeed, and therefore came I hither.
          Good gentle youth, tempt not a desperate man.
          Fly hence and leave me. Think upon these gone;   60
          Let them affright thee. I beseech thee, youth,
          Put not another sin upon my head
          By urging me to fury. O be gone!
          By heaven, I love thee better than myself
          For I come hither armed against myself.   65
          Stay not, be gone; live, and hereafter say
          A madman's mercy bid thee run away.

PARIS   I do defy thy conjurations
          And apprehend thee for a felon here.

ROMEO   Wilt thou provoke me? Then have at thee, boy!   70

They fight and Romeo kills Paris.

PAGE   O Lord, they fight! I will go call the watch.

Exit PAGE.

PARIS   (*Falling*) O I am slain! If thou be merciful,
          Open the tomb; lay me with Juliet.

ROMEO   In faith, I will. Let me peruse this face,
          Mercutio's kinsman, noble County Paris!   75
          What said my man when my betossèd soul
          Did not attend him as we rode? I think
          He told me Paris should have married Juliet.
          Said he not so? Or did I dream it so?
          Or am I mad, hearing him talk of Juliet,   80
          To think it was so? O give me thy hand,
          One writ with me in sour misfortune's book.
          I'll bury thee in a triumphant grave.
          A grave? O no, a lantern, slaughtered youth;
          For here lies Juliet, and her beauty makes   85
          This vault a feasting presence full of light.
          Death, lie thou there, by a dead man interred.

5.3 A churchyard containing the Capulet tomb

Romeo admires Juliet's beauty and, drinking the poison, he kisses her and dies. Friar Lawrence arrives outside the tomb, seconds too late.

89   **keepers** gaolers

90   **lightning** sudden light-heartedness

92   **honey** sweetness

94   **ensign** flag

96   **is not advancèd ...** has not reached it yet

99   **cut thy youth in twain** killed you when you were young

100   **To sunder ...** to cut in two the youth of the person who was your enemy

103   **unsubstantial** without a physical body

103   **amorous** in love

104   **abhorrèd** revolting, repulsive

105   **paramour** mistress

106   **still** for ever

107   **pallet** bed

111   **And shake the yoke ...** and shake off the oppressive weight of my unlucky fortune

115   **A dateless bargain** a contract which will never expire

115   **engrossing Death** death that consumes everything

116   **conduct** guide (the poison – which will guide him to another world)

117   **pilot** navigator

117   **run on** run aground on

118   **bark** ship

He lays PARIS beside JULIET's tomb.

How oft when men are at the point of death
Have they been merry, which their keepers call
A lightning before death! O, how may I   90
Call this a lightning? O my love, my wife!
Death, that hath sucked the honey of thy breath,
Hath had no power yet upon thy beauty.
Thou art not conquered; beauty's ensign yet
Is crimson in thy lips and in thy cheeks,   95
And death's pale flag is not advancèd there.
Tybalt, liest thou there in thy bloody sheet?
O, what more favour can I do to thee
Than with that hand that cut thy youth in twain
To sunder his that was thine enemy?   100
Forgive me, cousin. Ah, dear Juliet,
Why art thou yet so fair? Shall I believe
That unsubstantial Death is amorous,
And that the lean abhorrèd monster keeps
Thee here in dark to be his paramour?   105
For fear of that I still will stay with thee,
And never from this pallet of dim night
Depart again. Here, here will I remain,
With worms that are thy chambermaids. O, here
Will I set up my everlasting rest,   110
And shake the yoke of inauspicious stars
From this world-wearied flesh. Eyes, look your last;
Arms take your last embrace; and lips, O you,
The doors of breath, seal with a righteous kiss
A dateless bargain to engrossing Death.   115
Come, bitter conduct; come, unsavoury guide,
Thou desperate pilot, now at once run on
The dashing rocks thy seasick weary bark,
Here's to my love. (*Drinks the poison*) O true
   apothecary!
Thy drugs are quick. Thus with a kiss I die.   120

He dies.

Enter FRIAR LAWRENCE at the gate of the vault, with a lantern, crowbar and spade.

FRIAR   Saint Francis by my speed! How oft to-night
LAWRENCE   Have my old feet stumbled at graves! Who's there?

5.3 A churchyard containing the Capulet tomb

Balthasar informs the Friar that Romeo has been in the tomb for some time. The Friar is full of foreboding, which intensifies when he sees the blood on the tomb entrance. He enters and finds the bodies of Romeo and Paris.

Activities

Actors' interpretations (36): the Friar's haste

In pairs, discuss where in lines 121–136 the Friar begins to fear that something awful has happened. Then act out the scene. To create a sense of urgency, each actor should cut in with their line *just before* the other actor's speech has ended. This is known as 'cue-biting'; it takes a lot of concentration and practice, but is extremely effective in making speech sound natural.

125 **yond** that over there

125 **vainly** without much effect

126 **discern** make out

132 **My master knows not but** As far as my master is aware

133 **menace** threaten

136 **ill unthrifty thing** evil and unlucky happening

142 **masterless and gory** without their owners and bloody

BALTHASAR   Here's one, a friend, and one that knows you well.

FRIAR
  LAWRENCE   Bliss be upon you. Tell me, good my friend,
                   What torch is yond that vainly lends his light   125
                   To grubs and eyeless skulls? As I discern
                   It burneth in the Capels' monument.

BALTHASAR   It doth so, holy sir; and there's my master,
                   One that you love.

FRIAR   Who is it?
  LAWRENCE

BALTHASAR   Romeo.

FRIAR   How long hath he been there?
  LAWRENCE

BALTHASAR   Full half an hour.   130

FRIAR   Go with me to the vault.
  LAWRENCE

BALTHASAR   I dare not, sir.
                   My master knows not but I am gone hence,
                   And fearfully did menace me with death
                   If I did stay to look on his intents.

FRIAR   Stay then; I'll go alone. Fear comes upon me.   135
  LAWRANCE   O much I fear some ill unthrifty thing.

BALTHASAR   As I did sleep under this yew tree here,
                   I dreamt my master and another fought,
                   And that my master slew him.

FRIAR   Romeo!
  LAWRENCE   Alack, alack, what blood is this which stains   140
                   The stony entrance of this sepulchre?
                   What mean these masterless and gory swords
                   To lie discoloured by this place of peace?

  He enters the vault.

                   Romeo! O pale! Who else? What, Paris, too?

5.3 A churchyard containing the Capulet tomb

Juliet awakes and, hearing people approaching, the Friar tries to hurry her away. When she realises that Romeo is dead, she refuses to go and the Friar flees without her. She gives Romeo a final kiss and stabs herself with his dagger.

Activities

Character review: Juliet (14)

Niamh Cusack described her approach to Juliet's final moments like this: 'The first few seconds of waking up and believing it has all worked out must be played for all their happiness. The poison did not kill me, everything has gone according to plan, there is the Friar, and I am where I am supposed to be – all this, I think, has to be suggested in those moments though you have only just woken up and are a little bit dozy. Then you turn and see Romeo lying there dead,'

1. In pairs try acting out these moments in the way that Niamh Cusack describes (from the Friar's 'The lady stirs', 147–160).
2. What effect does an initially happy Juliet have on the audience, do you think?
3. What goes through Juliet's mind in those first few seconds?

145 **unkind** cruel and unnatural

146 **Is guilty of . . .** is responsible for this tragic happening (**lamentable chance**)

148 **comfortable** comforting, reassuring

152 **contagion** disease

153 **contradict** argue against

154 **thwarted our intents** prevented us from doing what we wanted to do

155 **in thy bosom** in your arms

156–157 **dispose of thee Among** find you a place with

162 **timeless** (1) everlasting; (2) untimely

163 **churl** ill-mannered person

165 **Haply** perhaps

166 **restorative** cure

169 **brief** quick

Olivia Hussey as Juliet and Leonard Whiting as Romeo in the 1968 film

And steeped in blood? Ah, what an unkind hour   145
Is guilty of this lamentable chance!

JULIET wakes.

The lady stirs.

JULIET   O comfortable Friar, where is my lord?
                I do remember well where I should be,
                And there I am. Where is my Romeo?   150

Approaching voices are heard.

FRIAR   I hear some noise, lady. Come from that nest
LAWRENCE   Of death, contagion, and unnatural sleep.
                A greater power than we can contradict
                Hath thwarted our intents. Come, come away.
                Thy husband in thy bosom there lies dead,   155
                And Paris too. Come, I'll dispose of thee
                Among a sisterhood of holy nuns.
                Stay not to question, for the watch is coming.
                Come, go, good Juliet; I dare no longer stay.

JULIET   Go, get thee hence, for I will not away.   160

Exit FRIAR LAWRENCE.

                What's here? A cup closed in my true love's hand?
                Poison, I see, hath been his timeless end.
                O churl! drunk all, and left no friendly drop
                To help me after? I will kiss thy lips:
                Haply some poison yet doth hang on them   165
                To make me die with a restorative.
                (*Kisses him*) Thy lips are warm.

The PAGE and the WATCH approach the vault.

FIRST   Lead, boy. Which way?
WATCHMAN

JULIET   Yea, noise? Then I'll be brief. (*She takes ROMEO's
                    dagger*) O happy dagger!
                This is thy sheath; there rust, and let me die. 170

She stabs herself, falls on ROMEO's body and dies.

5.3 A churchyard containing the Capulet tomb

Paris's page leads the watch to the tomb and they discover the bodies. As other watchmen bring in Balthasar and the Friar, the Prince arrives, closely followed by Juliet's parents.

173 **attach** arrest

180–181 **But the ... descry** But we cannot make out (**descry**) the real reason (**true ground**) for these pitiful sad sights without further facts (**circumstance**).

180 **ground** reason (*wordplay with ground on the previous line*)

187 **A great suspicion!** That looks extremely suspicious!

187 **Stay** hold

188–189 **What misadventure ...** what dreadful event has happened so early in the day?

190 **shrieked abroad** screamed in the streets

5.3

The PAGE and the WATCH enter the vault.

PAGE   This is the place; there, where the torch doth burn.

FIRST   The ground is bloody. Search about the churchyard.
WATCHMAN   Go, some of you: whoe'er you find, attach.

Some WATCHMEN go out.

            Pitiful sight! Here lies the County slain,
            And Juliet bleeding, warm and newly dead,   175
            Who here hath lain this two days burièd.
            Go, tell the Prince, run to the Capulets,
            Raise up the Montagues. Some others search

More WATCHMEN go out.

            We see the ground whereon these woes do lie,
            But the true ground of all these piteous woes   180
            We cannot without circumstance descry.

Re-enter some of the WATCH with BALTHASAR.

SECOND   Here's Romeo's man; we found him in the churchyard.
WATCHMAN

FIRST   Hold him in safety till the Prince come hither.
WATCHMAN

Re-enter another WATCHMAN with FRIAR LAWRENCE.

THIRD   Here is a Friar that trembles, sighs, and weeps.
WATCHMAN   We took this mattock and this spade from him,   185
            As he was coming from this churchyard's side.

FIRST   A great suspicion! Stay the Friar too.
WATCHMAN

Enter PRINCE ESCALUS and attendants.

PRINCE   What misadventure is so early up,
            That calls our person from our morning rest?

Enter CAPULET and LADY CAPULET.

CAPULET   What should it be that is so shrieked abroad?   190

211

5.3 A churchyard containing the Capulet tomb

As the watchman gives his report, Juliet's parents look with horror upon their daughter's body. Montague arrives to tell of his wife's death from grief at Romeo's exile and is shocked to find his son dead in the tomb.

Activities

Actors' interpretations (37): the final scene

In groups of ten, freeze-frame the scene as Montague enters (208). Each character then expresses their most important thought or feeling at that moment.

Shakespeare's language: wordplay (3)

The Prince's wordplay to Montague (208–209) can seem in very bad taste and yet Montague himself plays with the idea of his son jumping the queue and getting to the grave first (214–215). Discuss the possible reasons for Shakespeare including wordplay at this point.

194 **What fear ...?** What is this fearful event you are hearing about?

200 **instruments** tools

203 **has mista'en** is in the wrong place

203 **lo, his house** look, his sheath

207 **That warns ...** which summons me to my grave

209 **more early down** gone to sleep even early

210 **my liege** my lord

210 **is dead to-night** died during the night

214 **thou untaught** you ill-mannered boy

215 **press before** push in front of

216 **Seal up the mouth of outrage** Cease your expressions of anger

217 **clear these ambiguities** clear up these mysteries

218 **spring ... head ... true descent** origin, cause and true sequence of events

219 **will I be general of your woes** I will lead you in mourning

220–221 **Meantime forbear ... patience** In the meantime, control your feelings and use your patience to keep a hold on your misfortunes.

LADY CAPULET	O, the people in the streets cry "Romeo", Some "Juliet", and some "Paris", and all run With open outcry toward our monument.
PRINCE	What fear is this which startles in your ears?
FIRST WATCHMAN	Sovereign, here lies the County Paris slain; 195 And Romeo dead; and Juliet, dead before, Warm and new killed.
PRINCE	Search, seek, and know how this foul murder comes.
FIRST WATCHMAN	Here is a Friar, and slaughtered Romeo's man, With instruments upon them fit to open 200 These dead men's tombs.
CAPULET	O heavens! O wife, look how our daughter bleeds! This dagger has mista'en, for lo, his house Is empty on the back of Montague, And is mis-sheathèd in my daughter's bosom. 205
LADY CAPULET	O me! this sight of death is as a bell That warns my old age to a sepulchre.

Enter MONTAGUE.

PRINCE	Come, Montague; for thou art early up To see thy son and heir more early down.
MONTAGUE	Alas, my liege, my wife is dead to-night; 210 Grief of my son's exile hath stopped her breath. What further woe conspires against mine age?
PRINCE	Look, and thou shalt see.
MONTAGUE	(*Seeing* ROMEO) O thou untaught! what manners is in this, To press before thy father to a grave? 215
PRINCE	Seal up the mouth of outrage for a while, Till we can clear these ambiguities, And know their spring, their head, their true descent, And then will I be general of your woes, And lead you even to death. Meantime forbear, 220 And let mischance be slave to patience.

5.3 A churchyard containing the Capulet tomb

The Friar tells what he knows about the events that have led to the tragedy.

Activities

Plot review (14)

Use the Friar's and Balthasar's accounts (231–227) to write a report for the *Verona Independent* with the headline 'Friar involved in star-crossed lovers tragedy'.

222 **parties of suspicion** suspects

223 **I am the greatest** I am most liable to be suspected

225 **Doth make against me** throw suspicion on me

225 **direful** terrible

226 **impeach and purge** accuse and excuse

228 **in** of

229 **short date of breath** short time I have to live

233 **stolen** secret

237 **to remove that siege ...** to prevent her from being overwhelmed by her grief

238 **Betrothed** promised her in marriage

238 **perforce** forcibly

240 **devise some mean** think up some way

243 **tutored by my art** guided by my knowledge *(of herbs)*

245–246 **wrought on her ... death** gave her the appearance of being dead

247 **as** on

248 **borrowed** temporary

249 **the potion's force should cease** the effect should wear off

251 **stayed** delayed

253 **prefixèd** prearranged

255 **closely** in secret

Bring forth the parties of suspicion.

FRIAR LAWRENCE and BALTHASAR are brought forward.

FRIAR **LAWRENCE**	I am the greatest; able to do least,
	Yet most suspected, as the time and place

Doth make against me, of this direful murder;   225
And here I stand, both to impeach and purge,
Myself condemnèd and myself excused.

PRINCE   Then say at once what thou dost know in this.

FRIAR   I will be brief, for my short date of breath
LAWRENCE   Is not so long as is a tedious tale.   230
Romeo there dead, was husband to that Juliet;
And she, there dead, that Romeo's faithful wife.
I married them; and their stolen marriage day
Was Tybalt's doomsday, whose untimely death
Banished the new-made bridegroom from this city; 235
For whom, and not for Tybalt, Juliet pined.
You, to remove that siege of grief from her,
Betrothed and would have married her perforce
To County Paris. Then comes she to me,
And with wild looks bid me devise some mean   240
To rid her from this second marriage,
Or in my cell there would she kill herself.
Then gave I her, so tutored by my art,
A sleeping potion, which so took effect
As I intended, for it wrought on her   245
The form of death. Meantime I writ to Romeo
That he should hither come as this dire night
To help to take her from her borrowed grave,
Being the time the potion's force should cease.
But he which bore my letter, Friar John,   250
Was stayed by accident, and yesternight
Returned my letter back. Then all alone,
At the prefixèd hour of her waking,
Came I to take her from her kindred's vault,
Meaning to keep her closely at my cell   255
Till I conveniently could send to Romeo.
But when I came, some minute ere the time
Of her awakening, here untimely lay
The noble Paris and true Romeo dead.

5.3 A churchyard containing the Capulet tomb

When Balthasar and Paris's page have added their evidence, the Prince summons the fathers to view the terrible results of their hatred.

260 **entreated** begged

266 **is privy** shares the secret

266 **aught** anything

267 **Miscarried** went wrong

268 **some hour before his time** some time before I might have been expected to die

269 **Unto the rigour of . . .** in line with the strictest interpretation of the law

270 **still** always

273 **in post** in a great hurry

275 **early** as soon as I could

276 **going in** as he was going into

277 **If I departed not** unless I went away

280 **what made your master** what was your master doing?

283 **Anon** straight afterwards

284 **by and by** instantly

286 **make good the Friar's words** backs up what the Friar said

289 **therewithal** in possession of it

292 **scourge** punishment

293 **your joys** your children

294 **winking at your discords** turning a blind eye on your quarrels

295 **brace** pair *(Mercutio and Paris)*

	She wakes, and I entreated her come forth	260
	And bear this work of heaven with patience;	
	But then a noise did scare me from the tomb,	
	And she, too desperate, would not go with me,	
	But, as it seems, did violence on herself.	
	All this I know, and to the marriage	265
	Her Nurse is privy, and if aught in this	
	Miscarried by my fault, let my old life	
	Be sacrificed some hour before his time	
	Unto the rigour of severest law.	

PRINCE   We still have known thee for a holy man.   270
Where's Romeo's man? What can he say to this?

BALTHASAR I brought my master news of Juliet's death,
And then in post he came from Mantua
To this same place, to this same monument.
This letter he early bid me give his father,   275
And threatened me with death, going in the vault,
If I departed not and left him there.

PRINCE   Give me the letter; I will look on it.
Where is the County's page that raised the watch?

PAGE comes forward.

Sirrah, what made your master in this place?   280

PAGE   He came with flowers to strew his lady's grave,
And bid me stand aloof, and so I did.
Anon comes one with light to ope the tomb,
And by and by my master drew on him,
And then I ran away to call the watch.   285

PRINCE   This letter doth make good the Friar's words,
Their course of love, the tidings of her death;
And here he writes that he did buy a poison
Of a poor 'pothecary, and therewithal
Came to this vault, to die and lie with Juliet.   290
Where be these enemies, Capulet, Montague?
See what a scourge is laid upon your hate,
That heaven finds means to kill your joys with love.
And I, for winking at your discords too,
Have lost a brace of kinsmen. All are punished.   295

5.3 A churchyard containing the Capulet tomb

Capulet and Montague make peace, each one promising to raise a statue to the other's child. The Prince declares that some people will be punished and some pardoned.

Activities

Actors' interpretations (39): the ending

A Re-read lines 296–304. Write brief epitaphs on each of the two lovers to be inscribed at the feet of the statues.

B The ending of the play can be performed in many different ways. Act out these two interpretations, to see how well they work. The first is how it was done in the 1986 Stratford production; the second is from the 1997 film:

(a) Follow the Prince's speech with the Prologue (page 1), and perform it as though it were an official statement being read out in public, issued jointly on behalf of the two fathers.

(b) Give the Prince's last speech (305–310) to a television news presenter.

C What do you think of the gestures made by the two fathers?

Stage the final lines of the play (296–310) to bring out two different interpretations:

(a) that there will now be peace between the families;

(b) that people will soon forget about the deaths and the feud will start up again.

Stage any other possible interpretations and discuss which one seems to fit best your overall view of the play and its meanings.

297 **jointure** marriage-settlement *(the dowry which the father of the bride would be expected to pay)*

301 **figure** statue

301 **at such rate be set** be valued so highly

305 **glooming** gloomy, sad

5.3

CAPULET	O brother Montague, give me thy hand.
	This is my daughter's jointure, for no more
	Can I demand.

MONTAGUE	But I can give thee more,
	For I will raise her statue in pure gold,
	That whiles Verona by that name is known,
	There shall no figure at such rate be set
	As that of true and faithful Juliet.

300

CAPULET	As rich shall Romeo's by his lady's lie –
	Poor sacrifices of our enmity.

PRINCE	A glooming peace this morning with it brings;
	The sun for sorrow will not show his head.
	Go hence, to have more talk of these sad things.
	Some shall be pardoned, and some punishèd;
	For never was a story of more woe
	Than this of Juliet and her Romeo.

305

310

Exeunt.

Exam practice

Plot review (15)

To make the plot work, Shakespeare had to invent something which would prevent Friar John not only from delivering the letter to Romeo, but also from informing Friar Lawrence that he had not fulfilled his task. Some people are of the opinion that what Shakespeare came up with is a serious weakness in the plot, because it seems contrived and unlikely.

The two films of *Romeo and Juliet* have adapted this element of the plot and have in both cases represented the series of accidents without dialogue:

- In the 1968 Zeffirelli film, we see Balthasar riding off to inform Romeo that Juliet is dead and, a second later, Friar John coming round the corner on a (much slower) donkey.
- In the 1997 Baz Luhrmann film, Romeo is on the other side of his caravan as we see the mailman failing to deliver the letter and leaving a note which Romeo never finds. Balthasar then arrives, having seen the 'funeral'.

Discuss (a) whether you think Shakespeare's plot is contrived here; and (b) whether either of the film versions seems more satisfactory.

Actors' interpretations (40): Romeo's death

In many productions, the director decides to give us an ending slightly different from the one in Shakespeare's script.

1. Rehearse a performance of the lovers' deaths as Leonardo DiCaprio and Claire Danes acted them in the 1997 film:
   - Romeo walks slowly down the aisle of the church up to the alter where Juliet lies.
   - He sits by her body and speaks lines from 91 ('O my love . . .') to 105 ('. . . paramour').
   - He takes the ring she had given him, worn on a chain round his neck, and places it on her finger.
   - We see a shot of Juliet's head, and then her hand, moving slightly.
   - Romeo speaks lines 109–114 ('O, here . . . righteous kiss').
   - We see a shot of her eyes opening: she smiles at him, but he does not notice.
   - He speaks line 115 and drinks the poison.
   - Her hand touches his cheek and he reacts, shocked.
   - She says 'Romeo' and then, seeing the poison flask in his hand, speaks lines 161–167 ('What's here? . . . thy lips').

- Romeo speaks his last words: 'Thus with a kiss I die' (120).
- Juliet cries out in grief, takes his gun and shoots herself in the temple.
2. Do you prefer this sequence of events or those in Shakespeare's original script? Why? What are the strengths and weaknesses of each version?
3. Do you think it is right for a director to move Shakespeare's script around in this way?

Claire Danes as Juliet and Leonardo DiCaprio as Romeo in the 1997 film

Activities

Thinking about the play as a whole . . .

Actors' interpretations

1 **A** *A key moment*

Pick your favourite scene from the play and draw a sketch to show what a key moment might look like, adding notes to explain details of the characters' actions, expressions and gestures.

B *Contrasting moments*

Pick two contrasting moments from the play (perhaps one near the beginning and one near the end) and, using the plan on page 242, show how the moments might be staged to bring out the contrasts, writing annotations to explain your decisions.

C *Directing an extract*

Annotate a short scene or extract to show actors' movements, actions and reactions. Introduce it with a statement about the particular interpretation that you are aiming for (such as a pessimistic ending to the play).

2 **A** *Casting the play*

If you had the chance to direct a performance of *Romeo and Juliet* on stage, which actors and actresses would you cast in the various roles? Make decisions about each character, explaining why you think the particular performer would be right for the part.

B *A theatre programme*

Create a theatre programme for a production of *Romeo and Juliet*. This might include:

- a cast list with the names of the actors
- some background material (for example, on parents and children in Shakespeare's plays – see page 243; or articles on the wordplay or some of the major themes)
- details about Shakespeare and his plays (see page 255).

C *A newspaper review*

Write a review of *Romeo and Juliet*, as a response to an actual theatre performance, or any one of the video versions that you have seen.

3 There have been many different film adaptations of the Romeo and Juliet story: for example, *West Side Story* (1961), a musical version by Leonard Bernstein and Ernest Lehman, in which the warring families became the deprived white and Puerto Rican communities of New York; and two famous ballets with music by Tchaikovsky and Prokofiev. The best-known film versions of Shakespeares' play are those directed by Franco Zeffirelli (1968, with Olivia Hussey and Leonard Whiting) and Baz Luhrmann (1997, with Claire Danes and Leonardo DiCaprio).

Plan your own modern film adaptation of *Romeo and Juliet*, thinking about an appropriate setting (different from the 'Verona Beach' chosen by Baz Luhrmann).

- Make decisions about actors to play the roles and locations for the different scenes of the story.
- Storyboard one of the key sequences and bring out the special qualities of your new interpretation.
- Discuss which features of the play (not only the story, but its themes and language) you would hope to bring out most successfully and which would be harder to get across.

4 **A** *An advertisement*

Create a poster or magazine advert for a new production of *Romeo and Juliet*, featuring some of your favourite actors. First look at some examples in magazines, to see how images are used and what written material is included.

B *Video covers*

Discuss the two covers of video versions of *Romeo and Juliet* on page 224.

- Which features of the story do they seem to be concentrating on?
- Which characters have they decided to highlight?
- How have they arranged the images?
- What text have they used to 'sell' the product?

Create a video cover for your own screen production of the play (which might feature some of the performers chosen for activity A).

Activities

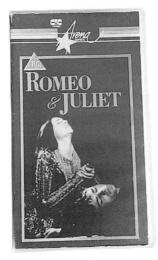 

G *A display*

Put together a classroom display on *Romeo and Juliet*, which would be interesting for a younger class approaching the play for the first time. Include:

- any drawings that you have done (stage designs, storyboards ...)
- other background work (letters; newspaper articles from the *Verona Independent*; diary entries ...)
- anything else you can think of (a poster advertising the play; cartoons of images ...)
- things that you have collected from productions (production postcards, programmes, reviews ...).

You will need to write some introductory material, explaining what the play is about and how the various elements of the display tie in.

Character reviews

5   Character profiles

Many actors write systematic notes about the characters they are preparing to play. Draw up a Character Profile form on a word-processor and then fill it in for any characters you are working on. Headings might be:

NAME:
SOCIAL POSITION:
SUPER-OBJECTIVE: (the character's overriding aim, which drives them on:
    e.g. 'to continue the feud against the Montagues')
LINE OF ACTION: (the practical things they must do to achieve that aim: e.g.
    'Challenge Romeo to a fight')
OBSTACLES AGAINST IT: (e.g. 'He is hiding somewhere')
WHAT THE CHARACTER SAYS ABOUT HERSELF/HIMSELF:
WHAT OTHER CHARACTERS SAY ABOUT HER/HIM:
IMPRESSION ON FIRST APPEARANCE:
RELATIONSHIPS WITH OTHERS:
OTHER INFORMATION:

6 Character review: Romeo

 Biography

Note down Romeo's major actions in the play. Then write a short biography
of him for the *Verona Encyclopedia*.

 Obituary

Draft an obituary on Romeo for the *Verona Independent*.

C *Your views*

Write about your views of Romeo, discussing the suggestion that 'Romeo's
emotions are so out of control and his actions so foolhardy that he forfeits
most of the sympathy that his fate as a "star-crossed" lover might
otherwise cause us to feel'.

7 Character review: Juliet

 Biography

Note down Juliet's major actions in the play. Then write a short biography
of her for the *Verona Encyclopedia*, to accompany the one on Romeo.

B *Recollections*

Imagine the Friar or Nurse were thinking about Juliet a year after her death.
Write down the recollections that either of them might have (starting with
the events which are portrayed in this play).

Activities

C *Your views*

Write about your views of Juliet, discussing Niamh Cusack's suggestion that 'Her passion is tempered with a practicality which is almost, but not quite, sensible ... Juliet has a great sense of reliance upon herself and confidence in her own point of view.'

8 Character review: Romeo and Juliet

A *Their relationship*

Look back at the scenes in which Romeo and Juliet appear together and jot down one or two statements per scene which reveal something about their relationship at that point in the play.

B *Their love*

Niamh Cusack said: 'Romeo and Juliet meet only five times in the play and if the audience doesn't believe utterly in their love, then the whole thing is a waste of time.' What do Shakespeare's lovers say and do which helps audiences to 'believe utterly in their love'?

C *Juliet's tragedy?*

Write about your views of Juliet, discussing the suggestion that 'Juliet is really the central character in the play: she is stronger than Romeo, and an altogether more interesting person: it is her tragedy that we feel keenly – not his.'

9 Character review: Mercutio

A *A letter*

Write a letter from Benvolio to a friend in which he expresses his feelings about Mercutio's death, but also reports on (a) Mercutio's attitudes towards Romeo's love affairs; and (b) Mercutio's views on the Capulet–Montague feud.

B *Thoughts and feelings*

Write brief notes on Mercutio's thoughts and feelings at four moments in the play: after 1.4, as they set off for the Capulet party; after 2.1, when Romeo has given him the slip; after he has left Romeo with the Nurse in 2.4; and at the beginning of 3.1, when he is walking around the streets of

Verona with Benvolio. Pick one of these moments and write his thoughts and feelings in detail. For example, you might begin: 'As he leaves the Capulet party, having failed to find Romeo ...'.

C *A study and discussion*

(a) Write a study of Mercutio which deals with the questions: what exactly does he add to the play? and why did Shakespeare kill him off halfway through, just when we have become interested in him?

(b) Discuss the interpretation held by some actors who have played Mercutio that his behaviour is motivated strongly by his love for Romeo:

- 'What I was seeing in Mercutio was his grief and pain at impending separation from Romeo ... He is hurt and jealous at Romeo's love for Rosaline ... The Queen Mab speech arises because Mercutio feels that Romeo, by placing his faith in dreams, feelings and love for women, is being inconstant to Mercutio: he is betraying a relationship based on a higher, truer love, the bond between men ... In Act 3 the thought begins to form in Mercutio's mind that he could fight Tybalt in Romeo's stead and win back Romeo by saving his life' (Roger Allam, 1983).

- 'it could be played that he has homosexual feelings for Romeo' (Chook Sibtain, 1998).

10 Character review: the Nurse

A *Her importance*

Look through the Nurse's appearances in this play and note briefly what she says and does to (a) help Juliet; and (b) influence Juliet's actions. Then discuss how important she is in affecting what happens to the lovers.

B *Defending herself*

Imagine that the Nurse has been asked by the Prince what part she played in the tragedy. Write down what she might say in defending her actions, focusing especially on her words to Juliet in 3.5.

C *Her role*

In 5.3 the Friar confesses his part in the tragedy and says: 'and to the marriage Her Nurse is privy'. Write an account of the Nurse's role in the play, which includes the fact that she is missing from the final scene and therefore does not have the opportunity to put her case.

Activities

11 Character review: Friar Lawrence

 Strong and weak points

List (a) the Friar's strong points; and (b) his weak points. Then discuss how far you think he was responsible for the deaths of Romeo and Juliet.

B *Autobiography*

Imagine that it is ten years after the tragedy and that the Friar sits down to write his autobiography. What does he write about his involvement with Romeo and Juliet?

C *Sympathetic or unsympathetic?*

What advice would you give to two actors who wanted to play the Friar as, respectively, a sympathetic and an unsympathetic character? Give examples of the features of his character and behaviour which could be emphasised in order to bring out one or other of the chosen interpretations.

12 Character review: Benvolio, Paris, Tybalt, the Prince, Capulet, Lady Capulet and Montague

 Discussion

Pick one of these characters and look back through their appearances in the play. Then discuss what part you think they played in causing the deaths of Romeo and Juliet.

B *Acting opportunities and diary*

(a) What opportunities are there for actors playing these characters? Pick one, look at the scenes in which she or he appears and describe what satisfaction or enjoyment exists in playing the part. (You could write this from the actor's point of view, using their 'voice'.)

(b) Write some entries from the diary kept by an actor playing one of these roles. Include their comments on which scenes they found difficult or interesting and what advice the director gave them on handling certain moments.

Different interpretations

Construct an argument for one or more of the following interpretations:

- a very weak and ineffectual Prince
- a Capulet and Lady Capulet for whom the audience has sympathy throughout
- an attractive and appealing Tybalt
- a highly sympathetic Paris.

Cite evidence from the script which would make such an interpretation possible and consider what might be gained and lost by such an approach in terms of the overall interpretation of the play.

Shakespeare's language

When you are thinking about the meanings of a Shakespeare play, it is helpful to understand how he uses language.

13   Language features

Look back through the play and find an example of each of the following:

- antithesis and oxymoron (look at the activities on pages 16, 72)
- imagery (see pages 14, 74, 142)
- wordplay (see pages 6, 36, 82, 212)
- dramatic irony (see page 98)
- bawdy innuendo (see page 102).

Create a poster for the classroom with the title 'Shakespeare's language in *Romeo and Juliet*', which includes the examples, with a brief written account and a drawing which explains how each one works.

Make sure that you explain what each example adds to the meaning of the play at the point where it occurs.

Activities

14 The sonnet

Read the section on Shakespeare's Verse (page 245–248) before
attempting the following activities on the sonnet:

 What is a sonnet?

To define what a sonnet is, answer the following questions:

- How many lines does it have?
- How many sections is it usually divided into?
- What rhyme scheme do Shakespeare's sonnets usually have?
- What are Shakespeare's sonnets usually about?

 Write an octave

Paris's speech (5.3.12–17) in which he mourns the death of Juliet takes the
form of the sestet (the last six lines) of a sonnet. Write an octave (the first
eight lines) which would lead up to it.

 Sonnets in the play

Write about the contribution that sonnets make to *Romeo and Juliet*.

Themes

15 A theme is an important subject which seems to arise at several times in
the play, showing in what the characters do and the language they use, so
that we receive different perspectives on it. Themes in *Romeo and Juliet*
include the following:

- Fate (see activities on pages 156, 160 and 190)
- Love (see activities on pages 26, 60, 66, 76 and 100)
- Violence (see activity on page 156)
- 'What's in a name?' (see activity on page 62).

There are also **oppositions** – antitheses and oxymorons – explored in the
play (see pages 16 and 72). These include: light and dark; youth and age;
dreams and reality.

A theme collage

Draw up a spider diagram which includes all the many references you can find to any one theme in the play. Then create a collage which illustrates how the theme is developed and explored.

 Analysing the theme

Select one theme and write about:

- how it is developed and explored in the play
- what it adds to your overall interpretation of the play's meanings.

 Themes and oppositions

Write an account of the themes and oppositions in *Romeo and Juliet*, showing how the themes and oppositions are developed and explored, in order to contribute to the overall meanings of the play.

Plot review

16 Who was to blame? (1)

 Diamond-ranking

Write the following names on nine pieces of thin card: Romeo; Juliet; the Prince; the Nurse; Mercutio; Tybalt; the Friar; Capulet; Montague. In pairs 'diamond-rank' the characters, in order of whom, in your opinion was most to blame for the lovers' deaths. Assume for this activity that 'Fate' was acting upon all of them equally. Diamond-ranking means placing the names in the following pattern:

```
        1           most responsible for the deaths
     2     3        equally second most responsible . . .
  4     5     6     equally fourth, etc.
     7     8        equally seventh, etc.
        9           least responsible
```

Place your cards on a desk where they can easily be seen and then walk around to compare your decisions with other people's. Finally discuss the differences, giving reasons for your judgements.

Activities

 Interviews

In groups of six, improvise a television current affairs programme, in which someone interviews the following characters and asks them some tough questions about their involvement in the tragedy: the Prince; Capulet; Lady Capulet; the Friar; the Nurse.

C *Coroner's report*

Hold an inquest into the deaths of Romeo and Juliet, in which all the characters are interviewed (including the ghosts of the lovers and of Lady Montague, Tybalt and Paris). At the end, write up the coroner's report, weighing the evidence and assigning responsibility for the deaths.

17   Who was to blame? (2)

Collect all the references to fate in the play (see activity 15 above) and all the examples of things that could be said to have happened by chance.

Hold a class discussion in which you debate the following motion: 'There was nothing that any of the characters could have done to avoid their deaths: they were preordained by fate.' Half the class finds arguments to support the motion and the other half finds arguments to oppose it.

18   Media reports

A *Newspaper headlines*

Write the series of headlines which might have appeared in the *Verona Independent* starting with the story of the riot (1.1) and finishing with the deaths of the lovers and their parents' reactions.

 Radio reports

Write a series of brief radio reports which might have been broadcast on Verona FM. Each one should be no more than two or three sentences long, but should summarise the most important news of the day. If possible, record your reports and include brief interviews where appropriate.

C *Television programme*

How might a serious television current affairs programme have handled the full story when it came out? Draft the script for a programme which includes factual reports from a correspondent in Verona and interviews with appropriate people. Finally perform the script.

19 Retell the story as one of the following

 An acrostic

Create a 'ROMEO AND JULIET' acrostic (in this case, a fourteen-line poem, the first line beginning with R, then O, then M ... and so on).

B *A mini-saga*

Write a mini-saga (a prose story of *exactly* fifty words, no more no less).

C *A sonnet*

Compose a sonnet similar to the Prologue of *Romeo and Juliet*, but including references to the Friar and Nurse, or any other significant details omitted from Shakespeare's own version.

20 Why did Shakespeare include comedy in a serious story?

Although *Romeo and Juliet* is a tragedy, there is a significant amount of comedy.

(a) Discuss the following possible reasons for Shakespeare having included comedy in the play:

- Audiences need a break from the tension: if they are allowed some comic relief, they will be able to concentrate on the serious scenes more effectively.
- Shakespeare knew that the less educated people in his audience need to be entertained.
- The comedy provides a contrast against which the serious parts of the play show up more strikingly.
- The comic scenes add to our understanding of the main themes, such as love.

(b) Then look back at the following scenes and briefly note the moments that might be played comically: 1.1; 1.3; 1.4; 2.1; 2.4; 2.5.

(c) Finally, discuss how many of the reasons listed in (a) apply to each of the scenes that you have looked at.

Background to Shakespeare

Do some research in an encyclopedia or CD-ROM to find out more about the background features highlighted in **bold**.
There are also activities for additional research.

Shakespeare's England

Shakespeare lived during a period called the **Renaissance**: a time when extraordinary changes were taking place, especially in the fields of religion, politics, science, language and the arts. He wrote during the reigns of **Elizabeth I** and **James I**.

Religion and politics

- In the century following the **Reformation** and England's break with Rome in the 1530s, people in Shakespeare's England began to view the world and their own place in it very differently.

- Queen Elizabeth restored the **Protestant religion** in England, begun under her father Henry VIII.

- England had become a proud and independent nation, and a leading military and trading power, especially after the defeat of the **Spanish Armada** in 1588.

- There were divisions in the Protestant Church, with extremist groups such as the **Puritans**, disapproving of much of what they saw in society and the Church.

- James I succeeded Elizabeth in 1603. He was a Scot, interested in witchcraft, and a supporter of the theatre, who fought off the treasonous attempt of the **Gunpowder Plot** in 1605.

- People began to question traditional beliefs about rank and social order – ideas that some people should be considered superior simply because they were born into wealthy families; or that those in power should always be obeyed without question.

- As trade became increasingly important, it was not only the nobility who could become wealthy. People could move around the country more easily and a competitive **capitalist economy** developed.

Science and discovery

- Scientists began to question traditional authorities (the accepted ideas handed down from one generation to the next) and depended instead upon their own observation of the world, especially after the development of instruments such as the telescope. **Galileo** came into conflict with the Church for claiming that the Earth was not the centre of the universe.
- Explorers and traders brought back new produce, such as spices and silks, and created great excitement in the popular imagination for stories of distant lands and their peoples.

Language

- The more traditional scholars still regarded **Latin** as the only adequate language for scholarly discussion and writing (and liked it because it also prevented many 'uncultured' people from understanding philosophy, medicine, etc.).
- A new interest in the **English language** came with England's growing importance and sense of identity.
- The Protestants favoured a personal relationship with God, which meant being able to read the Bible themselves (rather than letting priests interpret it for them). This led to the need for a good version in English, and **The Authorised Version of the Bible** (the 'King James Bible') was published in 1611.
- **Grammar schools** sprang up after the Reformation which increased literacy (but mostly among males in the middle and upper classes, and mainly in London).
- The invention of the **printing press** in the 1450s had led to more people having access to information and new ideas – not just the scholars.
- The English language began to be standardised in this period (into **Standard English**), but it was still very flexible and there was less insistence on following rules than there is nowadays.

- There was an enormous expansion in **vocabulary**, which affected every area of daily life: crafts, sciences, technology, trade, philosophy, food . . .
- English vocabulary was enriched by numerous **borrowings** from other languages. Between 1500 and 1650, over 10,000 new words entered the language (though many later fell out of use). Some 'purists' (who disliked change) opposed the introduction of new words.
- Shakespeare therefore lived through a time when the English vocabulary was expanding amazingly and the grammar was still flexible, a time when people were intensely excited by language.

Shakespeare's plays reflect this fascination for words. Do some research to find examples of: Dogberry's slip-ups in *Much Ado About Nothing*; Shylock's fatal bond and Portia's 'escape clause' in *The Merchant of Venice*; the puzzling oracle in *The Winter's Tale*; and Bottom's problems with words ('I see a voice!') in *A Midsummer Night's Dream*.

Plays and playhouses

The theatre was a very popular form of entertainment in Shakespeare's time, with audiences drawn from all classes of people. The theatre buildings and the companies of actors were different from what we are used to today.

The theatres

- Theatre companies were based almost exclusively in London, which had around 200,000 inhabitants in 1600.
- It was often under attack from the **Puritan**-dominated Guildhall, which wanted to abolish the theatres totally because, in their opinion, they encouraged sinful behaviour.
- Acting companies first performed in the courtyards of coaching inns, in the halls of great houses, in churches, at markets and in the streets. The first outdoor purpose-built playhouse was The Red Lion, built c.1567 (when Shakespeare was three).

- By 1600, there were six purpose-built outdoor theatres, including **the Rose**, the Swan and the Globe (Shakespeare's theatre).
- **The Globe** opened in 1599 on Maiden Lane, Bankside, and was destroyed by fire during a performance of *Henry VIII* in 1613. (No one was killed, but a bottle of ale was needed to put out a fire in a man's breeches!). See pages 239–242.
- Some outdoor theatres held audiences of up to 3,000.
- Standing room was one penny; the gallery twopence; the 'Lords' Room' threepence; and it was more expensive still to sit on the stage. This was at a time when a joiner (skilled carpenter) might earn 6s to 8s (72 to 96 pence) per week. By 1614, it was 6d ($2^1/_2$ pence) for the newly opened indoor Hope theatre.

Work out whether it was cheaper or more expensive to go to the theatre in Shakespeare's time than it is today. (To do the comparison, you will need to find out (a) how much the cheapest and most expensive tickets are at the Royal Shakespeare Theatre, Stratford-upon-Avon, for example; and (b) what a skilled worker might earn nowadays.)

- Outdoor theatre performances usually started about 2 pm or 3 pm (there was no artificial light).
- The season started in September, through to the beginning of Lent; then from after Easter to early summer. (Theatres were closed during outbreaks of **the plague**: 11,000 died of the plague in summer 1593 and the theatres remained almost completely closed until 1594.) Some companies went on summer tours, playing in inns, etc.
- Several theatres were closed during the **Civil War** (1642–51), and most of the playhouses were demolished by 1656.
- There were some indoor theatres (called 'private' or 'hall' theatres) such as the **Blackfriars**, which was used up to 1609 almost exclusively by child actors (the minimum entrance fee of 6d indicates a wealthier audience). Plays developed which were more suited to the more intimate atmosphere, with the stage illuminated by artificial lighting.
- The star actor **Richard Burbage** and his brother Cuthbert had the lease of the Blackfriars from 1596 and Shakespeare's later plays were performed there.

Work out from page 255 which of Shakespeare's plays might have been written with the indoor Blackfriars theatre in mind.

The actors

- In 1572 parliament passed an Act 'For the Punishment of Vagabonds'. As actors were classed as little better than wandering beggars, this Act required them to be attached to a theatre company and have the patronage (financial support and protection) of someone powerful. This meant that companies had to keep on the right side of patrons and make sure they didn't offend the Master of the Revels, who was responsible for **censorship**.

- Major companies in Shakespeare's time included the Admiral's Men and the Queen's Men. **The Lord Chamberlain's Men** (the group that Shakespeare joined, later known as **the King's Men** when James came to the throne) was formed in 1594 and was run by shareholders (called 'the housekeepers').

- The Burbages held 50 per cent of the shares of the company; the remaining 50 per cent was divided mainly between the actors, including Shakespeare himself, who owned about 10 per cent – which helped to earn him a comfortable regular income.

Acting

- There was very little rehearsal time, with several plays 'in repertory' (being performed) in any given period.

- We don't actually know about the style of acting, but modern, naturalistic, low-key acting was not possible on the Globe stage. At the same time, Shakespeare appears to be mocking over-the-top delivery in at least two of his plays.

Read *Hamlet* 3.2 (Hamlet's first three speeches to the First Player) and *A Midsummer Night's Dream* (especially Act 5).

- Actors certainly needed to be aware of their relationship with the audience: there must have been plenty of direct contact. In a daylight theatre there can be no pretence that the audience is not there.

Publishing

- Plays were not really regarded as 'literature' in Shakespeare's lifetime, and so the playwright would not have been interested in publishing his plays in book form.
- Some of Shakespeare's plays were, however, originally printed in cheap 'quarto' (pocket-sized) editions. Some were sold officially (under an agreement made between the theatre company and the author), and some pirated (frequently by the actors themselves who had learned most of the script by heart).
- In 1623, seven years after Shakespeare's death, two of his close friends, John Heminges and Henry Condell, collected together the most reliable versions of the plays and published them in a larger size volume known as the **First Folio**. This included eighteen plays which had never before appeared in print, and eighteen more which had appeared in quarto editions. Only *Pericles* was omitted from the plays which make up what we nowadays call Shakespeare's 'Complete Works' (unless we count plays such as *The Noble Kinsmen*, for which Shakespeare is known to have written some scenes).

The Globe theatre

No one knows precisely what Shakespeare's Globe theatre looked like, but we do have a number of clues:

- a section of the foundations has been unearthed and provides an idea of the size and shape of the outside walls
- the foundations of the Rose, a theatre near the Globe, were excavated in 1988–89
- a Dutch visitor to Shakespeare's London, called Johannes de Witt, saw a play in the Swan Theatre and made a sketch of the interior.

Using much of the evidence available, a reconstruction of Shakespeare's Globe theatre has been built in London, not far from the site of the original building.

The facts

From what you can learn from these photographs:

- Roughly what shape is the theatre, looked at from above?
- How many storeys does it have?
- In which areas can the audience (a) stand, and (b) sit?

- What is behind the stage?
- How much scenery and lighting are used?
- What other details can you pick out which seem to make the Globe different from an indoor theatre (which has a stage at one end, similar to many school assembly halls)?
- Find a copy of Shakespeare's *Henry V* and read the opening speech (by the Chorus) to see what phrase Shakespeare himself famously used to describe the shape of an earlier theatre, the Curtain.

 Using the stage

Copy the plan on page 242. Then, using the staging guidelines provided, sketch or mark characters as they might appear at crucial moments in *Romeo and Juliet* (such as the arrival of the Prince after Romeo has killed Tybalt in 3.1).

 The actor–audience relationship

In what ways is the design of Shakespeare's Globe ideally suited to the performance of his plays?

- How might the open stage and the balcony be useful? (Refer to moments in *Romeo and Juliet* or other Shakespeare plays that you know.)
- What might be interesting about the way in which Shakespeare's actors – and those on the reconstructed Globe today – might interact with the audience? (Which moments in *Romeo and Juliet* seem to require a performance in which the audience are very close to the actors, for example?)

Background to Shakespeare

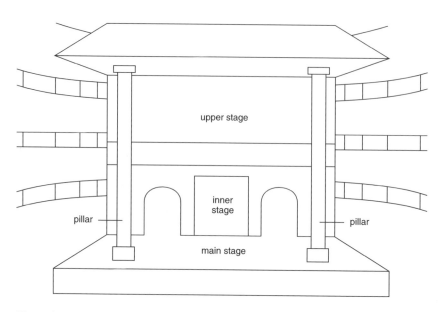

Above: front on view of the stage, as seen by the audience.

Below: bird's-eye view of the stage for positioning of characters.

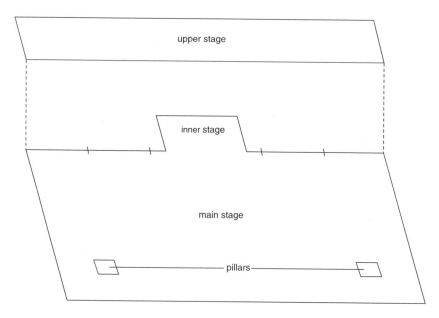

The social background

Parents and children in Shakespeare's plays

- Many of Shakespeare's plays show conflicts between parents and their children, especially fathers and daughters. In many of the societies that Shakespeare describes, daughters seem to be regarded as property to be given in marriage to the most suitable man who comes along.
- You can gain a good idea of the power that fathers have in Shakespeare's plays by looking up the following:
  (a) *A Midsummer Night's Dream*: Egeus threatens to have his daughter Hermia executed if she refuses to marry the man he has chosen for her (1.1).
  (b) *The Taming of the Shrew*: Baptista refuses to allow his younger daughter to marry until someone has married his older daughter, Kate (1.1).
  (c) *King Lear*: the old king casts off his youngest daughter, Cordelia, because she refuses to declare her love for him publicly (1.1).
  (d) *The Merchant of Venice*: Portia is not allowed by the terms of her dead father's will to make her own choice of a husband (1.2).
  (e) *Cymbeline*: the king imprisons his daughter Innogen (sometimes called Imogen) for marrying the man she loves (1.1).

Honour

It is a misplaced sense of family honour, and the belief that wrongs have to be avenged, which keeps the feud going between the Montagues and the Capulets.

- Many plays from Shakespeare's lifetime deal with the question of honour, the importance to individuals of their personal pride and reputation.
- Very often this sense of honour leads to revenge and violence, as it certainly does in Romeo's case:

> This gentleman, the Prince's near ally,
> My very friend, hath got this mortal hurt
> In my behalf, my reputation stained
> With Tybalt's slander . . .

>   ... O sweet Juliet,
> Thy beauty hath made me effeminate,
> And in my temper softened valour's steel. (3.1.113–119)

- In Shakespeare's plays honour can be a very powerful force, as you can see by reading the following scenes:

  (a) *Henry IV Part 1* (1.3): Hotspur is greedy for honour:

  > By heaven, methinks it were an easy leap,
  > To pluck bright honour from the pale-faced moon

  and he later dies in hand-to-hand combat with Prince Hal (5.4).

  (b) *Troilus and Cressida* (2.2): Troilus argues that they should not hand Helen back to the Greeks (she has been stolen from her husband by Troilus's brother, Paris, and this has led to a bloody war), even if it means that many Trojans will die, because Helen is 'a theme of honour and renown'.

  (c) *Hamlet* (1.5): The prince is told by the ghost of his murdered father that he must avenge his death and, urged on by a sense that it is something he has to do, finally kills the murderer, his uncle Claudius.

- One famous character in Shakespeare who is deeply cynical about honour is the fat knight Falstaff. Thinking about the possibility of being wounded or killed in the coming battle, he asks, 'Can honour set to a leg? No. Or an arm? No ... What is honour? A word ... I'll none of it (*Henry IV Part 1,* 5.1). Falstaff's views of honour contrast with Hotspur's in the same play – see above.

Fate and tragedy

Romeo and Juliet are famously described as 'star-crossed lovers', a phrase which suggests that they are simply fated to die.

- Fate played a major part in the tragedies written by the ancient Greeks of classical Athens.

- One of the best known tragedies was written by Sophocles (pronounced 'Soffer-cleese', he died in 406 BC), who retold the story of Oedipus. When Oedipus is born, the oracle foretells that he will one day kill his father and marry his mother, the King and Queen of Thebes. To prevent this happening, the parents arrange for the baby to be abandoned on a mountainside and left to die. However, he is found by a shepherd and taken to the King and Queen of Corinth, who adopt him, and Oedipus grows up believing that he is their son. One day, when Oedipus is a young man, he learns about the prophecy and, thinking that it refers to the loving couple who have brought him up, he runs away, in an attempt to prevent it all from coming true. He decides to head for Thebes, but on the road, he meets a man, gets into a fight and kills him, not realising that it is his father. When he arrives at Thebes, the city is in turmoil. Not only have they just lost their king, but they are being threatened by the monstrous sphinx. Oedipus saves them by solving the sphinx's riddle, and the people, in their gratitude, ask him to marry their recently widowed Queen. Many years later Oedipus discovers the truth of what has happened and plucks out his eyes in horror and guilt.

- Fate is a powerful force in these other plays by Shakespeare:
  Julius Caesar: look at the prophecy concerning the Ides of March, for example.
  Macbeth: one interpretation is that the Witches simply tell Macbeth what is fated to happen anyway; 'weird sister' means 'sister of destiny or fate'.
  The Winter's Tale: the oracle foretells that 'the king shall live without an heir if that which is lost be not found' (3.2).

Shakespeare's verse

Metre

It is possible to describe where the heavy stress falls in any English word. For example, these three words (from 1.1) have their heavy stress on the first syllable: **collar**; **weakest**; **Sampson**; while in these the heavy stress is on the second syllable: dis**grace**; a**gain**; ap**roach**.

All Shakespeare's verse has a pattern of light and heavy stresses running through it, known as the metre. You can hear the metre if you read these lines out loud, overemphasising the heavily stressed syllables:

- If **ev**er you dis**turb** our **streets** a**gain** (1.1.94)
- He **swung** a**bout** his **head** and **cut** the **winds** (1.1.109)
- And **makes** him**self** an **arti**ficial **night** (1.1.138)

No actor would ever perform the lines in that monotonous way, but they would certainly be aware that the metre was always there, helping to give the verse form and structure.

Sometimes, to point out that a syllable which does not carry a stress in modern English is stressed in Shakespeare's line of verse, it will be accented, like this:

- Profaners of this neighbour-stainèd steel (1.1.80)

> (a) Mark the heavy stresses in that line of the Prince's (1.1.80).
> (b) The four lines above are all totally regular in their metre: what do you notice about: the pattern of short and heavy stresses? The number of syllables?

Varying the metre

Most of the lines in Shakespeare's plays are not as regular as the four quoted above. In fact, most will have an irregular stress pattern, like this one, where the three heavy stresses at the beginning (and the total of six heavy stresses, rather than the usual five) perhaps help the actor to emphasise the seriousness of the repeated riots:

- **Three civ**il **brawls bred** of an **airy word** (1.1.87)

A collection of heavy stresses together can add emphasis. The three words 'add more grief' sound like hammer-blows:

- Doth **add more grief** to **too much** of mine **own** (1.1.187)

Occasionally a line will contain an extra syllable (11 rather than 10):

- Being one too many by my weary self (1.1.126)

Here the actor can either try to deliver 'Being' as though it were one syllable – *be'ng* – (making it a regular line), or emphasise the slowness of the phrase, perhaps underlining Benvolio's weariness.

Some lines stand out, because they are clearly short:

- In love?
  Out –
  Of love? (1.1.163–165)

This quick exchange makes Romeo's point very effectively and prepares us for the wordplay to come.

Dividing the line into feet

Just as music has a number of beats in a bar, so Shakespeare's verse has five 'feet' in a complete line. A five-feet line is called a 'pentameter' (pent = five; meter = measure).

A single foot can contain syllables from different words, and any one word can be broken up by the foot divisions:

- And **hear** | the **sen** | -tence of | your **mov** | -èd **Prince** (1.1.86)

This is why a single line of verse is sometimes set out rather oddly in different lines of print, if it is shared between two or more characters, as happens in 2.2:

JULIET	Romeo!		] three speeches
ROMEO		Madam?	] make up
JULIET		What o'clock tomorrow	] line 167
	Shall I send to thee?		] two speeches make
ROMEO		By the hour of nine.	] up line 168

Iambic pentameter

A foot which contains an unstressed syllable followed by a stressed one (the standard 'beat': *dee-**dum*** is called an 'iamb'. Verse which has five iambs per line as its standard rhythm is called an 'iambic pentameter'. This is Shakespeare's standard verse form.

Iambic pentameter which does not rhyme is also sometimes known as 'blank verse'.

(a) Bearing in mind that the iambic pentameter line goes: dee-***dum***, dee-***dum***, dee-***dum***, dee-***dum***, dee-***dum***, make up some of your own 'Shakespearean' verse. To start off, write a line on each of the following: love, violence and fate.
(b) Copy out the following lines from 1.2 and divide them into five feet; then mark the heavy stresses: lines 5, 11, 13, 20 and (more difficult) 87 'Sups the fair Rosaline whom thou so loves').
(c) Do the same with these key lines: 1.1.6; 1.4.53; 1.5.94–95 ('If I profane ... is this'); 2.2.1; 2.2.33; 2.3.94; 3.1.20 ('Mercy ... kill'); 3.2.1. Pick one and show how the rhythm helps the meaning.

Rhyme

Romeo and Juliet is unusual because it contains a number of passages written in rhyming verse. 1.1 is part rhyme, part blank verse; sometimes a whole section will rhyme regularly (such as 215–222: chaste – waste, etc.); sometimes there will be a non-rhyming word in the middle of a rhymed section (such as 182–196, where 190 is the odd line).

Shakespeare also uses rhyme for the ends of scenes, where a 'rhyming couplet' can have the effect of rounding things off, as it does in 1.1.

Find the other scenes which end with a rhyming couplet and discuss what the effect might be in each case.

Verse and prose

It is never totally clear why Shakespeare chooses to write some scenes, or passages, in verse, and others in prose. Although there are many examples where the more serious scenes, involving great passions, are in verse while those about ordinary people and comedy are in prose, there are also significant examples throughout Shakespeare's plays where this is not the case.

Find the prose scenes in *Romeo and Juliet* and try to work out why Shakespeare did not write them in verse.

The plot of *Romeo and Juliet*

Act 1

The Chorus delivers a Prologue which sets the scene in Verona and outlines the story of the two 'star-crossed lovers'.

1.1: A street fight breaks out between servants of the feuding families, the Capulets and Montagues. Benvolio, a Montague, tries to stop the riot, but is attacked by one of the leading younger Capulets, Tybalt. As the heads of the Montague and Capulet households join the fray, the Prince enters and threatens them with the death penalty if they disturb the streets in this way ever again.

Benvolio and Lord and Lady Montague discuss Romeo's melancholy behaviour, and when Romeo enters, he reveals to Benvolio that he is in love, but that the girl (who, we learn later, is called Rosaline) is rejecting him.

1.2: Count Paris visits Lord Capulet to ask for his daughter Juliet's hand in marriage. Capulet points out that she is not yet fourteen, but agrees to let Paris woo her, and invites him to a party to be held that night.

Peter ('the Clown'), the Capulet servant, is walking the streets with a list of the people he has to invite to the party. His problem is that he cannot read, and, seeing Romeo, he asks him to help. Learning that Rosaline is to be among the guests, Benvolio suggests that they gate-crash the party, so that Romeo can see that there are many girls in Verona more beautiful than Rosaline.

1.3: After the Capulet Nurse has reminisced about Juliet's childhood, Lady Capulet informs her daughter of Paris's request. Juliet has not considered marriage, but dutifully promises to accept Paris as a suitor.

1.4: Romeo and Benvolio are joined by Mercutio, a friend of theirs and kinsman to the Prince. They have prepared a masque – a short entertainment – for the Capulet party, but Romeo has an uneasy feeling about the whole thing. When he explains that he had a dream, Mercutio tells them about Queen Mab, who comes to people in their sleep and causes, strange fantasies. They set off for the Capulet feast, Romeo still full of foreboding.

1.5: Capulet welcomes his guests and sits reminiscing with his cousin. Romeo enters and is immediately struck by Juliet's beauty. Tybalt recognises Romeo, but Capulet refuses to let him challenge Romeo, as he is behaving courteously. Tybalt goes off threatening revenge.

Romeo meets Juliet and they fall in love. Juliet is called away to speak to her mother and the Nurse reveals to Romeo that Juliet is a Capulet. After he and his friends have left, Juliet learns that Romeo is a Montague.

Act 2

Prologue: The Chorus talks about the difficulties the lovers will have to overcome before they meet.

2.1: Having left the party, Romeo turns back and refuses to come out of hiding when Mercutio mockingly calls him.

2.2: Inside Capulet's garden, Romeo sees Juliet at a window and hears her declare her love for him, despite the fact that he is a Montague. He surprises her by calling out and offering to change his name if it offends her. Realising that Romeo has already learned the secret of her love for him, Juliet, despite misgivings that it is all happening too fast, asks Romeo to send a message the next day telling her when and where they can be married.

2.3: Romeo visits Friar Lawrence, who, as his confessor, has heard all about his heartaches and at first assumes that Romeo has been with Rosaline. When Romeo tells him about Juliet, he chides Romeo for being so changeable in his feelings, but agrees to marry them, as it might help to heal the enmity between the feuding houses.

2.4: Mercutio jokes with Benvolio but tells him what a dangerous fencer Tybalt is. Romeo joins them and after some light-hearted and witty exchanges, the Nurse enters and becomes the target for some of Mercutio's jokes. Left alone with the Nurse, Romeo asks her to tell Juliet to meet him at the Friar's that afternoon, where they can get married. Romeo's servant will give the Nurse a rope-ladder, by which Romeo will climb to Juliet's room that night.

2.5: When the Nurse finally returns to an impatient Juliet, she passes on Romeo's instructions, but only after delaying the news by grumbling about her aches and pains.

2.6: Friar Lawrence advises Romeo to be more moderate in his emotions, but then hurries the lovers away to be married.

Act 3

3.1: Benvolio is anxious, walking around the streets of Verona while the Capulets are about, but Mercutio ignores his warnings and they meet Tybalt who is looking for Romeo. When Romeo arrives, Tybalt tries to provoke him into a fight, but Romeo refuses and tries to placate him. Angered that Romeo should put up with Tybalt's insults, Mercutio challenges Tybalt himself, and, as Romeo tries to stop the fight, Mercutio is wounded. Tybalt runs away and Mercutio is carried off, cursing the Montague–Capulet feud. When Romeo learns that Mercutio has died, he is appalled at his earlier peacemaking, fights with Tybalt and kills him. When

Michael Kitchen as Mercutio and Hugh Quarshie as Tybalt in the 1986 RSC production

the Prince arrives, Benvolio reports what has happened and, as punishment, Romeo is exiled from Verona.

3.2: Juliet impatiently awaits night, when Romeo will visit her, but the Nurse arrives to report that Romeo has killed Tybalt and has been banished from the city. Juliet grieves for her cousin, but is distraught at the thought of Romeo's banishment, and she asks the Nurse to take a ring to Romeo and bring him to her.

3.3: Romeo, hiding at the Friar's cell, is desperate at the idea of having to leave Juliet and is obsessed with thoughts of banishment. When the Nurse arrives, the Friar lists all the reasons Romeo has for being thankful, and Romeo's spirits are lifted when he receives Juliet's ring and realises that he can see her once more.

3.4: Capulet tells Paris that Juliet is mourning for the death of Tybalt, but he decides that the best cure for her sadness will be for her to get married the following Thursday (in three days' time).

3.5: The following dawn, Juliet urges Romeo to be gone from her room before he is captured.

As soon as he leaves, Lady Capulet enters to inform her daughter that she is to marry Paris on Thursday. Lord Capulet comes into the room, and when Juliet refuses to marry the count, Capulet flies into a rage and tells her that she will either obey him or be thrown out on to the streets.

When Juliet's parents have gone, the Nurse advises Juliet to marry Paris, given that there is no chance that Romeo will ever be able to return to Verona. Juliet realises that she can no longer share her secrets with the Nurse and plans to seek help from the Friar.

Act 4

4.1: When she arrives at the Friar's cell, Juliet meets Paris, who has come to make arrangements for the marriage.

Realising how desperate Juliet is, the Friar suggests a plan, which Juliet accepts. She is to return home and pretend to agree to the marriage. That night she will take a potion which will make her appear to be dead. She will be placed in the Capulet family tomb and, when she awakes, the Friar and Romeo will be there to carry her off to Mantua, the city where Romeo has taken refuge. Meanwhile the Friar will send a letter to Romeo informing him of the plan.

4.2: Following the Friar's advice, Juliet returns home, apologises for having been disobedient and pretends to agree to the marriage with Paris. Capulet delightedly brings the wedding forward a day (it is now arranged for the next morning, Wednesday) and plans to stay up all night supervising preparations.

4.3: That evening Juliet says goodnight to her mother and the Nurse and, after terrifying visions of what might go wrong with the Friar's plan, she drinks the potion.

4.4: Early next morning the Capulet household is still bustling around, getting everything ready for the wedding, and Capulet gives orders that Juliet should be woken up.

4.5: Coming to wake Juliet, the Nurse finds her apparently dead: the potion has taken effect. The Capulets and Paris mourn for Juliet and the Friar attempts to console them as arrangements are made for the funeral.

Act 5

5.1: In Mantua Romeo waits for news from Friar Lawrence, but his servant Balthasar arrives to report that Juliet is dead. Romeo desperately resolves to join Juliet in the Capulet tomb that night and kill himself. He visits a poor apothecary, buys poison from him and departs for Verona.

5.2: Friar Lawrence learns to his dismay that the letter he had written to Romeo has not been delivered because the bearer, Friar John, has been shut up in a house suspected of the plague. Juliet is due to awake within three hours and Friar Lawrence rushes off to the tomb.

5.3: Paris arrives at the tomb, bringing flowers to place by Juliet. He tells his page to wait outside, but, as he is about to enter, hears someone approaching. It is Romeo, saying goodbye to Balthasar. Paris tries to arrest Romeo, they fight, and Paris is killed. Romeo then realises who he has killed and carries the body into the tomb to lie with the Capulets. Romeo gazes on Juliet for the last time, kisses her and drinks the poison.

Friar Lawrence arrives, questions Balthasar and enters the tomb to find Romeo dead. Juliet awakes, the Friar tires to explain what has happened, but, hearing the watch approaching, runs away. Juliet stays behind and, after kissing Romeo, stabs herself and dies.

The watch discover the bodies. The Prince and Juliet's parents arrive, and then Romeo's father enters to report that his wife has died of grief from her son's banishment. The Friar gives an account of what has happened, and Paris's page and Balthasar add further details. In their grief, Capulet and Montague make peace with each other. The Prince, promising that some people will be pardoned and some punished, closes the play.

Study skills: titles and quotations

Referring to titles

When you are writing an essay, you will often need to refer to the title of the play. There are two main ways of doing this:

- If you are handwriting your essay, the title of the play should be underlined: <u>Romeo and Juliet</u>.
- If you are word-processing your essay, the play title should be in italics: *Romeo and Juliet*.

The same rules apply to titles of all plays and other long works including novels and non-fiction, such as: *Animal Farm* and *The Diary of Anne Frank*. The titles of poems or short stories are placed inside single inverted commas; for example: 'Timothy Winters' and 'A Sound of Thunder'.

Note that the first word in a title and all the main words will have capital (or 'upper case') letters, while the less important words (such as conjunctions, prepositions and articles) will usually begin with lower case letters; for example: *The Taming of the Shrew* or *Antony and Cleopatra*.

Using quotations

Quotations show that you know the play in detail and are able to produce evidence from the script to back up your ideas and opinions. It is usually a good idea to keep quotations as short as you can (and this especially applies to exams, where it is a waste of time copying chunks out of the script).

Using longer quotations

There are a number of things you should do if you want to use a quotation of more than a few words:

Background to Shakespeare

1. Make your point. —— **Lady Capulet accuses Benvolio of having a one-sided account:**

2. A colon introduces the quotation.

3. Leave a line ————

4. Indent the quotation. —— **He is a kinsman to the Montague.** —— 5. No quotation marks.

6. Keep the same —— **Affection makes his false . . .**
line-divisions as
the script.

7. Three dots show that the quotation is incomplete.

8. Continue with a —— **The Prince cannot ignore**
follow-up point, **this accusation and . . .**
perhaps
commenting on
the quotation
itself.

Using brief quotations

Brief quotations are usually easier to use, take less time to write out and are much more effective in showing how familiar you are with the play. Weave them into the sentence like this:

- Since we know from the outset that the 'star-crossed lovers' are to die . . .

If you are asked to state where the quotation comes from, use this simple form of reference to indicate the *Act, scene* and *line*:

- If we take the view that the story has 'much to do with hate, but more with love' (1.1.173), it might be argued that . . .

In some editions this is written partly in Roman numerals – upper case for the Act and lower case for the scene; for example: (I.i.173) or (I.1.173).

William Shakespeare and *Romeo and Juliet*

A first version of *Romeo and Juliet* was published in 1597, but the script that we now use is based mainly on a revised edition of 1599.

Shakespeare's life and career

No one is absolutely sure when he wrote each play.

1564   Born in Stratford-upon-Avon, first son of John and Mary Shakespeare.

1582   Marries Anne Hathaway from the nearby village of Shottery. She is eight years older and expecting their first child.

1583   Daughter Susanna born.

1585   Twin son and daughter, Hamnet and Judith, born.

Some time before 1592 Shakespeare arrives in London, becomes an actor and writes poems and plays. Several plays are performed, probably including the three parts of *Henry VI*. Another writer, Robert Greene, writes about 'Shake-scene', the 'upstart crow' who has clearly become a popular playwright.

By March 1595 he is a shareholder with the Lord Chamberlain's Men (see page 238) and has probably written *Richard III*, *Comedy of Errors*, *Titus Andronicus*, *Taming of the Shrew*, *Two Gentlemen of Verona*, *Love's Labours Lost*, *Romeo and Juliet*, *Richard II* and *A Midsummer Night's Dream* (as well as contributing to plays by other writers and writing the poems 'Venus and Adonis' and 'The Rape of Lucrece').

1596   Hamnet dies, aged 11.

1597   Buys New Place, one of the finest houses in Stratford.

1599   Globe theatre opens on Bankside.

By 1599: *King John*, *Merchant of Venice*, the two parts of *Henry IV*, *Merry Wives of Windsor*, *Much Ado About Nothing*, *Julius Caesar* and *Henry V* (as well as the Sonnets).

1603   King James I grants the Lord Chamberlain's Men a Royal Patent and they become the King's Men (page 238).

By 1608: *As You Like It, Hamlet, Twelfth Night, Troilus and Cressida, All's Well That Ends Well, Measure for Measure, Othello, Macbeth, King Lear, Antony and Cleopatra, Pericles, Coriolanus* and *Timon of Athens.*

1608   The King's Men begin performing plays in the indoor Blackfriars theatre (page 237).

By 1613: *Cymbeline, The Winter's Tale, The Tempest, Henry VIII, Two Noble Kinsmen* (the last two probably with John Fletcher).

1613   Globe theatre destroyed by fire.
1614   The rebuilt Globe theatre opens.
1616   Dies, 23 April, and is buried in Holy Trinity Church, Stratford.
1623   Publication of the First Folio (page 239).

Shakespeare's times

1558   Elizabeth I becomes queen.
1565   The sailor John Hawkins introduces sweet potatoes and tobacco into England.
1567   Mary Queen of Scots is forced to abdicate in favour of her year-old son, James VI.
1567   The first-known playhouse in London, the Red Lion, is built.
1568   Mary escapes to England and is imprisoned by Elizabeth.
1572   Francis Drake attacks Spanish ports in the Americas.
1576   James Burbage opens the Theatre in London.
1580   Francis Drake returns from the first English circumnavigation of the world.
1582   Pope Gregory reforms the Christian calendar.
1587   Mary Queen of Scots executed for a treasonous plot against Elizabeth; Drake destroys two dozen Spanish ships at Cadiz and war breaks out with Spain.
1588   Philip II of Spain's Armada is defeated by the English fleet.
1593   Plague kills 11,000 Londoners.
1593   Playwright Christopher Marlowe killed in a pub brawl.
1595   The Earl of Tyrone leads a new rebellion in Ireland.
1596   Tomatoes introduced into England; John Harington invents the water-closet (the ancestor of the modern lavatory).
1599   The Earl of Essex concludes a truce with Tyrone, returns home and is arrested.
1601   Essex is tried and executed for treasonous plots against Elizabeth.
1603   Elizabeth I dies and is succeeded by James VI of Scotland as James I of England.

1603   Sir Walter Raleigh is jailed for plotting against James.

1604   James is proclaimed 'King of Great Britain, France and Ireland'; new Church rules cause 300 Puritan clergy to resign.

1605   Gunpowder Plot uncovered.

1607   First permanent English settlement in America at Jamestown, Virginia.

1610   Galileo looks at the stars through a telescope; tea is introduced into Europe.

1611   The Authorised Version of the Bible published.

1618   Raleigh executed; physician William Harvey announces discovery of blood circulation.

1620   Pilgrim Fathers sail from Plymouth to colonise America.

1625   James I dies and is succeeded by Charles I.

Index of activities